P6,8,15,20,71

P69

The Later Affluence of W. B. Yeats and Wallace Stevens

The Later Affluence of
W. B. Yeats and
Wallace Stevens

Edward Clarke

First published 2012 by
PALGRAVE MACMILLAN

Palgrave Macmillan in the UK is an imprint of Macmillan Publishers Limited, registered in England, company number 785998, of Houndmills, Basingstoke, Hampshire RG21 6XS.

Palgrave Macmillan in the US is a division of St Martin's Press LLC, 175 Fifth Avenue, New York, NY 10010.

Palgrave Macmillan is the global academic imprint of the above companies and has companies and representatives throughout the world.

Palgrave® and Macmillan® are registered trademarks in the United States, the United Kingdom, Europe and other countries.

ISBN 978–0–230–29668–8

This book is printed on paper suitable for recycling and made from fully managed and sustained forest sources. Logging, pulping and manufacturing processes are expected to conform to the environmental regulations of the country of origin.

A catalogue record for this book is available from the British Library.

A catalog record for this book is available from the Library of Congress.

10 9 8 7 6 5 4 3 2 1
21 20 19 18 17 16 15 14 13 12

Printed and bound in Great Britain by
CPI Antony Rowe, Chippenham and Eastbourne

The scholar busies himself with investigations into language, and if it be his desire to go farther afield, he works on history, or, if he would extend his range to the farthest limits, on poetry. But which of these paves the way to virtue? Pronouncing syllables, investigating words, memorizing plays, or making rules for the scansion of poetry, – what is there in all this that rids one of fear, roots out desire, or bridles the passions?

(*Seneca*, Epistles, *LXXXVIII. 3*)

I resolved thereupon to bend my studies towards the Holy Scriptures, that I might see what they were. But behold, I espy something in them not revealed to the proud, not discovered unto children, humble in style, sublime in operation, and wholly veiled over in mysteries; and I was not so fitted at that time, as to pierce into the sense, or stoop my neck to its coming. For when I attentively read these Scriptures, I thought not then so of them, as I now speak; but they seemed to me far unworthy to be compared to the stateliness of the Ciceronian eloquence. For my swelling pride soared above the temper of their style, nor was my sharp wit able to pierce into their sense. And yet such are thy Scriptures as grew up together with thy little ones. But I much disdained to be held a little one; and big swollen with pride, I took myself to be some great man.

(*Augustine*, Confessions, *III. v*)

Contents

Acknowledgements

For their advice, conversation and support, I wish to thank Jerome Boyd-Maunsell, Terence Brown, David Clarke, Sherille Clarke, Peter Claus, Andy Cooke, Hugh Dancy, Ralph Dennison, Ned Denny, Alexander Fiske-Harrison, Steve France, Emma Griffin, Paul Griffin, Lee Jenkins, Francesca Magnabosco, Stephen Matterson, Robin Powley, Paul Saville, Francesca Southerden and the late Jonathan Wordsworth. I would also like to thank Felicity Plester and Catherine Mitchell at Palgrave Macmillan as well as Christine Ranft for all of their help during the production of this book.

The author and publishers wish to thank the following for permission to reproduce copyright material: 'Not Ideas about the Thing but the Thing Itself', 'Of Mere Being' from *The Collected Poems of Wallace Stevens* by Wallace Stevens, copyright 1954 by Wallace Stevens and renewed 1982 by Holly Stevens. Used by permission of Alfred A. Knopf, a division of Random House, Inc., and Faber and Faber Ltd. 'Cuchulain Comforted' and 'The Black Tower' from *The Collected Poems of W. B. Yeats*, 2nd edn, Macmillan (1950) used with the permission of A P Watt Ltd on behalf of Gráinne Yeats. Reprinted with the permission of Scribner, a division of Simon & Schuster, Inc., from *The Collected Works of W. B. Yeats, Volume I: The Poems, Revised* by W. B. Yeats, edited by Richard J. Finneran. Copyright © 1940 by Georgie Yeats, renewed 1968 by Bertha Georgie Yeats, Michael Butler Yeats, and Anne Yeats. All rights reserved.

A version of Chapter 4 of this work appeared originally as '"The cry that contains its converse in itself": Voices in the Poem at the End of Wallace Stevens's *Collected Poems*', in *The Modern Language Review* (2010) 105: 345–65, and is reprinted with their permission.

Note on Texts

Although the following two books are by no means definitive by the standards of modern scholarship, I usually quote from *The Collected Poems of W. B. Yeats* (*YCP*) and *The Collected Poems of Wallace Stevens* (*SCP*). Both poets gave thought to the idea of, while helping to prepare, their respective *Collected Poems*, and both editions are usefully inadequate for someone interested in their late work: their very flaws are matters of interest for interpretation. Requisite modern editions of both poets that address these shortcomings present their own problems.

We should question the arrangement and editing of *The Poems of W. B. Yeats* (1949), undertaken after Yeats's death, upon which the texts for the later poems in the 1950 expanded 'Second Edition' of Yeats's 1933 *Collected Poems* are mainly based (see Finneran 1990: 3). As James Pethica is 'concerned to show', 'The history of the transmission of the texts' of Yeats's last poems 'between their form in the latest manuscript or typescript draft that now survives for each poem, and their supposedly "canonical" form in *The Poems* (1949), was . . . a saga involving errors, misreadings, and posthumous editorial alterations of various kinds by George Yeats and Thomas Mark' (1997: liv). Nonetheless Yeats had worked with these two before, and would have relied upon them again while preparing the texts of his recent poems, had he lived (see Gould 1996: 706). My main concern with the 1950 *Collected Poems* is its grouping of the last poems that Yeats composed with the poems from *New Poems* (1938). I accept the different ordering of Yeats's very last poems in the 1939 *Last Poems and Two Plays*, published posthumously by Cuala Press, identical to 'a manuscript table of contents for an untitled volume' that 'Yeats must have written . . . in the last week or two of his life' (Finneran 1997: 688).

In April 1954 Stevens consented to Alfred A. Knopf's proposal to publish a collected edition of his poetry (see *SL*: 829). Stevens 'asked that it include a section of new poems in addition to the poetry that had appeared in previously published volumes' and 'initially proposed calling this section "Amber Umber," but then decided to use "The Rock" as its title' (*CPP*: 972; see *SL*: 833). A number of poems, composed after publication of his previous collection, *The Auroras of Autumn* (1950), and published in periodicals or anthologies, were not chosen by Stevens for 'The Rock'. At least one of these poems had been left out of this final section through the poet's negligence (see *SL*: 881). Stevens also continued to write poems after the publication of his *Collected Poems* and some of these remained unpublished at his death (see *CPP*: 972–3). Milton J. Bates's revised edition of *Opus Posthumous* (*OP*) is, therefore, indispensable.

It is often safer to use first or other appropriate early editions when discussing the relations between more than two writers from different periods and I usually prefer reading texts up close without modern editorial interventions. Unless otherwise stated, Shakespeare quotations are from Folio or Quarto editions, and their titles and act, scene and line numbering from 'The Globe Edition' (1891); Bible quotations in English are from the King James Version (KJV), and in Latin from the 2007 *Biblia Sacra Vulgata*, 5th edn (Stuttgart: Deutsche Bibelgesellschaft). In all quotations from early editions, I use normalized modern typography. I will always present translations of foreign texts; for different reasons, I will sometimes present those texts or portions of those texts in the original language. In references, the Roman numerals after a comma denote book, chapter, act or scene divisions and Arabic numerals, line numbers; after a colon, Roman numerals denote volume numbers and Arabic numerals, page numbers.

List of Abbreviations

Au	W. B. Yeats (1955) *Autobiographies* (London: Macmillan).
BCP 1549	Church of England (1549) The Booke of the Common Prayer and Administracion of the Sacramentes and Other Rites and Ceremonies of the Churche (London: Edward Whitchurch, STC 16272).
BCP 1928	Church of England (1928) The Book of Common Prayer with the Additions and Deviations Proposed in 1928 (London: Eyre and Spottiswoode).
Blake	William Blake (2001) *The Complete Illuminated Manuscripts* (London: Thames and Hudson).
Cary	H. F. Cary (trans.) (1908) *The Vision of Dante Alighieri* (London: Dent).
CPP	Wallace Stevens (1997) *Collected Poetry and Prose*, ed. Frank Kermode and Joan Richardson (New York: Library of America).
E&I	W. B. Yeats (1961) *Essays and Introductions* (London: Macmillan).
Erdman	David V. Erdman (ed.) (1988) *The Complete Poetry & Prose of William Blake*, rev. edn (New York: Doubleday).
Ex	W. B. Yeats (1962) *Explorations* (London: Macmillan).
F	Charlton Hinman (ed.) (1996) *The First Folio of Shakespeare: The Norton Facsimile*, 2nd edn (New York: Norton).
Iliad	Homer (2003) *The Iliad*, trans. E. V. Rieu, rev. Peter Jones and D. C. H. Rieu (London: Penguin).
Inferno	Robert M. Durling (ed. and trans.) (1996) *Inferno*, vol. 1, *The Divine Comedy of Dante Alighieri*, 3 vols (Oxford: Oxford University Press).
KJV	Gordon Campbell (ed.) (2010) The Holy Bible: Quartercentenary Edition, an exact reprint in Roman type, page for page and line for line, of the King James Version (1611) (Oxford: Oxford University Press).

L&S	Charlton T. Lewis and Charles Short (1879) *A Latin Dictionary* (Oxford: Clarendon Press).
LB1	William Wordsworth and Samuel Taylor Coleridge (2002) *Lyrical Ballads (1798)* (Otley: Woodstock).
LB2	William Wordsworth (1997) *Lyrical Ballads (1800)* (Poole: Woodstock).
M	W. B. Yeats (1959) *Mythologies* (London: Macmillan).
NA	Wallace Stevens (1960) *The Necessary Angel: Essays on Reality and the Imagination* (London: Faber and Faber).
Odyssey	Homer (2003) *The Odyssey*, trans. E. V. Rieu, rev. D. C. H. Rieu (London: Penguin).
OED	http://www.oed.com (accessed 5 February 2011) *Oxford English Dictionary* (Oxford: Oxford University Press).
OP	Wallace Stevens (1990) *Opus Posthumous*, ed. Milton J. Bates, 2nd edn (London: Faber and Faber).
Paradiso	Robert M. Durling (ed. and trans.) (2011) *Paradiso*, vol. 3, *The Divine Comedy of Dante Alighieri*, 3 vols (Oxford: Oxford University Press).
PL	John Milton (1674) *Paradise Lost*, 2nd edn (London: Printed by S. Simmon) in Harris Francis Fletcher (ed.) (1943–8) *John Milton's Complete Poetical Works in Photographic Facsimile*, 4 vols (Urbana: University of Illinois Press).
Purgatorio	Robert M. Durling (ed. and trans.) (2003) *Purgatorio*, vol. 2, *The Divine Comedy of Dante Alighieri*, 3 vols (Oxford: Oxford University Press).
Q 1600	William Shakespeare (1880) *Shakespeare's Midsummer Night's Dream. The First Quarto, 1600: a fac-simile in photo-lithography* (London: Griggs).
Q 1604	William Shakespeare (1964) *Shakespeare's Hamlet: the Second Quarto. Reproduced in facsimile from the copy in the Huntingdon Library*, special edn (San Marino: Western Federal Savings).
Q 1609	William Shakespeare (1926) *Shake-speares Sonnets. Never before Imprinted (1609)* (London: Noel Douglas).
SCP	Wallace Stevens (1954) *The Collected Poems of Wallace Stevens* (New York: Knopf).

SL	Holly Stevens (ed.) (1996) *Letters of Wallace Stevens* (London: Faber and Faber).
U	Shree Purohit Swāmi and W. B. Yeats (trans) (1937) *The Ten Principal Upanishads* (London: Faber and Faber).
VA	George Mills Harper and Walter Kelly Hood (eds) (1978) *A Critical Edition of Yeats's A Vision (1925)* (London: Macmillan).
VB	W. B. Yeats (1962) *A Vision*, 2nd edn (London: Macmillan).
Virgil	Virgil (1999) *Eclogues, Georgics, Aeneid*, trans. H. R. Fairclough, rev. G. P. Gould, 2 vols (Cambridge: Harvard University Press).
VP	Peter Allt and Russell K. Alspach (eds) (1956) *The Variorum Edition of the Poems of W. B. Yeats* (London: Macmillan).
YCP	W. B. Yeats (1950) *The Collected Poems of W. B. Yeats*, 2nd edn (London: Macmillan).
YL	Allan Wade (ed.) (1954) *The Letters of W. B. Yeats* (London: Rupert Hart-Davis).
YPl	W. B. Yeats (2001) *The Plays*, ed. David R. Clark and Rosalind E. Clark (Basingstoke: Palgrave Macmillan).
1645	John Milton (1970) *Poems (1645). Lycidas (1638)* (Menston: Scolar).
1671	John Milton (1968) *Paradise Regained. Samson Agonistes (1671)* (Menston: Scolar).
1673	John Milton (1673) *Poems &c. upon several occasions* (London: Printed for Tho. Dring, Wing M2161A).
1798	William Wordsworth, *1798 Prelude* in Jonathan Wordsworth (ed.) (1995) *The Prelude: The Four Texts* (London: Penguin).
1799	William Wordsworth, *1799 Prelude* in Jared Curtis (ed.) (2009) *The Poems of William Wordsworth*, 2nd edn, 3 vols (HEB).
1805	William Wordsworth, *1805 Prelude* in Ernest de Selincourt (ed.) (1926) *The Prelude* (Oxford: Oxford University Press).

1807   William Wordsworth (1997) *Poems in two volumes (1807)* (Poole: Woodstock).

1815   William Wordsworth (1989) *Poems (1815)*, 2 vols (Oxford: Woodstock).

1849–50   William Wordsworth (1849–50) *Poetical Works*, 6 vols (London: Edward Moxon).

1850   William Wordsworth (1850) *The Prelude* (London: Edward Moxon).

1895   W. B. Yeats (1895) *Poems* (London: T. Fisher Unwin).

Prologue: 'Of the planet of which they were part'

The last two Romantics

Our world today is a labyrinth: it is time that we found our way out. Among poets of the twentieth century, I take Yeats and Stevens to be our best guides. Their poems remind us, in distinct ways, of an inward covenant written in our hearts. Stevens saw that our unfaithful age had put the gods to flight, but he also felt the need to write, near the end of his life, 'We say God and the imagination are one . . . ' (*SCP*: 524). The gods and God have vanished into the imagination and its literature, and criticism must set about consulting with them. Introducing his work as an old man, Yeats invoked the Upanishads because he would seek, in 'age-long memoried self' (*Au*: 272), the living and the dead, to gain more than the world gives. This deathless spirit, unaffected by fear and to be distinguished from our everyday selves, is revealed in the style of a poem, but it is always within us. The poems explored in this book are each at the end of one kind of time that precedes the beginning in another. By engaging with the forms of these late works that follow different paths back through western literature, we find ourselves on the threshold of tradition that gathers in the future, and from within, as revelation.

Nested within broader analyses of Yeats's and Stevens's later works, the central chapters of this book are concerned with four poems. 'Cuchulain Comforted' and 'The Black Tower' are Yeats's last two poems, dated '*January* 13, 1939' and '*January* 21, 1939', respectively, in the 1950 *Collected Poems*. At the age of seventy-three, he was to die on 28 January. 'Not Ideas about the Thing but the Thing Itself' was composed by Stevens in March 1954 for a special issue of a local literary magazine, published to celebrate his forthcoming seventy-fifth birthday. 'Of Mere Being', written at some point during the following spring or summer, turned out to be the final poem of his life, since he died on 2 August 1955. The historical circumstances of these poems mean that only one of them, 'Not Ideas', was seen through to publication by its poet. Both poets were dying, whether they knew it or not, as they composed these poems: each writes on the cusp of this world, gathering a lifetime's work in poems that speak of that which is beyond the grave.

In the winter of 1938 and 1939, Yeats was 'in the final phase of his . . . extraordinary creativity' (Brown 1999: 375), composing his last play, *The Death of Cuchulain*, as well as his final poems. By the end of 1938 he had left Ireland for the sake of his health, and he was staying in the aptly named Hôtel Idéal Séjour in Roquebrune-Cap-Martin on the Côte d'Azur, where he was to die, attended by his wife, George, among others. On one of Dorothy Wellesley's early 1939 visits to the hotel, he read to her the prose theme for what became 'Cuchulain Comforted'. On the bitter, brilliant 21 January, when the poet recited his last poem to Wellesley and other assembled guests, he seemed 'as well as we had ever seen him, full of ideas about his theories of words for songs'; he asked Hilda Matheson to write a tune for the poem he had read; 'He was wearing his light brown suit, blue shirt and handkerchief. Under the lamp his hair seemed a pale sapphire blue.' A few days later, when Wellesley visited again, 'He was very ill, in fact I saw he was dying, and I saw he knew it' (Wellesley 1964: 194 and 195). But as early as 4 January, Yeats had written to Lady Elizabeth Pelham:

> I know for certain that my time will not be long. . . . It seems to me that I have found what I wanted. When I try to put all into a phrase I say, 'Man can embody truth but he cannot know it.' I must embody it in the completion of my life. The abstract is not life and everywhere draws out its contradictions. You can refute Hegel but not the Saint or the Song of Sixpence . . . (*YL*: 922)

In the autumn of 1954, Stevens's *Collected Poems* was published to coincide with his birthday on 2 October. 'Not Ideas' was chosen by the poet to conclude the volume; it is the last poem of a previously unpublished collection of new poems included at the end, called 'The Rock'. In the spring of 1955, surgery revealed that he was suffering from terminal stomach cancer. Apparently, 'The doctors advised and Holly agreed that it would be best not to tell her father of his condition' (Richardson 1988: 423). 'Of Mere Being' was written either before Stevens was admitted to hospital in April or after he was discharged, when he lived at home on Westerly Terrace for a spell, even venturing back to his office at the

Hartford Accident and Indemnity Company, on a part-time basis for a few days. Afraid that he would encumber his frail wife, Elsie, he spent time at the Avery Heights Convalescent Home, just around the corner from his Hartford home, before he was finally admitted to St Francis Hospital where he was to die. Stevens explained, in a letter to Sister M. Bernetta Quinn on 21 April 1954, the day before he would agree to a collected volume of his poems:

> The office has been rather overwhelming of late and in general there has been a bit too much of everything, too many books to read etc. But suddenly spring begins to look like summer and the space of summer may mean more time, more room. One should have eyes all the way round one's head and read in all directions at once. (*SL*: 828)

This book contemplates Yeats and Stevens as embodying truth in their final years, writing poems that, like the Song of Sixpence, cannot be refuted, and, therefore, must be read 'in all directions at once'. I have chosen to devote chapters to four of their final poems because one should read them as if one has 'eyes all the way round one's head'. Like Stevens, 'I believe in pure explication de texte. This may in fact be my principal form of piety' (*SL*: 793). These poems need room to unfold, making the ostensible concern of an essential part of my study carefully specific. In this book, called *Later Affluence,* about poems that I call 'Songs of Sixpence', I hope that I am not short-changing the reader. Is there 'Abundant recompence' (*LB1*: 206) in spending time with a select number of poems? Close and extended attention to a poem permits my scrupulous mode of scrutiny, slowing down our engagements with poetry. I hope that my readers return to Yeats's and Stevens's respective collected works, refreshed to notice new things, in the light of my detailed explications. In order to discern poetic relations, my tight focus adjusts itself, during each extended reading, to afford broader views of Yeats, Stevens and western literature as part of tradition, conceived as the continual renewal of divine revelation in time. The space that I give to each poem distinguishes my methodology from much current criticism. This book is the first to concentrate on Yeats and Stevens together in such detail; while uncovering their different relations to earlier poets, I have time to attend to the way in which the work of tradition is constructed out of the materials of the past. But the works of these two latecomers transform, in turn, the way in which we read their predecessors. I am most concerned to demonstrate, not only how Yeats and Stevens learned from earlier poets, but how they make us see hidden aspects of their poems as revelation.

My style of explication is twofold because I balance close readings with larger surveys. I also see each poem as making twofold sense. If I am at all concerned with these poets as worldly contingencies, with their lives and love affairs, their socio-historical contexts and their politics, it is because of their poems. Dante understood that one cannot reach the heights of anagogy without establishing first a foothold on something of literal substance. But the literal sense, that can take account of a poem's everyday circumstances, so essential for poet and reader, only exists in relation to its threefold spiritual sense. If meaning is not twofold then we are not dealing with a poem. 'A poet writes always of his personal life', admits Yeats, introducing his own work near the end of his life, but 'even when the poet seems most himself . . . he is never the bundle of accident and incoherence that sits down to breakfast; he has been reborn as an idea, something intended, complete' (*E&I*: 509). This fourfold method of interpretation, which I develop in Chapter 3, is of use in understanding the late work of Yeats and Stevens. A reading that takes account of a poem's threefold spiritual sense is always tropological: it seeks to understand a poet 'in terms of his own deepest knowledge', by being 'prepared to learn *from* and not merely *about* . . . his store of deep wisdom' (Raine 1999: 3). Typology illuminates such a store, by making parallels between texts, so that we find anagogy, the secret sense of words, arising from their future in eternity, which turns out to precede and to transform all of the other senses, including the poem's literal meaning, or our worldly premises.

I advocate interpretation that focuses on the poems themselves, because I believe that truly great poems are endlessly fascinating (they are much more interesting than poets) and not to be consumed so easily as some might think on the march of their arguments that often look elsewhere for their substance. In my book, arguments spiral around poems; poems must be put first by giving them time. In his defence of the critical approach pursued in *Mimesis*, Erich Auerbach refers to

> modern philologists who hold that the interpretation of a few passages from *Hamlet*, *Phèdre*, or *Faust* can be made to yield more, and more decisive information about Shakespeare, Racine, or Goethe and their times than would a systematic and chronological treatment of their lives and works.

Along with *Mimesis*, 'the present book may be cited an illustration' (2003: 547–8). But I consider a few poems specifically in relation to other works that need further room for explication. Surveys of late Yeats and late Stevens also point back to their earlier works, and lead to paths that wind around the whole of western literature, bordered by 'the Perennial Philosophy' (Raine 1991: 3).

My tight focus in central chapters turns out to be the magnification of a panoramic view. As we step back for an outlook, we find that each poem literally takes in the vista: it is a unique gathering of tradition at the end as it foresees our future in a hypostatic present. I talk of true time or the arrival of that which has been, not what is past, but 'the gathering of essential being, which precedes all arrival in gathering itself into the shelter of what it was earlier, before the given moment'; 'die Versammlung des Wesenden, die aller Ankunft voraufgeht, indem sie als solche Versammlung sich in ihr je Früheres zurückbirgt' (Heidegger 1971: 176–7; Heidegger 2007: 57). I am writing about that which Heidegger would have considered as a great turning point in destiny: 'The end precedes, namely as the end of the decaying kind, the beginning of the unborn kind'; 'Das Ende geht, nämlich als das Ende des verwesenden Geschlechtes, dem Anbeginn des ungeborenen Geschlechtes vorauf' (adapted from Heidegger 1971: 176; Heidegger 2007: 57). This change, which I explore in Chapter 4 by according Stevens's 'Not Ideas' to the phrasing taken by Heidegger from Georg Trakl, is at once sudden and gradual, and so my style is by turns focused and systematic. Chapters devoted to single poems are complemented by framing chapters that allow larger views by engaging in broader analyses of Yeats's and Stevens's later work. Throughout I relate later developments in both poets to their earlier material.

I see the four poems interpreted in the middle of this book as forming an at once fortuitous and inevitable sequence at the end of a much longer story. After all I do not explicate a few passages chosen at random, and four is a significant number in vision at the end. Although their poets can never have intended these poems to be read together, they seem to me to form a kind of apocalyptic post-or-pre-passion cycle. They are linked because they were all composed at, or near the end of, their poets' lives, and they consequently share, as we shall see, the themes and motifs common to death-bed or near-death poems. But there are still stronger undercurrents pulling them together. While both Yeats and Stevens were 'looking back a little enviously to the uncomplicatedness of the Romantic border impulse', they nonetheless made border poetry, obeying, even amid the scepticism, materialism and modernism of the twentieth century, an impulse that 'seems at some level to be more optimistic, implying that the poetic spirit, and not just the poetry, may be transcendent' (Jonathan Wordsworth 1984: 7 and 6); among less capable examples, they are our last two great Romantics[1] and so the poems explored in this book just may be, for now, chronologically speaking, the last notable Romantic poems to have been written.

Stevens half-light-heartedly has us 'hear the poet's prayer' in 'Sailing after Lunch':

> The romantic should be here.
> The romantic should be there.
> It ought to be everywhere.
> But the romantic must never remain,
> Mon Dieu, and must never again return.

> (*SCP*: 120)

'It is the nature of Romanticism', acknowledges Jonathan Wordsworth, 'that its promptings are distinct, individual, at odds with the standards of the day' (1991: 1), especially if those standards are first of all a debased mode of Romanticism, and then an even more debased generational reaction against that, as during the lifetimes of Yeats and Stevens. Since their deaths, no such poet has been published. My book is designed to show just how at odds with the standards of their day were Yeats and Stevens; both end up making 'antiquated romantic stuff' (*YPl*: 545) that has a shocking freshness; the poets writing after them have remained too current, 'sharing to a large extent the values and assumptions of their audience' (Jonathan Wordsworth 1991: 1), to be of any consequence. My selection of works is therefore polemical. Indirectly, I am also asking whether anything of the canon has been written since. Do these poems mark the end of a certain way of writing that 'must never again return'? And the beginning of another yet to come?

Reading Yeats, Seamus Heaney says, we have a

> sense of confronting a prepared position, of coming up against an opus that is disposed with almost military forethought to take the force of posterity's hordes, its poet spies and intellectual guerrillas, that is one of the greatest consolations of Yeats's *Collected Poems*.

Stevens's poems, on the other hand, share 'the deliquescent ease' Heaney sees 'that Robert Frost knew as a poem came slipping free "like a piece of ice on a hot stove"' (1984). The poems by Stevens that I explore in this book have a different relation to being than the poems by Yeats. But the relationship that each poet establishes within language is equally valid. As prepared as Yeats's position seems to posterity's hordes, the symbolism takes over from the poet in each of his poems, and his wilful attention to form allows Yeats to lose his ordinary sense of self, to find himself again in 'age-long memoried self'; as each poem by Stevens slips upon its human meaning, he is always there to catch us, as we eavesdrop upon its 'inhuman meditation' (*SCP*: 521). Both poets are attentive to 'the more than human "It" (*das "Es"*) which speaks whenever man speaks' (Caputo 1987: 290): in different ways, both understand, and often write about, '*Negative Capability*' (Keats 2002: 41) that is required for the careful disposing of words; both are 'awake and asleep', at the 'moment of revelation, self-possessed in self-surrender' (*E&I*: 524).

The later poems of Yeats and Stevens demonstrate both their differences and similarities in technique. Yeats's poetry inhabits a massive variety of old verse forms, which is a mode of allusion, and he writes, as he says, to 'the dance music of the ages' (Wellesley 1964: 114). Without his rigorous attention to form, his poems would not have their spiritual capability. In a sense the struggle between meaning and form is the subject of Yeats's work: the hypostatic relation that is man; the fact that God is in man. Stevens finds this theme at the end too, but by inventing form. He eschews rhyme and finds peculiar rhythms in loose lines. Much of his later work after *Notes toward a Supreme Fiction* (1942) is arranged in unrhymed tercets, although there is a greater diversity of form in his earlier and very late material.

Yeats's 'Cuchulain Comforted' is written as an iambic pentameter adaptation of the *terza rima* form invented by Dante, and 'The Black Tower' is a style of ballad: it is a song with six line verses made up of a basically iambic, perfect tetrameter quatrain and rhyming couplet, and a metrically varied, imperfect tetrameter quatrain chorus; a version of a form that has been 'sung by the roadside' (*M*: 139) for generations upon generations. Stevens's 'Not Ideas' and 'Of Mere Being' are six and four stanza poems, respectively; their tercets, of unrhymed, rhythmically loose, trimeters, tetrameters and, occasionally, pentameters, have no precedent in folk art or literature, unless you try to relate them to *terza rima*, which I see as a tenuous connection without the concatenating rhyme and longer line.

We do not know if Yeats ever read Stevens, there is no indication that he did, certainly he did not include him in his *Oxford Book of Modern Verse*, although he had 'confined' his selections there 'to those American poets who by subject, or by long residence in Europe, seem to English readers a part of their own literature' (Yeats 1936: xlii); Stevens rarely mentions Yeats in his letters, his only major allusion in his poetry being quotations from 'The Lake Isle of Innisfree' in 'Page from a Tale' (see *YCP*: 44 and *SCP*: 421–3). But Stevens could have just as easily have said, as

Yeats does, 'I must seek, not as Wordsworth thought, words in common use, but a powerful and passionate syntax' (*E&I*: 521–2). Enjambment and caesuras are used to great effect by both poets as their sometimes complex but always vigorous sentences run on through lines and stanzas. Both poets understood too that 'all that is personal soon rots; it must be packed in ice or salt', the method of preservation varying in each case. I sometimes wonder when reading Stevens whether he comes close to Yeats's description of 'The translators of the Bible, Sir Thomas Browne, certain translators from the Greek when translators still bothered about rhythm', who 'created a form midway between prose and verse that seems natural to impersonal meditation' (*E&I*: 522). Yeats, on the other hand, has been 'cast up out of the whale's belly', he still remembers 'the sound and sway that came from beyond its ribs, and, like the Queen in Paul Fort's ballad, I smell of the fish of the sea'. Yeats is on the side of traditional songs and dances, his poetry is rooted in the soil of folk art. But I would argue, 'What moves' both Yeats and Stevens, and their hearers, 'is a vivid speech that has no laws except that it must not exorcise the ghostly voice' (*E&I*: 524).

Later affluence

It is fascinating to bring Stevens and Yeats together as two gate-keepers of the past because, although they are 'of kind the same' (*PL*, v. 490), in detail they differ in degree. Since neither poet seemed especially important to the other, their unity of insight fostered instead by disparate kinds of relations with certain precursors, my study of Yeats and Stevens involves itself with different styles of imitation, allusion and influence. While Yeats's imagination is 'essentially dramatic' (Brown 1999: x), he has written us poems 'Where the symbolic rose can break in flower' (*YCP*: 226). As Kathleen Raine has pointed out, he

> disguises profound metaphysics and essential clues and indications – signposts – in casual allusions – so that they are not apparent to the common reader but immediately illuminating to those who have begun to explore the terrain of the *sophia perennis* on which he draws. (1999: 29)

On occasion, Yeats proclaims his masters. At the end 'that William Blake' (*YCP*: 347) remains as significant a teacher as at the beginning when Yeats joined with Edwin J. Ellis to edit his work in the 1890s. Yeats sets his work in deliberate, and sometimes deliberately hidden, but clueful, relation, to his wide and profound reading of writers from western literature and tradition. Sometimes he will have a character in a poem, like Michael Robartes in 'The Phases of the Moon', dramatically and affectionately mock his mode of reference, while guiding us explicitly to, say, Percy Bysshe Shelley's 'Prince Athanase' or John Milton's 'Il Penseroso'. We will always do well to search out and reread these allusions, as I often do in this book. But Yeats's symbolic mode of writing means that his poems are made to have a life of their own. They will always mean more than the poet intended them to mean, because their symbolism comes from 'age-long memoried self' that is greater than the conscious self that wills the poem's ostensible or literal meaning into being: 'their precision is multiple' (Raine 1986: 89). Yeats's poems are designed to escape their author, however controlled their inception. Taking up the poet's seemingly fanciful clues, we should have several books open, mentally or literally; and his poems' meanings flicker across their thresholds. In Chapter 1, I listen to the ghosts of William Wordsworth and others that come perhaps unbidden to Yeats's poems and it becomes necessary to ask, whose voice is sent through the generations?

Not just fanciful readers of poems often wonder whether or not a poet intended a meaning or an allusion that we understand, and whether or not he was also alert to an echo that we hear. Stevens grumbled to one of his earliest commentators, Bernard Heringman, 'While, of course, I come down from the past, the past is my own and not something marked Coleridge, Wordsworth, etc. I know of no one who has been particularly important to me' (*SL*: 792). Although Stevens makes very few overt references to other poets, to my ears his work generates hidden but creative conversations with Walt Whitman, John Keats, Samuel Taylor Coleridge, Wordsworth, Blake, Milton, William Shakespeare, Prudentius, Virgil and so on. If we can say that Stevens is making allusions, then we must admit that these are submerged. If these submerged allusions are indeed unconscious echoes, then we must consider the nature of such underground influence. Stevens's late poems give themselves over to another mode of coherence in a different way to Yeats. A scheme of influence that still believes in the primacy of cause and effect would say that Stevens's poems do not move from the outside, inside, or from consciousness to the unconscious: they well up from the unconscious to become conscious of themselves; they move from the inside, outside.

Lucy Newlyn admits, 'There are aspects of poetic influence which no amount of source-hunting can adequately explain, and which would appear to support Harold Bloom's claim that "criticism is the art of knowing the hidden roads that go from poem to poem"' (Newlyn 1993: 1;

Bloom 1973: 96). In order to apprehend the oracular substance of a given poem, we must comprehend the auricular paths between poems that are sometimes blocked by their ostensible content: that which we seek tricks us in its 'manifold lurking-places' (Jones 1974: 9). The hidden roads that go from poem to poem may be discovered through 'pure explication de texte', but we usually seek to understand imitation, allusion and influence in literature according to the 'causality principle', asserting that 'the connection between cause and effect is a necessary one'. Acknowledging that Yeats and Stevens have made allusions to others with deliberation, and that sometimes they may have been unconsciously influenced by poems they had once read, I also see many of the correspondences between poets traced in this book according to a literary version of the 'synchronicity principle', which 'asserts that the terms of a meaningful coincidence are connected by *simultaneity* and *meaning*'. C. G. Jung argues that 'besides the connection between cause and effect there is another factor in nature which expresses itself in the arrangement of events and appears to us as meaning' (1985: 95).

I contend that this other 'factor in nature' is at work too in literature and expresses itself in the arrangement of poems across the generations, appearing to us as meaningful affluence, or an abundance of poems that gathers toward 'a Moment' (Blake, *Milton*, plate 35: 283) of our apprehension. Such affluence is a 'wave' that does not leave its original site behind, 'in its rise' causing, if that is the right word, 'all the movement of Saying to flow back to its ever more hidden source' (Heidegger 1971: 160), a site that is within 'the Human Imagination' (Blake, *Jerusalem*, plate 5: 302), 'gone over' (Psalm 42. 7) the distances of everyday selfhoods. This site should be understood with regard to time; it is 'a Moment' in our engagement with a text that 'renovates every Moment' of that text and others 'if rightly placed' (Blake, *Milton*, plate 35: 283). When poems correspond it is often the case that their poets are corresponding with this other 'factor' or 'ever more hidden source', which disrupts causality: 'Deepe calleth unto deepe at the noyse of thy water-spouts: all thy waves, and thy billowes are gone over me' (Psalm 42. 7).

One of the themes of this book is that interpretation can, knowingly and unknowingly, become all too easily entrenched in Aristotelian teaching to do justice to the poems it serves. Peter Struck makes a distinction between two kinds of criticism in the ancient world: 'analytical' criticism 'that is primarily dedicated to locating and mastering various classifications and characteristics of poetry, considered as *techne* with unique rules and specifications'; and 'interpretive' criticism 'that sees the text primarily as a repository of hidden wisdom and envisions its task as the extraction of these meanings'. Struck sees 'an analogue here . . . to the relationship between modern formalist criticisms and those approaches based on hermeneutics' (2004: 3). I would agree, to a degree: the old division remains but Aristotelian criticism has become pre-eminent, even determining our interpretive criticism, despite the contentions of contemporary theory.

The Aristotelian approach to the text of a poem assumes, as its premise, causality, and it relies on categories of discourse; reasonably, it will not apprehend the synchronicity and symbolism of secret wisdom. In this book I develop a mode of criticism in which interpretation transmutes analysis; that which is divined from a text changes our apprehension of its form. 'Whereas the rhetorical [or analytical] approach shares tools and assumptions in common with oratory . . . the allegorical [or interpretive] approach shares conceptual tools with other well-attested fields of interpretive inquiry in the ancient world, including divination, magic, religious rite, and certain traditions of esoteric philosophy.' An ancient allegorist, like a Romantic of our modern era, would have viewed the poet as 'a kind of prophet' (Struck 2004: 4). In order to do justice to the work of Yeats and Stevens, we must treat their work as prophecy and open our explications to fields of interpretive inquiry excluded from current trends of criticism. We must learn to read in all directions at once.

Newlyn opens her foreword to a recent collection of essays on Romantic influence by asking, 'Do poems refer to the world, to each other, or to their authors?' (2006: vii). A Romantic poet would have asked, where is God or the 'secret Strength of things'? (Shelley 1967: 535). Where is that which would make Newlyn's unholy trinity whole again? Surely poems are also 'exalted by an underpresence, | The sense of God, or whatsoe'er is dim | Or vast in its own being' (*1805*, xiii. 71–3)? If we are to love one another, and poetic imitation, allusions and influence are, I would argue, a kind of love, we must know and feel what love is through loving what is unfathomable and mysterious. I would qualify Newlyn's question by admitting with Yeats:

> I know now that revelation is from the self, but from that age-long memoried self, that shapes the elaborate shell of the mollusc and the child in the womb, that teaches the birds to make their nest; and that genius is a crisis that joins that buried self for certain moments to our trivial daily mind. (*Au*: 272)

By forgetting that poems are also in relation to the ineffable, modern criticism proves Wordsworth's sad insight that 'The world is too much with us'. In a faithless manner, we are too concerned with ourselves; 'We have given our hearts away' (*1807*: i. 122), overlooking the learning of the imagination: that the soul's 'sweet will is Heaven's will' (*YCP*: 214).

With Yeats and Stevens as guides, my book sets out in part to explore the relation of imitation to allusion and influence. I sometimes wonder if there is a transition from conscious imitation to knowing allusion to unconscious influence as we move from the Renaissance through the decorous eighteenth century to the Romantics. Does a poet's growth mirror this transition of relationships to the past? Looking back, or reading poems together, what is the use of such a classification? Francis Turner Palgrave opens the fourth and final section of *The Golden Treasury* with Blake's 'To the Muses'. I consider the allusions that poets make as such a calling at such a belated beginning, or whenever the 'ancient melody' has ceased. An allusion for a Romantic poet is an invocation, a calling to an older master for an incentive to continue; a looking before to tradition, or the unfolding in time of divine revelation, in order to look after. Unconscious influence, on the other hand, is when the divine calls to a poet through tradition, awakening his verse out of a subject now conjoined with a transcendental or 'age-long memoried self'. For what we sometimes mistake as allusion is in fact symptomatic of a more profound anamnesis when we remember the soul's pre-existent state, prompting us today to apprehend its future in eternity. Such correspondences between poems are inevitably fortuitous. As with tradition it is the theme or the symbol or the 'something far more deeply interfused' (*LB1*: 207) that summons us, gathering voices together, so that we discover affluence.

Although I offer these definitions of allusion and influence, which contradict others that have emerged out of this kind of criticism, I do not believe that classifications help us very much to think about correspondences between poets. No doubt Christopher Ricks is right to say that 'There is a spectrum in these matters, from the diction, or furniture, or topoi, of a particular period or of a particular poet . . . ; through unconscious reminiscence; to allusion, the calling into play of the words or phrases of another writer. A source may not be an allusion. An allusion always predicates a source' (1996: xxv). But Ricks often reveals himself to be an 'analytical' critic of the highest order. Analytical allusion criticism, also practised by Gian Biagio Conte (1986), John Hollander (1981), among others, and neatly summarized by Eleanor Cook (1998), tends to preoccupy itself about the classification of different kinds of borrowings, subdividing echo and finding differences in degrees of allusion. Such critics tend to rely on rhetorical terms for their definitions and classifications, and they tend to view the whole process of one poem relating to another as a highly conscious activity: the poets they consider are, in these analytical critics' opinions, masters of the game of allusion, the rules of which they are in the process of identifying or establishing. Ricks's scrupulous essays on the subject are exemplary: he often deals with allusions made by poets in the contexts of topics, that is, themes or motifs, that can be associated with the process of allusion, such as inheritance and succession, and he also develops a good working definition of allusion in terms of 'the similarity within difference' (2002: 12) apparent in its art.

Harold Bloom, on the other hand, could be described as the first 'interpretive' critic of influence. Like a classical allegorist, he tends to look outside of oratory for ways of exploring the 'labyrinth' (Bloom 1970: 4) of poetic influence, and he tends to see the creation of poetic relations as an unconscious process. Although Bloom organizes *The Anxiety of Influence* according to rhetorical classifications, this hangover from analytical criticism is overshadowed by the book's recourse to Freud, who offers a modern, albeit overly materialist, version of the fields of inquiry from which ancient allegorists picked up their interpretive tools. Michael O'Neill and Newlyn (1993) are two 'post-Bloom' critics who usefully redeem Bloom's inhibiting paradigm of 'a quasi-Freudian struggle between male egos' to find, for example, 'an interplay between indebtedness and individuation' (O'Neill 2007: 15). Intertextuality is a theoretical version of interpretive criticism, but based on materialist premises.

In my opinion, both kinds of allusion and influence criticism are valid, and of course each critic whom I have too neatly classified offers much more than either category indicates, but they are still at early stages of development. It is important not to become fixated by rhetorical classifications and I consider Freud's and other fashionable and usually materialist theories as dangerous diversions for the practice of literary criticism. My work is an attempt to draw out the spiritual affluence of two twentieth-century poets through close explication de texte and by looking at their work in relation to western literature conceived as part of tradition. I see the relation between unconscious influence and conscious allusion as central to this project, but I am also interested in any reader's uncertainties about these categories. I welcome the possibilities of chance in my readings because I have come to understand that there are relations between poets that have very little to do with cause and effect, the principle that makes us worry about authorial intention.

Ricks warns, 'Coincidence does not lend itself to unmitigated pronouncement. For not only is it the nature of coincidence to resist the schematic, the philosophical, the theoretical, but coincidence with its evidential consideration, is no less resistant to theory's less ambitious sibling, principle' (1998: 4). But I believe Ricks's reticence, as well as his peculiar meticulousness, to be caused by his love of T. S. Eliot, his favourite poet of the twentieth century, whose scrupulous but descriptive poetry is 'Formd by the Daughters of Memory'. My masters, Yeats and Stevens (both largely ignored by Ricks in his criticism), both write 'Surrounded by the daughters of Inspiration' (Erdman: 554). Under the tutelage of these poets it is necessary for me to address that which resists theory and principle, and I do so with the aid of Augustine's meditations on time (in my epilogue), by considering that which Heidegger calls 'the site of the unspoken statement' (Heidegger 1971: 161) of poetry (especially in Chapter 2), with recourse to Chinese thinking (in Chapters 1 and 5), and by adapting and exploring throughout Jung's investigation of the phenomenon of synchronicity. My acceptance of acausal, that is, meaningful but chanceful, relations between poets predicates my belief in the 'secret Strength of things' or 'age-long memoried self'.

Raine argues:

> Irreconcilable with atheist humanism is the teaching that the soul is immortal; has existed before birth, and will continue after death. Virtually all the great works of human intellect and imagination prior to Whitehead's 'provincial centuries' have rested upon the knowledge of immortality. It must be obvious that the entire self-awareness of human beings must be different not only in certain respects and in certain situations, but in all respects and in every situation, according to whether the atheist or the traditional belief is held. And so also it must be with our ability to respond to every art in which mankind has expressed his natural and supernatural intuitions and aspirations. (1974: 11)

Stevens said, teasingly and half in dismay, that 'the soul no longer exists' (*NA*: 4), but his poems understand the necessity of 'a Supreme Fiction' (*SCP*: 380) for mankind and art. Yeats spent his whole adult life investigating and learning from the supernatural. I contend that both Yeats and Stevens would have advocated, especially by the ends of their lives, a traditional method of interpretation of their work that rests 'upon the knowledge of immortality'. In this book, therefore, the traditional belief is held. The poems that we are dealing with here are generated out of a twentieth-century dialectic, an argument between atheism and traditional belief, but both Yeats and Stevens emerge from our 'provincial centuries', having questioned traditional sanctity, all the more ready to teach us that the soul is immortal. I have found that their poems are endlessly fascinating and available for startling interpretation when I accept such teaching. If their poems have any intention it is to make us question scepticism itself and intentionality so that we may discover who we are. When I began reading these two poets I did not consciously hold the traditional belief, or even understand the distinction between prophetic knowledge of immortality and atheist materialism, but I have come to recognize that I and my culture have rejected our 'natural and supernatural intuitions and aspirations' at our own peril; nonetheless 'they come back to us with a certain alienated majesty' (Emerson 1883–4: ii. 48). This book is in some respects the record of my realization that each of its poets was fulfilling an ancient function in educating a modern ephebe.

Just what has this modern ephebe learnt? I have been prompted by both Yeats and Stevens to read ancient texts from distant cultures, now widely available in numerous translations, but difficult to obtain when some of them were first translated into English in the late eighteenth and nineteenth centuries, and to be found usually in Watkins Books in London or through agents during Yeats's and Stevens's lifetimes. As foreign as those books appear to me with my essentially Aristotelian training in a decayed Christian culture, I find that their insights are already within us, our religion, and English literature if its works are 'rightly placed'. As sceptical as my habits of mind are, I have come to understand that scepticism as a historical phenomenon, and I find myself acknowledging an undercurrent of perennial wisdom that flows through the generations. Beginning with this earth and its human counterpart, this body, then moving through water (human seed), fire (speech), wind (breath), sun (the eye), quarters (the ear), moon (the mind), lightning (the light of the body), thunder (the voice), air (the hollow of the heart), law (the law in the body), truth (the truth in man), and mankind (a man), a mantra in the Brihadāranyaka-Upanishad ends with Self:

Self is the honey of all beings; all beings the honey of Self. The bright eternal Self that is everywhere, the bright eternal Self that lives in a man, are one and the same; that is immortality, that is Spirit, that is all.

This Self is the Lord of all beings; as all spokes are knit together in the hub, all things, all gods, all men, all lives, all bodies, are knit together in that Self. (*U*: 135)

Any demonstration of the Self at work in tradition is inevitably syncretic; the very image of spokes and a hub that is used for us to discover Self allows my turning to Lao-tsu:

> We put thirty spokes together and call it a wheel;
> But it is on the space where there is nothing that the usefulness of the wheel depends.
> We turn clay to make a vessel;
> But it is on the space where there is nothing that the usefulness of the vessel depends.
> We pierce doors and windows to make a house;
> And it is on these spaces where there is nothing that the usefulness of the house depends.
> Therefore just as we take advantage of what is, we should recognize the usefulness of what is not. (Waley 1934: 155)

Jung comments, '"Nothing" is evidently "meaning" or "purpose," and it is only called Nothing because it does not manifest itself in the world of the senses, but is only its organizer' (1985: 97–8): 'The relation between meaning (Tao) and reality cannot be conceived, either, under the category of cause and effect' (Wilhelm 1922: 15, quoted in Jung 1985: 98). Chang Chung-yuan explains:

> The spokes of the wheel . . . indicate particularity. The wheel . . . refer[s] to the unity of multiplicity. When things are differentiated, they are called individual things. When things are united, none of them functions any longer as an individual being. Each becomes a member of the unity. This is the aspect of non-being. (1975: 30)

The hub of the wheel functions like the 'site' of the poet's 'unspoken statement', in this world giving and taking 'meaning' from this world. Meister Eckhart called it 'a strange land, a wilderness'. He recognized that in 'created things', that is, individual, differentiated things,

> there is no truth. But there is something which is above the created being of the soul and which is untouched by any createdness, by any nothingness. . . . It is like the divine nature; in itself it is one and has nothing in common with anything. . . . It is a strange land ['ein ellende'], a wilderness ['ein wüestenunge'], being more nameless than with name, more unknown than known. If you could do away with yourself for a moment ['einen ougenblik'], even for less than a moment,

then you would possess all that this possesses in itself. But as long as you have any regard for yourself in any way or for anything, then you will not know what God is. As my mouth knows what colour is and my eye what taste is: that is how little you will know what God is ['als mîn munt weiz, waz varwe ist, und als mîn ouge weiz, waz smak ist: als wênic weist dû und ist dir bekant, waz got ist']. (Eckhart 1994: 121–2; Eckhart 1993: i. 322)

Eckhart's mind is also syncretic, for he continues his sermon by saying, 'Now at this point we hear Plato, the great priest ['der grôze pfaffe'], speaking to us of great things [von grôzen dingen']. He speaks of a purity ['einer lûterkeit'] which is not in the world' (Eckhart 1994: 122; Eckhart 1993: i. 322). This current of perennial wisdom is, according to Thomas Taylor, 'coeval with the universe itself' (1969: 345), and it emerges in the west, after Plato and the 'Middle Platonism' of Apuleius, the Gospel of John, and the Epistles of Paul, with Plotinus. His work sustains Augustine and Boethius, the Proclian Pseudo-Dionysius, and Arabs such as Alfarabi and Avicenna. Different strains of Neoplatonism inspired the great early Gothic cathedrals, influenced even Aquinas, and underpin Dante's work (see *Paradiso*: 741–9). We see such thinking flourish in the fifteenth century in the work of Marsilio Ficino and the Florentine school. Michelangelo's work is its supreme expression in his generation. It is evident too in English literature of the early modern period. In *A Midsummer-Night's Dream*, Bottom awakes from a vision of non-being, a dream of the hub of the wheel:

I have had a most rare vision. I had a dreame, past the wit of man, to say, what dreame it was. Man is but an Asse, if he goe about to expound this dreame. Me-thought I was, there is no man can tell what. Me-thought I was, and me-thought I had. But man is but a patch'd foole, if he will offer to say, what me-thought I had. The eye of man hath not heard, the eare of man hath not seen, mans hand is not able to taste, his tongue to conceive, nor his heart to report, what my dreame was. I will get *Peter Quince* to write a ballet of this dreame, it shall be called *Bottomes Dreame*, because it hath no bottome; and I will sing it in the latter end of a play, before the Duke. Peradventure, to make it the more gracious, I shall sing it at her death. (*F*; IV. i. 210–28)

Shakespeare's comical use of 1 Corinthians 2. 9–10 did not lay him open to charges of heresy as Eckhart's mysticism had led to official questioning a few hundred years before. But both deny synaesthesia by alluding to Paul in order to declare how little we know God, newly and audaciously named '*Bottomes Dreame*', if we remain preoccupied by our everyday selves. The comic confusion of Bottom's misremembering of the vision registers our age's tragic passage into its 'provincial centuries' of scientific materialism. In *King Lear* the discrepancy between perennial wisdom and the contemporary world is more marked and desperate; King Lear unable to accept 'nothing' as he gives away everything, although there is just time enough for him to come to some self-knowledge during the play. The current of perennial wisdom was still near the surface of English culture in the seventeenth century, and is especially evident in the work of John Donne, Milton, Henry Vaughan and Thomas Traherne. Run underground in the eighteenth century, it rises in the work of the Romantics in the late eighteenth and nineteenth centuries, and in Stevens and Yeats in the twentieth century.

My listing of writers, artists and thinkers provides historical evidence for this perennial wisdom. In our sceptical age we also need philosophical or ontological evidence. How could anyone possibly object to the passages of ancient wisdom that I have quoted? Catherine Belsey complains:

> Subjectivity . . . is linguistically and discursively constructed and displaced across the range of discourses in which the concrete individual participates. It follows from Saussure's theory of language as a system of differences that the world is intelligible only in discourse: there is no unmediated experience, no access to the raw reality of self and others. (1985: 380–1)

Belsey refuses to know any other self than the everyday self that 'sits down to breakfast' (*E&I:* 509) with others and her understanding of a text is also confined:

> The unconscious of the work (*not*, it must be insisted, of the author) is constructed in the moment of its entry into literary form, in the gap between the ideological project and the specifically literary form. Thus the text is no more a transcendent unity than the human subject. (1985: 387)

The modern western mind, whether it believes in the fiction of its own subjectivity, surrounded by objects, or operates within Belsey's horrifying 'concrete individual', displaced across her discourses, across our modern concrete cities, has difficulty with tradition's unfolding of the acausal relation between nothing and existence. The changing, but always acausal, relation between this perennial wisdom and the worldly discourses of the different ages, in which it also must become manifest, typifies the relation itself that tradition appreciates between non-being and beings. Tradition already comprehends fashionable, modern and materialist theories because it knows Self, which they ignore or seek to deny. In earlier ages in the west, Christianity provided a contemporary framework to which perennial wisdom could be fitted. Our culture was then more hub-like than today. This tradition 'continued to be, both outside and within Christianity, the mainstream of European civilization until superseded by the modern scientific school' (Raine 1991: 3). With the onset of our sceptical age, our materialist culture began to contradict or to ignore this perennial wisdom, forcing it underground to flow unheeded. Western minds have become increasingly particular, or spoke-like, and as they spin they deny or ignore the existence of their hub. During four centuries of rapid multiplication, we have become more ingenious in describing our ignorance.

The recent phenomenon of literary theory foregrounded ideology and language to understand how the subject is constructed by society. But self-knowledge that is merely based on social factors can only be limited knowledge of the conscious ego. If we are to confront the very pressing problems that our world faces today each man must first come to know his profounder self; he must learn to consult his divine imagination with intellectual love. The world's problems and divine solutions are already within each of us and it is our responsibility first of all to address them there. As Wordsworth understood:

> Here must thou be, O Man!
> Strength to thyself; no Helper hast thou here;
> Here keepest thou thy individual state:
> No other can divide with thee this work,
> No secondary hand can intervene
> To fashion this ability; 'tis thine,
> The prime and vital principle is thine
> In the recesses of thy nature, far
> From any reach of outward fellowship,
> Else is not thine at all.

(1805, xiii. 188–97)

Wordsworth is not advocating solipsism because in this 'work' each loses an everyday self to discover that greater Self, 'Ever expanding in the Bosom of God, the Human Imagination' (Blake, *Jerusalem*, plate 5: 302). In a dark age, Yeats consoled himself by giving thought to the slow-moving gyres of history. It is possible that our age is at an end that precedes a beginning; it is certainly the case for every man and woman alive. If we become industrious, as Blake, Wordsworth, Yeats and Stevens each set about his work, our multiplicity at the end of the decaying kind precedes a vision of nothingness or meaning that is the beginning of the unborn kind. Each of us has a responsibility to make our soul. When each man knows himself, 'far | From any reach of outward fellowship', he discovers a greater unity: he understands that Self to be 'within us and abroad' (Coleridge 2001: i. 233); he comes to know himself in the world from the inside out, rather than in the limited terms of the world, which will always provide us, sooner or later, with lonelier circumstances.

King Lear is initially appalled that he has 'no Helper' but his eventual acceptance of this state is the beginning of a profounder self-knowledge and acknowledgement of the suffering of other 'Poore naked wretches', (F; *King Lear*, III. iv. 28). Ultimately poets cannot undertake this work for us, but they can prompt each of us to begin to know 'the bright eternal Self that lives in man' by recognizing 'the usefulness of what is not' in this world: both Yeats and Stevens understood such guidance to be the poet's ancient and modern function just as writing poetry helps each to make his soul. The perennial wisdom re-emerged in the work of Yeats and Stevens at the onset of a late phase in an ironic and materialist age, just before some thinkers were about to foreground language as something with an ideological function, intent to know primarily their diffuse social selves. This atmosphere, a still prevailing materialism that keeps generating new theories, might appear at first inhospitable to tradition and poetry; it turns out to have much to teach us about non-being. The initial chapters in this book focus on irony in Yeats and Stevens because that kind of ingenuity, if lightly disposed by poets with an understanding of tradition, provides a fresh way of apprehending non-being. Language so questioned is readied for possibilities of deliverance.

Wordsworth announced magnificently in his preface to his first collected poems:

> The grand store-house of enthusiastic and meditative Imagination, of poetical, as contradistinguished from human and dramatic Imagination, is the prophetic and lyrical parts of the holy Scriptures, and the works of Milton, to which I cannot forbear to add those of Spenser.

'Of the human and dramatic Imagination the works of Shakespear are an inexhaustible source' (*1815*: i. xxix and xxx), he adds. Blake's *Milton* is composed to transform a seventeenth-century Christian epic into a magically regenerative book. Blake, Wordsworth, Yeats and Stevens would all 'say' that 'God and the imagination are one'. By also understanding that certain English poems are repositories of divine knowledge, Romantic poets have discovered for us, not the cause, but the 'moving soul' (*1805*, xiii. 171) of our literature, something already within us that judges our everyday selves, which are ensnared by our age's relatively recent but overriding belief in causality (see Jung 1985: 96). Romantic poets have elevated forever certain strains of English poetry to tradition, or that which delivers spiritual knowledge, so that poems flow together in 'a Moment' of explication to be consulted, as, say, the Chinese consult the *I Ching*. The late poems of Yeats and Stevens also teach us that the divine is within us and within our literature, and each can unlock the other, if we negotiate the exchange in the right way. Interpretation can gather us today to question a body of work with a soul, a conversation animated by supernatural beings we thought we had dismissed from our modern world. Such conversation readies each of us to confront without any more help the hidden recesses of our nature, so that we may return to a more integrated way of being in the world and of reading our literature. The activity of 'pure explication de texte' that occurs within Stevens's poems, as his work interprets earlier poems in a creative manner, and Yeats's seemingly casual references to writers from tradition and western literature, make of our literature an oracular canon that can be consulted, if we learn how to formulate the questions. Both poets seem haunted by the unbidden ghosts of earlier poets because their work has conjoined them with that buried self, the 'Divine Humanity' (Raine 1991: 94). Their chanceful correspondences with other poets prove that each man must discover for himself that which he shares with others.

I think, in general, the modern critic would do well to learn from Yeats's style of interpretation in his essays. Criticism that is concerned with the historical context of a poem is valid and useful, but it is a method of only single vision; it deals merely with literal, contingent, accidental sense. A poem is a twofold thing, and criticism must remember the threefold, intended, complete, spiritual sense of works of literature. In an early essay, 'The Philosophy of Shelley's Poetry', Yeats steps back from his discussion, of the difference between the symbols of cave with river and tower, to reflect on symbolic poetry:

It is only by ancient symbols, by symbols that have numberless meanings besides the one or two the writer lays an emphasis upon, or the half-score he knows of, that any highly subjective art can escape from the barrenness and shallowness of a too conscious arrangement, into the abundance and depth of Nature. The poet of essences and pure ideas must seek in the half-lights that glimmer from symbol to symbol as if to the ends of the earth, all that the epic and dramatic poet finds of mystery and shadow in the accidental circumstances of life. (*E&I*: 87)

My reading of Stevens's poems will question Yeats's assertion that it is only by symbols that a subjective art can escape into the 'depth of Nature'. I will argue that criticism can discover abundance also in Stevens's 'pure explication de texte' without symbolism, which occurs within his poems. But my book does itself have a presiding twofold symbol: the cave with a tree on top and water welling within, which is an inversion of the riverside tower struck by lightning. Since my work is concerned with echoes, a term that might cover unconscious influence and intentional allusion, I suggest that a poem is a cave with two mouths and waters flowing through it, like the cave of the nymphs in Book XIII of *The Odyssey* that so delighted the ancient allegorist Porphyry:

> and at the head of the harbor is a slender-leaved olive
> and near by it a lovely and murky cave
> sacred to the nymphs called Naiads.
> Within are kraters and amphoras
> of stone, where bees lay up stores of honey.
> Inside, too, are massive stone looms and there the nymphs
> weave sea-purple cloth, a wonder to see.
> The water flows unceasingly. The cave has two gates,
> the one from the north, a path for men to descend,
> while the other, toward the south, is divine. Men do not
> enter by this one, but it is rather a path for immortals.

> (xiii. 102–12, in Porphyry 1983: 21)

Odysseus has just been returned to the shore of Ithaca and, when he wakes up, he leaves his goods of gold, bronze and fabric, acquired from those who bore him there, in this cave. A poem is full of treasure; more importantly, it allows for communication between mortals and immortals: as Yeats says of genius, it is a conjoining of 'that buried self for certain moments to our trivial daily mind'. As long as we inhabit poems they, in turn, inhabit us and, in Byron's words, 'thought seeks refuge in lone caves'

(2000: 105). This book is concerned with the different ways in which the later poems of Yeats and Stevens allow for such communication, as their poets at once fill and empty the cave; it discovers different kinds of affluence: material treasure and spiritual influence that 'flows unceasingly' in 'bounty . . . as boundlesse as the Sea' (*F*; *Romeo and Juliet*, II. ii. 133).

By considering Yeats's later poems, I take up the subject of the perennial symbolic language that he shares and deepens with Blake and Shelley and their emblematic poetry. As Raine says, in her essay 'Yeats's Debt to Blake':

> Such symbols are not less exact for being unspecific: their precision is multiple. . . . Such questions as whether Blake (or Yeats, for that matter) learned the symbol of the world-cave from Plato or from Porphyry . . . are not of an importance comparable with the great question (which no textual source-hunting will answer): is the poet speaking the symbolic language of tradition, or is he not? (1986: 89)

Her question echoes throughout my book as I measure against each other different modes of allusion and influence and wonder about acausal affluence. The cave in Homer that Porphyry interprets can be considered in relation to Yeats's central symbol of his tower on a river; we can think of the two symbols together in terms of Dante's descent through the circles of Hell and his subsequent ascent around the mountain of Purgatory, or Yeats's interlocking gyres as outlined in *A Vision*. Yeats would have been aware of the relationship: in 'Coole Park and Ballylee, 1931', he meditates on the river that runs under his tower with its winding stair, and drops to 'Run underground' (*YCP*: 275). Both symbols and their relationship are endlessly fascinating in their multiple precision; conjoining by contrasting art and nature, consciousness and unconsciousness, or even Heidegger's 'world' and 'earth' (see Heidegger 2002: 26), they work in the same manner as Yeats who constructed sturdy, realistic looking, poems above hidden currents of tradition. They can also be made to represent the relation between Yeats and Stevens.

If Yeats constructs towers in his poems, from which he can meditate upon underground currents, Stevens's late poems seem to open out of the same region as the cave, as if they are created by an 'Art | That Nature makes' (*F*; *The Winter's Tale*, IV. iv. 91–2). Stevens and Yeats reveal the same circumstances from different directions. Other poets are not hidden in Stevens like a store of reminders, inorganically, in the manner that Odysseus stowed the Phaeacians' gifts in the cave. Organically, each of Stevens's poems seems to grow out of the ground of other poems, putting out roots into English literature to find the hidden waters of tradition, like 'The palm at the end of the mind' (*OP*: 141) or the slender-leaved olive tree near the cave on the shore of Ithaca. I have argued elsewhere that Stevens's poems remember, they help the poet remember, and remind others to respond, by fructifying in the future (see Clarke 2006: 31). I used to emphasize that, in Stevens's poems, others' poems are remarkable makings as, for Wordsworth, 'the earth | And common face of Nature spake to me | Remarkable things' (*1805*, i. 614–16), seeking to distinguish such things from other memorials such as wreaths, epitaphs or precious gifts. I still believe that Stevens's poems vivify the souls of poets who have followed the same track before, as his poems recollect theirs, allowing them to respond from beyond the grave. Certainly his poems also renovate the soul of any after-reader, still following the same track of growing older, while watching the tender growth of his reminders. But now I discern another factor, before memory hand in hand with 'Nature', at work gathering others to his poems.

Part of my concern in this book is the dynamic relationship itself between the perennial symbolic language shared by the consciously emblematic poetry of Blake, Shelley and Yeats, and the operation of unconscious influence in the more organic poems of Wordsworth, Keats and Stevens. But my interest in this ambiguous relationship has led me to acknowledge another kind of correspondence between poems, occurring before allusion and influence as they are usually conceived. Today this acausal phenomenon, like wisdom, 'cryeth at the gates, at the entrie of the citie, at the comming in at the doores', since we are not listening very hard for it, but the Lord 'possessed' it, like wisdom or the wilderness of 'non-being' or 'meaning', 'in the beginning of his way, before his works of old'. If we become attentive, it still walks with us and wisdom 'in the midst of the pathes of judgement, That I may cause those that love me, to inherit substance: and I will fill their treasures' (Proverbs 8. 3, 22, and 20–1). The non-substantial substance that love of wisdom causes us to inherit is not effected by causality as we understand that principle ordinarily. We can discover such spiritual affluence, 'gone over' to overwhelm our everyday selves, in the late work of Yeats and Stevens since they do not just remember earlier works: they write 'Surrounded by the daughters of Inspiration who in the aggregate are calld Jerusalem' (Erdman: 554).

Labyrinth and rainbow

Two short poems by Blake and Wordsworth, and lines from the end of the penultimate book of Milton's *Paradise Lost*, delineate an animating difference between Yeats and Stevens. Above the prologue 'To the Christians' of the fourth and final book of his culminating prophecy, *Jerusalem: The Emanation of The Giant Albion*, Blake inserts a discrete four line poem:

> I give you the end of a golden string,
> Only wind it into a ball:
> It will lead you in at Heavens gate,
> Built in Jerusalems wall.

(Blake, *Jerusalem*, plate 77: 374)

Once upon a time Theseus entered the labyrinth. During his fight with the Minotaur, at the centre of Daedalus' dark passages, the end of Ariadne's thread was lost. These four mythological characters are in us all; they are psychological archetypes that correspond to Blake's 'four Zoas': Theseus is Orc, the fiery spirit of energy; the Minotaur is heavy and slothful Tharmas; Daedalus is Urizen, the tyrant reason; and Ariadne is Los, the spirit of inspiration. Such figures also tell the whole of mankind's story: since the beginning of civilization we have progressed further and further into a technological labyrinth of our own making, locked in mortal combat with our materialism, and only inspired art can help us out. Blake uses elemental geometrical symbols, a line that can be wound into a sphere so that a labyrinth becomes a spiral, to focus his message: his verse could be transcribed as a yantra. In just four lines the poet unites 'the general and gregarious advance of intellect' through the generations with 'individual greatness of Mind' (Keats 2002: 90), and he traverses two traditions; from the labyrinth of pagan mythology, he passes into the heavenly city of Christian prophecy, guiding us to an integrated future in eternity. At the same time, his poem is wonderfully uncomplicated and immediately accessible.

Blake describes an inner landscape and he teaches us how to read his work. His most exacting readers trust in him as a guide. Aware of the 'insufficiency' of 'modes of thought and critical criteria that unwove all rainbows that drew me to Blake, whose world was so totally beyond the scope of these measures', Raine 'began to wind Blake's "Golden String" into a ball'. She began to pursue clues in Blake's poems and to read all of the books that he had read, attempting to learn from them as much as she could learn about them: 'The length of that string and its many windings astonished me then; the golden simplicity of the sphere that remains in my hands amazes me now' (1991: 1–2). Yeats also undertook that journey. Like Raine, I believe that interpretation of both Blake and Yeats must begin by trusting in them as guides, otherwise we merely

besiege their poems that become resistant to our attack, as we shall see
Yeats allegorize in 'The Black Tower'.

Both Yeats and Blake are gate-keeper poets. They put us to school, and
once we have begun to follow paths out of today's labyrinth, winding
lines of their poems into a golden ball, we discover a greater freedom
than an immediately antithetical reading of either could have vouchsafed. What seems constraining at first, our following of the poet's
intentions, becomes liberating: both Blake and Yeats open unexpected
modes of understanding and interpretation, as long as we are prepared
to take our first steps hand in hand with them. The symbols and forms
of their poems, as well as the books to which they lead us, teach us to
recognize within ourselves much that our culture has rejected in the last
three hundred years or so. Criticism of either that takes account only of
historical or biographical or even formal circumstances will only make it
so far through the dark passages. Single vision, or literal interpretation,
will soon lose its way, unless it becomes twofold: to find a way through it
must acknowledge the intended threefold spiritual sense that ultimately
takes over the literal sense of the poems of Yeats and Blake. Wordsworth
and Stevens are also gate-keepers. Although less exacting in their expectations of us initially, on our paths of explications of their poems, they
come to present the difficulties of interpretive freedom granted early on.

Wordsworth chose to open his first collected poems, *Poems* (1815),
a book that has, he tells us, 'a beginning, a middle, and an end' (*1815*: i. xiv),
with another superficially simple poem that promises, or at least 'could
wish' for, illumination at the end of a dark time:

> My heart leaps up when I behold
>   A Rainbow in the sky:
> So was it when my life began;
> So is it now I am a Man;
> So be it when I shall grow old,
>   Or let me die!
> The Child is Father of the Man;
> And I could wish my days to be
> Bound each to each by natural piety.

> (*1815*: i. 3)

The last three lines serve as the epigraph to the final poem of that collection, 'Ode. Intimations of Immortality', in which 'The Rainbow comes
and goes' (*1815*: ii. 347), making it, nonetheless, the overarching natural
and imaginative sign of his book, at the end of which, we find Romantic

affluence. The flood has come before. Wordsworth celebrates an atmos-
pheric phenomenon that is 'the token of the Covenant' between God and
man after Noah had left the ark in Genesis (9. 12). His poem claims to be
inspired first of all by nature, but his language comes from 'the grand store-
house of enthusiastic and meditative Imagination': the poem recalls the
'ancient sire' Noah as described in Michael's vision in *Paradise Lost* when

> with uplifted hands, and eyes devout,
> Grateful to Heav'n, over his head beholds
> A dewie Cloud, and in the Cloud a Bow
> Conspicuous with three listed colours gay,
> Betok'ning peace from God, and Cov'nant new.

> (*PL*, xi. 863–7)

The double position that 'The Rainbow' holds in *Poems* 1815 brings
out the doubleness in Wordsworth's allusion to the episode from the
first book of the Bible, which is also the point at which Milton chose to
divide the final book of *Paradise Lost* for its second edition. The later poet
emulates the earlier poet's use of the rainbow to prelude the end of his
work, but he also discovers for us greater sense in his predecessor's work.
Wordsworth's 'behold' at the end of the first line of his poem alludes to
Milton's end word 'beholds'. Noah, beholding, remains mute, under his
'uplifted hands'; Wordsworth, beholding, writes that his 'heart leaps up':
one expression echoes the other; '*hear*t *leap*s *up*' resounds, or sounds in
reverse, '*upli*fted *ha*nds', containing and modifying its sense, as a voluntary exterior movement becomes an involuntary interior pulsation.

The same process is described in the next lines of *Paradise Lost*; Adam
is moved by the vision and speaks to the archangel:

> Whereat the heart of *Adam* erst so sad
> Greatly rejoyc'd, and thus his joy broke forth.
> > O thou who future things canst represent
> As present, Heav'nly instructer, I revive
> At this last sight[.]

> (*PL*, xi. 868–72)

Wordsworth's 'heart' that leaps up comes from 'the heart of *Adam* erst
so sad' that forgot temporarily its newly fallen predicament and 'Greatly
rejoyc'd'; his poem has adopted our first father's register of spontaneous
effusion, his joyous way of speaking words that 'broke forth' from sorrow

like a rainbow from clouds, to celebrate, not a supernatural vision but a natural rainbow: 'I revive | At this last sight' becomes 'I behold | A rainbow'. Wordsworth's large present tense that attempts to represent past and future things in the poem is from Adam's reviving, and marvelling, at the angel's powers of prophecy 'who future things canst represent | As present'. Adam rejoices, not in the rainbow, but:

> For one Man found so perfet and so just,
> That God voutsafes to raise another World
> From him, and all his anger to forget.
>
> (*PL*, xi. 876–8)

The final three lines of 'The Rainbow' sound as if they have been voiced by Adam after he witnessed Michael's vision of Noah who is described by Adam inadvertently as an antetype of Christ. From the future we see that Adam's description is greater than he knows. Wordsworth's poem reworks the three cross-generational steps from Adam to Noah to Christ in order to describe the tripartite life of a man. Now Milton's lines make Wordsworth's lines greater than they seemed at first: Christ, who is God born of a woman, will regain the blissful seat lost by Adam who was created a man by God: 'The Child is Father of the Man'. Noah stands in the middle under the apex of a rainbow that stretches from Adam to Christ. Wordsworth stands at the end of another kind of rainbow that stretches to a future represented as present.

Adam comments on the archangel's vision and Wordsworth's poem is a veiled explication of Milton's lines: it finds meaning out of their position within the poem and the dramatic situation that they conjure, while using some of their words and parts of words. The relationship between Adam, Noah and Christ also parallels to a degree the relationship between Genesis, *Paradise Lost* and *Poems* (1815). Wordsworth's poem grows out of Milton's reworking of *Genesis*, but it transforms, in turn, the way that we read the earlier books: he writes of the inner pulsation that leaps from Milton to the Bible to later readers. I do not believe that Wordsworth made his poem with *Paradise Lost* open at his elbow on the evening of 26 March 1802, as Dorothy 'was getting into bed' (Dorothy Wordsworth 2002: 82), but neither was it composed under an actual rainbow. He draws on his memory of *Paradise Lost*, which has influenced him in the same manner that deep feelings have impressed natural forms on his mind from an early age, to rework an old token for a new way of being in the world, and for his poetry that can help revive us to that state.

If we understand Christ as an emblem of 'the "Divine Human", "Jesus the Imagination"' (Raine 1991: 13), the one that is now in all of us, then another rainbow leaps to the future for us to behold with our inner sense. The speaker of 'The Rainbow', and the speaker of Blake's poem who gives us the end of a golden string, serve as paradigms of this conjoining of every day selves with 'age-long memoried self'. Each poem thus gathers other figures in an eternal present, in the life of a man, considered from a visionary viewpoint. The final lines of the penultimate book in the second edition of *Paradise Lost* incorporate a lyrical part of the first book of the Old Testament and look forward to the final book of the New:

> Day and Night,
> Seed time and Harvest, Heat and hoary Frost
> Shall hold thir course, till fire purge all things new,
> Both Heav'n and Earth, wherein the just shall dwell.

> (*PL*, xi. 898–901)

Milton moves from water to fire when he recalls The Revelation of St John the Divine immediately before what becomes the final book of his poem. At both the beginning and the end of his collection, Wordsworth 'could wish my days to be | Bound each to each by natural piety'; like Adam he feels 'The Link' or 'Bond of Nature draw' him (*PL*, xi. 914 and 956): he writes from within the story begun by Adam. Blake also recalls the final book of the Bible at the beginning of the final book of his culminating prophecy. Like Blake, Wordsworth connects the generations of man with the life of a man. His poem also looks forward at its end to future days by establishing a carefully delineated and complex set of relations with earlier works. In each case we do well to return to the different traditions brought into play; each poem stands alone but they are both possessed of a 'fructifying virtue' (*1799*, i. 290) when we pursue their allusions. Making our way around the labyrinth of one, we step into 'the grand store-house' from which the other also draws. In different ways, both Blake and Wordsworth internalize the apocalypse; they discover a new time of poetry for us which disrupts causality, a condition brought upon man by Adam. Wordsworth establishes a conversation with Milton's reworking of Genesis to step into 'the grand store-house of enthusiastic and meditative Imagination'. Blake shows us a way out of the labyrinth of one tradition to step into the gate of his own radical reading of the Bible.

Yeats's mode of allusion can be conscious, symbolic, Blakean. When we have learned to discern his often disguised allusions to a wide range of authors from western literature and tradition, we follow the covert directions to discover abundance at the ends of the earth. Stevens is more of a Wordsworthian poet but not because he takes from 'the grand store-house' of the imagination in exactly the same manner as Wordsworth. It is tempting to say that Stevens's work draws from wells of unconscious influence that Wordsworth has already dug. Often Stevens himself seems unaware that he is establishing submerged and creative conversations with earlier poets, although he sets out to write poetry that is greater than he knows: he half-fulfils Wordsworth's hopes for his poems that he writes 'for the sake | Of youthful Poets, who among these Hills | Will be my second self when I am gone' (*LB2*: ii. 201). Stevens does unconsciously that which Wordsworth consciously prepared for, and as his work moves between reality and imagination its project, like Blake's, is 'to open the immortal Eyes | Of Man inwards into the Worlds of Thought: into Eternity | Ever expanding in the Bosom of God, the Human Imagination' (Blake, *Jerusalem*, plate 5: 302); Yeats consciously follows Blake's conscious journey into the divine unconscious, but there is a sense that his poems also love this world, and sometimes we hear the ghost of Wordsworth. Both paths of conscious allusion and unconscious influence lead us to the pre-existent and acausal realm of affluence.

In his poems, Yeats is adept at reading prepared prophecy to us, constructing seemingly realistic work upon foundations of ancient symbols. Stevens happens upon prophecy during the composition of a poem, as it slips with deliquescent ease from human meaning, to discover appropriate images in the world around the poet. In many respects it is too neat, but helpful at this stage, to say that Shelley comes between Yeats and Blake; Keats between Wordsworth and Stevens. I must emphasize that to think of Yeats in terms of Blake, and Stevens in terms of Wordsworth, marks just one stage in a much more nuanced argument, and certainly I hear Blake and Shelley in Stevens, and Wordsworth and even Keats in Yeats. The comparisons should be helpful as preliminary sketches but they should not inhibit the larger pictures formed in this book. Both Yeats and Stevens find for us Romantic affluence, as long as we follow them out of our labyrinth. My concern is to trace the different paths that their poems follow as they come from and return to that which Yeats called 'age-long memoried self' and Stevens, 'being' (see *SCP*: 444–5 and *OP*: 141).

Since the time of Blake and Wordsworth, we have been determined to understand a rainbow as an arch of concentric coloured bands formed when sunlight shines through rain droplets in the atmosphere. Yeats and

Stevens, along with Blake and Wordsworth, remind us of promises made in folklore; their poems know the necessity of believing in such things as pots of gold at the ends of rainbows that span the generations. They represent two kinds of prophecy in the modern world. The major difference between their work is the interpretive time that each allows the reader initially. Turning from Stevens, and the freedoms he seems to grant us, to Yeats, can seem like returning to school. But, having trusted in Yeats's intentions at the outset, we find amazing opportunities for interpretation in his poems later on, as we learn his lessons; besides, once we have begun to pursue the multiplicity of meanings in Stevens's poems, we realize that we have set out upon a peculiar and demanding path of explication, and one that had been expected of devoted readers all along. There is no escaping the 'Learning of the Imagination' (Raine 1999: 21) when reading great poets; each teaches us using different methods. I am interested in this book in the relation between Stevens's and Yeats's techniques of guidance. Ultimately both poets have the same lesson for us; what sets them apart from their contemporaries, and makes them Romantic poets, is that they 'chose for theme | Traditional sanctity' (YCP: 276), leading us to 'say' with them that 'God and the imagination are one'.

Yeats's understanding at the completion of his life that 'Man can embody truth but he cannot know it', so that 'You can refute Hegel but not the Saint or the Song of Sixpence', is reiterated by 'Ariel' in Stevens's late poem, 'The Planet on the Table'. Ariel, who sees himself and the sun as one, also understands that it was not important that his poems, as 'makings' of both, should survive:

> What mattered was that they should bear
> Some lineament or character,
>
> Some affluence, if only half-perceived,
> In the poverty of their words,
> Of the planet of which they were part.
>
> (SCP: 532–3)

To the end of his life Stevens remained, like Wordsworth, 'A lover'

> of all the mighty world
> Of eye and ear, both what they half-create,[2]
> And what perceive; well pleased to recognize
> In nature and the language of the sense,

> The anchor of my purest thoughts, the nurse,
> The guide, the guardian of my heart, and soul
> Of all my moral being.

> (*LB1*: 207–8)

Ricks has also noticed that 'In due course, Wallace Stevens was to do some half-creating along Wordsworth's lines' (2002: 116): 'Stevens was glad Wordsworth had written his poem, "Whose dwelling is the light of setting suns". This we can at least half-perceive, here where affluence meets influence, enriching with allusion what might otherwise be a poverty of words' (2002: 117; *LB1*: 207). But is Stevens making an allusion here? Ricks's explication leaves me uncertain about the relation between allusion and influence. Just how conscious was Stevens of Wordsworth's influence? Strangely, Stevens's 'allusion', 'where affluence meets influence', seems to include our uncertainty about his making of an allusion. I have argued elsewhere that Stevens's 'half-perceived' in 'The Planet on the Table' turns about Wordsworth's 'half-create | And what perceive', establishing a relation, which Newlyn believes Wordsworth intended, 'between nature's formative influence over [Wordsworth], and the influence his poetry has on the minds of his readers' (Newlyn 2000: 127; see Clarke 2006: 41). Can Wordsworth really be equating 'nature and the language of the sense' with 'The bright eternal Self that is everywhere, the bright eternal Self that lives in man'? Nature is the expression of that Self on earth. What is the 'planet' of which Ariel's 'makings of the sun' were also 'part'? I hear Blake murmur, 'There is no such Thing as Natural Piety Because The Natural Man is at Enmity with God' (Erdman: 665). This book will argue that the relations between Yeats and Wordsworth and Stevens and Wordsworth transcend the 'natural piety' (*1815*: i. 3 and ii. 346) that Wordsworth intended his poems to stir up unconsciously in future poets.

What is 'the language of the sense'? Language from the sense? Language about the sense? Language spoken by the sense? Or language spoken by what we sense, 'Wakening a sort of thought in sense' (as Shelley believes: see 1967, 'Peter Bell the Third', IV. x. 312: 353)? We bear in mind the matter of the language of the sense. Something written not just 'with inke, but with the spirit of the living God, not in tables of stone, but in fleshy tables of the heart' (2 Corinthians 3. 3). Behind Stevens's 'What mattered was' in 'The Planet on the Table', what matters, what is important, is the Latin obtrusion, *materia*: the building material that can bear, the stuff of which poems are made, the language that is 'vitally metaphorical' because it bears 'the before unapprehended relations of things' (Shelley

2003: 676). Of what is this matter? In philosophical use, matter is in con-
tradistinction to mind or to form, although matter is also subject matter.
Like sense it contains two different meanings.

Like Wordsworth, Yeats and Stevens comprehend the language of the
sense at the end of the decaying kind, but to 'half-create' poems that
apprehend the sense of another matter altogether at the beginning of the
unborn kind. Their poems are 'of the letter' and 'of the spirit' that 'giveth
life' or 'quickneth' (2 Corinthians 3. 6); they magnify the 'vivifying
Virtue' of Wordsworth's 'spots of time' (*1805*, xi. 260 and 258), by helping
us to find and rightly place 'a Moment' in each day that 'renovates every
Moment of the Day' (Blake, *Milton*, plate 35: 283). Their work looks in two
directions, admitting Self, which exists only as it withdraws from our per-
ceptual and phenomenological grasp, to look after the world that comes
before, making of that world a new planet, a 'new heaven' on our 'first
earth' (Revelation 21. 1). 'Some affluence' is when all comes together,
from earth (body) to Self (Self in man): it is the time and place of creative convergence that plays with agency, 'crowd on curious crowd' (*SCP*:
342), making us perceive that which poets half-create out of one kind of
matter, chancefully correspond about another. Ricks sees the 'dwelling' of
'Tintern Abbey' as 'the light of setting suns'; the rising sun can be viewed
as 'a round Disk of fire somewhat like a Guinea' or 'an Innumerable
company of the Heavenly host crying Holy Holy Holy is the Lord God
Almighty' (Erdman: 565–6). What of Yeats's and Stevens's 'makings of
the sun' (*SCP*: 532), their late Songs of Sixpence at the ends of cross-
generational rainbows? We half-perceive, 'In the poverty of their words',
prophecy at the end, pervading all that they gather, as pure being.

This book is designed to be read through to Yeats's and Stevens's very
last poems, but each chapter can also stand alone, and you may even read
the epilogue first, if you would prefer a theoretical emphasis. In Chapter 1,
I trace Yeats's late development from *The Tower*, published in 1928, to
his very last poems. As I range through his later poems, I consider, with
recourse to Kierkegaard, Yeats's uses of irony and mockery, and I detect
the ghostly presence of Wordsworth. The symbols of the tower and the
river become of increasing importance. In Chapter 2, which traces the
late development of Stevens from *Transport to Summer*, published in
1947, to his very last poems, I discover a different kind of irony, with
the help of Heidegger, and another relationship with Wordsworth. We
follow Stevens's rivers as I explore the role that chance has to play when
his work corresponds with earlier poems. Chapter 3 focuses on Yeats's
'Cuchulain Comforted', drawing in his own earlier engagements with
the Cuchulain story, with the help of Maurice Blanchot, and then the

Gospel of John, Apuleius, Dante and Shelley, among others. A theoretical section, 'Now must we sing', at the centre of the book, develops the fourfold method of interpretation, which is of use also in understanding Stevens's late work. Stevens's 'Not Ideas about the Thing but the Thing Itself' is scrutinized in Chapter 4 with reference to *Macbeth*, Milton, Ralph Waldo Emerson and Whitman, at the end of the decaying kind, and Prudentius and Ambrose as contained in *Hamlet* at the beginning of the unborn kind. Stevens's late poem also gathers his own earlier work but in order to apprehend that which Blake called 'Vision'. Yeats's and Stevens's very last poems are the subject of the final chapter. I consider 'The Black Tower' in relation to Dante, Virgil and Homer, among others. 'Of Mere Being' is understood by establishing its different kinds of affinities with Virgil. The epilogue begins with Augustine's meditations on time at the end of his *Confessions* to gather the book's prolonged meditations on the sometimes acausal nature of poetic relations.

1
Yeats from *The Tower* to the Last Poems

Irony in Yeats

Assessing *The Tower* (1928), Terence Brown says that 'power celebrated and exercised in this self-consciously masterful book is in no way immune to an ironic vision' (1999: 316). We shall see an 'ennobling interchange' (*1850*, xiii. 375) between irony and conviction from *The Tower* to Yeats's posthumously published *Last Poems* (1939). His last collections make their way out of this modern dialectic, this conflict of scepticism and belief, which spans from the dramatic or comic irony of Theseus' disbelief in 'anticke' (*F*) or 'antique' (*Q* 1600) 'fables' in *A Midsummer-Night's Dream* (V. i. 3) to Stevens's decision to say 'We say', at once affirming and qualifying a belief that 'God and the imagination are one' (*SCP*: 524). Irony takes on different aspects in later Yeats, as his poems range from dramatized Socratic dissimulation, inducing revelation, to mockery. Brown observes that 'the emotional force' of *The Tower* 'is dependent on a drama in which power is humiliated by decline, decay, disintegration and catastrophe' (1999: 316), and Yeats pulls a kind of irony out of his 'desire to write the body' (1999: 320). But the poet also makes regenerative use of figures of speech in which the intended meaning is the opposite of that expressed by the words used. Yeats understood 'that poets were good liars who never forgot that the Muses were women who liked the embrace of gay warty lads' (Wellesley 1964: 63). Writing in an ironic age, like Kierkegaard, he masters the attitude of irony once it has been pushed to its limits to become 'infinite absolute negativity' (1989: 261). A resource of the self, irony is expended in Yeats's relation to Wordsworth, in 'The spiritual intellect's great work' (*YCP*: 394), when Yeats makes his stanzas or 'incitements to generous self-transcendence' (Heaney 2000: xxv).

At the beginning of 'The Tower', the speaker does not share, but wishes upon himself, the predicament of Coleridge in 'Dejection: an Ode'. Prompted by an old-fashioned prognosis based on a phase of the moon, as well as Wordsworth's 'Ode', Coleridge dwells on his afflictions. They not only 'rob me of my mirth', but suspend 'what nature gave me at my birth':

> My shaping spirit of Imagination.
> For not to think of what I needs must feel,
>   But to be still and patient, all I can;
> And haply by abstruse research to steal
>   From my own nature all the natural Man –
>   This was my sole resource, my only plan:
> Till that which suits a part infects the whole,
> And now is almost grown the habit of my Soul.

>   (2001: i. 700)

Also beset by a catalogue of afflictions, which are no doubt exacerbated by his 'Excited, passionate, fantastical | Imagination', Yeats toys with what had been Coleridge's 'only plan':

> It seems that I must bid the Muse go pack,
> Choose Plato and Plotinus for a friend
> Until imagination, ear and eye,
> Can be content with argument and deal
> In abstract things; or be derided by
> A sort of battered kettle at the heel.

>   (*YCP*: 218–19)

But the collection proves that this is not the poet's 'sole resource'. Yeats is being ironic. He knows that the imagination is not found or given by nature: it is that which he creates. The pretence of only now practising Neoplatonic philosophy is in creative conflict with the derision of physical feebleness, which seems to drive the poet forward, clattering at the heel. Without his 'desire to write the body' and to embrace his fantastical imagination, among all their attendant ironies, Yeats might have come upon merely 'a metaphysical Bustard'; instead he discovers all sorts of poetic 'Game' (Coleridge 1956–71: ii. 814). Another plan unfolds for the 'natural Man' or everyday self. Since he had not died young, like Keats, Shelley or Byron, from the 1920s Yeats was determined not to wither 'into eighty years, honoured and empty-witted' (*M*: 342), like Wordsworth, and he would not commit himself to metaphysics, like Coleridge after his ode of 1802. He will continue himself to 'remake', like 'that William Blake | Who beat upon the wall | Till Truth obeyed his call' (*YCP*: 347). What role does mocking have to play in such remaking? By the end of 'The Tower', the poet declares his 'faith':

> I mock Plotinus' thought
> And cry in Plato's teeth,
> Death and life were not
> Till man made up the whole,
> Made lock, stock and barrel
> Out of his bitter soul,
> Aye, sun and moon and star, all,
> And further add to that
> That, being dead, we rise,
> Dream and so create
> Translunar Paradise.

> (*YCP*: 223)

Both Kierkegaard and Yeats use and come to an understanding of irony as they take issue with Hegel's idea of world-historical progress. Kierkegaard sees that an ironic figure like Socrates is a gift of the gods; he is a turning point in which the existing comes into conflict with the new order. In our own 'turning point in history' (1989: 260), when irony becomes more than mere mockery, but a way of being in the world, the ironist is caught in 'infinite absolute negativity': 'For the ironic subject, the given actuality has lost its validity entirely; it has become for him an imperfect form that is a hindrance everywhere. But on the other hand, he does not possess the new' (1989: 261). The ironic subject is alien to existence, both in its old and new dispensations, and his relation to language is also foregrounded and disturbed. Yeats strives to master irony, using irony, ironically, to do so. Like Blake and Kierkegaard, his work exploits 'fictional strategies of deception' to come upon 'language as a living truth' (Lorraine Clark 1991: 155) because he understands the value of irony as a figure of speech in overcoming an ironic way of being in the world: 'And further add to that | That, being dead, we rise', he commands, repeating 'that', over the line, to provide an ironic step out of irony.

In his own dialogue with Hegel, Yeats also asserts that our age is utterly decrepit, that is, fallen into 'infinite absolute negativity', at the end of the decaying kind. How can we wake up to the beginning of the unborn kind? Braving, by mocking, this modern world, Yeats tells his readers to:

> Mock mockers after that
> That would not lift a hand maybe
> To help good, wise or great
> To bar that foul storm out, for we
> Traffic in mockery.

> (*YCP*: 236)

When the poet traffics in mockery, which means to have dealings with our age and to 'write the body', among other things, he is helping 'good, wise or great', not 'To bar that foul storm out', but to find, like King Lear, self-knowledge in that storm, which leads to self-transcendence. At the end of the everyday self's ironies, when Yeats braves, rather than evades, the ruin of the 'natural Man', letting that foul storm in, the writing of his poem, rather than his reading of Plato and Plotinus, allows an apprehension that 'Death and life were not | Till man made up the whole' because our immortal soul is itself truth: 'for axioms in philosophy are not axioms until they are proved upon our pulses' (Keats 2002: 88). The revelation is essentially dramatic, born out of conflict.

In a wonderfully ironic interchange, Yeats imagines Balzac, 'that great eater', answering the Hegel of 1818, who expounds history with a 'head full of the intellectual pride of the eighteenth century' and who is 'Indifferent, as always, to the individual soul': 'There is a continual conflict – I too have my dialectic – the perfection of Nature is the decline of Spirit, the perfection of Spirit is the decline of Nature.' In the syncretic Renaissance, our spiritual dawn, 'Europe might have made its plan, begun the solution of its problems, but individualism came instead; the egg, instead of hatching, burst' (*E&I*: 466–8). Yeats's attempt to master irony, his desire to 'write the body' so that 'Nature' speaks through his work as well as the infinite, acknowledges the twofoldness of both man and language: 'What was, before man stood up, an impulse in our blood, returns as an external necessity.' When he masters irony, the poet remakes his decrepit readers out of the perennial conflict between 'Nature' and 'Spirit', outside and inside, end and beginning, and we apprehend our dull selves at a turning point in world history: 'As we grow old we accumulate abstract substitutes for experience, commodities of all kinds, but an old pensioner that taps upon the ground where he once crawled is no wit the wiser for all his proverbs' (*E&I*: 468).

The absolute ironist is old and ailing. Out of such 'dull decrepitude', such 'Testy delirium' (*YCP*: 224), Yeats finds for us the beginning of the unborn kind. Poems like 'The Tower', written by a raging and rambling 'old pensioner', are made out of such a dialectic, in order to force ironic readers from what Kierkegaard calls an aesthetic attitude through deft use of their irony. I believe that Yeats's poetry like Blake's, 'calls to the reader to rouse himself from his slumbers of passivity to action and to life – to the activity of interpretation' (Lorraine Clark 1991: 153). Yeats, Kierkegaard and Blake deploy irony as Jesus deploys allegory in the gospels: 'And he said, Unto you is given to know the mysteries of the kingdome of God: but to others in parables, that seeing, they might not see, and hearing, they might not understand' (Luke 8. 10). As we shall see in 'The Black Tower', Yeats's poetry is often deliberately cryptic, but we complete or dispose of irony as well as parabolic allegory through active interpretation, by becoming initiated into the mysteries through 'pure explication de texte' (*SL*: 793), as 'the old must be displaced' and 'the new must forge ahead' (Kierkegaard 1989: 335).

Irony is an excellent guide since it has the same relation to a human life as doubt to science: 'it is not the truth but the way' (Kierkegaard 1989: 327), and if the poet recognizes it as such he can use it to take in his readers to find the truth. Irony, as deployed by Jesus, Blake, Kierkegaard or Yeats, I hesitate to say Socrates, engages fallen understanding in order to lift us out of an ironic or sceptical way of being in the world; undertaking 'The spiritual intellect's great work', it engages the reader in order to deceive him out of his selfhood. The story has already been told, albeit cryptically, and we can suddenly wake up to its meaning. The reader's fully engaged interpretation makes a new order: 'Who in our day thinks of wasting any time on the curious idea that it is an art to be a good reader, not to mention spending time to become that? Of course, this deplorable state has its effect on an author who, in my opinion, very properly joins Clement of Alexandria in writing in such a way that the heretics are unable to understand it', opines Kierkegaard pseudonymously (1983: 225). When the speaker paces upon the battlements of his tower in 'The Tower', he joins Kierkegaard and Clement of Alexandria.

If a reader wishes to become initiated, as a preliminary step she may look outside of the poem, taking Yeats's clue of the 'bewitched' cards (*YCP*: 220), and turn to the Tarot pack, realizing that 'there is, in the Tower symbol which Yeats made his own, that element of *hybris* reflected in his choice of Self rather than Soul [in 'A Dialogue of Self and Soul'], the human condition rather than release from the wheel of death and birth' (Raine 1986: 244). All symbols are 'somewhat animate', according to

Daniel Albright, in late Yeats, 'not so much donors of meaning as receivers of it' (1994: 637 and 633). I would argue that they give and take meaning, having inner and outer senses, that seeing, we might not see, and hearing, we might not understand: most readers think initially of Yeats's tower as symbolizing power and permanence, but he admitted later:

> In mockery I have set
> A powerful emblem up,
> And sing it rhyme upon rhyme
> In mockery of a time
> Half dead at the top.

(*YCP*: 267)

The tower in the Tarot pack symbolizes the ego or everyday self, but lightning 'shatters' the top of this 'edifice of human knowledge' (Raine 1986: 245), descending 'through our souls and our bodies' (Yeats, *Is The Order of R.R. and A.C. to remain a Magical Order?* quoted in Raine 1986: 245). The ironies of art, of the self and of the body are likewise consumed on the path of self-transcendence that Yeats dramatizes in poems from *The Tower* onwards. Although his age, which is also Blake's, Kierkegaard's and our age, had lost its validity for Yeats, he is not an absolute ironist because he takes care to make poems that can bring about a new age in the reader. Even the 'unconsoled modernity' at the end of 'The Man and the Echo', which means 'Yeats abides many of our questions' (Heaney 2000: xxiv) at the beginning of the twenty-first century, may be a hook, operating like irony, to pull in and so renew the modern ironist or deconstructionist; to transform the testy, dull and decrepit reader who is unable to escape without help a bleakly materialist philosophy made out of 'a discrepancy between sign and meaning' (Preminger and Brogan 1993: 635). The everyday self may seem to have the last word in poems like 'A Dialogue of Self and Soul' but Yeats's work as a whole is made to elevate its reader for the lightning strike of renewal, as he makes his interpretations at the ruined top of the everyday self's ironies. Ironically the poet already stands there, pathetically beset by afflictions, mocking emblematically a decrepit and ironic age, fulfilling his role as our conductor and the lightning's. As we labour to join him there, our reward might just be a tower broken by a strike of lightning as a soul is made out of the wreck of the 'natural Man' and his accumulated wisdom. We shall see in Chapter 5 another side to the tower symbol in the light from Milton's Il Penseroso's window.

Irony and declaration, scepticism and faith, are but the two interlocking gyres of strife and love, objectivity and subjectivity: 'the Concord of Empedocles fabricates all things into "an homogeneous sphere", and then Discord separates the elements and so makes the world we inhabit, but even the sphere formed by Concord is not the changeless eternity, for Concord or Love but offers us the image of that which is changeless' (*VB*: 67–8). Empedocles' Concord 'fabricates', that is, it makes, but it also 'makes up', 'all things into "an homogeneous sphere"', and such invention is dependent upon Discord. Hence the 'ennobling interchange' of conviction and irony: without the way of seeming, the way of truth is but half a metaphysics. Yeats takes up Blake's protest in *The Marriage of Heaven and Hell* 'against an error found in "All Bibles or sacred codes" – and he must have included Platonism – that there are two "existing principles" and that evil is "alone from the Body"'. Both Yeats and Blake proclaim 'this harmony of opposites, "as above, so below" – the philosophy of Alchemy' (Raine 2002: 49): 'O may the moon and sunlight seem | One inextricable beam, | For if I triumph I must make men mad', wishes Yeats in 'The Tower' (*YCP*: 220), remembering 'an alchemical emblem of perfection' (Jeffares 1996b: 503). Irony, the discourse of modern sceptical materialism, the derision of the body, undoes creatively the fabrication of Concord's homogeneous sphere. But each is dependent on the other just as the soul must move in its cycles between generation and eternity. Yeats's verse is forged out of this harmony of opposites, and not least because, from a Neoplatonic perspective, language is always ironic. Caught up in his desire to 'write the body', the poet also asks, 'What is stirring in these words? Whose voice speaks?' (Caputo 1987: 290): 'Listen to presences inside poems, | Let them take you where they will' (Rumi 1995: 99). Language is twofold: it is of the body and of the soul. Ironically, as Stevens also understood, truth as freshness is 'accessible only in the most furtive fiction' (*OP*: 120).

In an 'oddly unhelpful' (Brown 1999: 322) footnote to 'The Tower', Yeats admits 'When I wrote the lines about Plato and Plotinus I forgot that it is something in our own eyes that makes us see them as all transcendence' (*YCP*: 533). Such an admission, which stands in all editions from *October Blast* to the 1933 *Collected Poems*, means that Yeats is being ironic when he says that he will choose Plato and Plotinus for friends *and* when he declares that he mocks Plotinus' thought and cries in Plato's teeth. The poet is practising a complex form of dissimulation. It seems that his lines have a Socratic irony that registers the poet's deepening engagement with Plato and Plotinus. But an 'ironic vision' can give way to mockery. Yeats's footnote inadvertently brings out the older meaning of mock, latent in the line: not so much, I deride, but I impose upon, or even disappoint, Plotinus' thought. At the end of *The Winter's Tale*, we 'prepare | To see the Life as lively mock'd, as ever | Still Sleepe mock'd Death' (V. iii. 18–20). To what degree does late Yeats merely parody or mimic Neoplatonic thought? Is there a more than auricular relationship between mocking and making in his late work? We find a transition from one mode to the other at the end of 'The Tower' as Yeats readies or composes his soul for death:

> Now shall I make my soul,
> Compelling it to study
> In a learned school
> Till the wreck of body,
> Slow decay of blood,
> Testy delirium
> Or dull decrepitude,
> Or what worse evil come –
> The death of friends, or death
> Of every brilliant eye
> That made a catch in the breath –
> Seem but the clouds of the sky
> When the horizon fades;
> Or a bird's sleepy cry
> Among the deepening shades.

> (*YCP*: 224–5)

The mocking in Yeats is involved with, but the opposite of, his project through verse to make his soul. Such is the dramatic power of Yeats's late work. Brendan Kennelly stresses, 'The thought is obviously important; but equally, and perhaps more, important is the image, the poem's blood-life, its packed emotional vitality, its resonant and concentrated drama' (1975: 100). Pragmatically, irony can be used by a poet to deceive readers into the truth, and it is also a vivifying discipliner of the poet since its pruning of the 'wild shoots' (Kierkegaard 1989: 328) of spiritual enthusiasm helps them to fructify. The tension between the often ironic blood-life of poems and their often ironic thought, gives Yeats's work in the world its soul-making capability. 'Call the world if you Please "The vale of Soul-making" Then you will find out the use of the world', requests Keats, admitting human nature 'to be immortal': 'Do you not see how necessary a World of Pains and troubles is to school an Intelligence and make it a soul? A Place where the heart must feel and suffer in a thousand diverse ways!' (2002: 232–3). In what kind of school is Yeats compelling his soul to study? In Blake's and Keats's time, 'educated people believed that they amused themselves with books of imagination, but that they "made their souls" by listening to sermons and by doing or by not doing certain things'. It may be that the poetry of Wordsworth and Keats changed that. In 1897, 'we are agreed that we "make our souls" out of some one of the great poets of ancient times, or out of Shelley or Wordsworth . . . while we amuse ourselves, or, at best, make a poorer sort of soul, by listening to sermons or by doing or by not doing certain things' (*E&I*: 111–12). Was this still true in 1928? And how have things changed today?

Raine understands that:

> The challenge to Plato and Plotinus [in 'The Tower'] would seem to be because the Greek philosophers, like the Christian theologians, have not attained the realisation of the Indian scriptures, that Spirit is 'that which has value in itself' and that the purified 'soul itself is truth'. To Aristotle and Christian orthodoxy, Yeats comments that for them 'only God has value in himself, even Spirit is contingent'. It seems that in the name of the Vedic tradition he challenges even Plato and Plotinus on similar grounds. (1999: 79)

But in his footnote, Yeats quotes from a part of Plotinus he had apparently forgotten when writing the verse: soul 'is the maker of the sun'. Yeats will, ironically, make the maker; through his poetry he will give 'rhythmic motion' to that which 'is a principle distinct from all these to which it gives law and movement and life' (*YCP*: 533). As Stevens says, pseudonymously of his own work, 'His self and the sun were one | And his poems, although makings of his self, | Were no less makings of the sun' (*SCP*: 532). Keats elucidates:

> I say '*Soul making*' Soul as distinguished from an Intelligence – There may be intelligences or sparks of the divinity in millions – but they are not Souls ~~the~~ till they acquire identities, till each one is personally itself. I[n]telligences are atoms of perception – they know and they see and they are pure, in short they are God – how then are Souls to be made? How then are these sparks which are God to have identity given them – so as ever to possess a bliss peculiar to each ones individual existence? How, but by the medium of a world like this? (2002: 232).

Such a distinct soul is not contingent: it puts the divine to work, which makes it correspondent with other such individuated souls. We find affinities between great poets because the labour of their 'secret discipline' (*YCP*: 150) is one way in this world for a divine intelligence to acquire a correspondent identity, a 'purified' soul, not distinct from, but in, God: 'I know now that revelation is from the self, but from that age-long *t*

memoried self . . . ; and that <u>genius is a crisis that joins that buried self</u>
<u>for certain moments to our trivial daily mind</u>' (*Au*: 272). Out of 'the lan-
guage of the sense' (*LB1*: 208) the soul of a poet is made as he makes the
'moving soul' (*1805*, xiii. 171) of a poem, each putting the other to work.
We can learn to consult such souls as we each make our own soul in this
world, such consultation can indeed prompt soul-making, as long as we
understand 'that the purified "soul itself is truth"', and that 'No other can
divide with thee this work' (*1850*, xiv. 212): a poem can put a reader to
work but it cannot intervene to aid the labour of soul-making. Keats talks
of making a soul out of a 'pure' intelligence in this world: such a soul
is 'purified' out of perception; 'Spirit is "that which has value in itself"'.
Intelligences are God but only individual souls are 'Ever expanding in the
Bosom of God': <u>the more distinct in his soul focus the poet, the more fit-</u>
<u>tingly his work corresponds with other such committed souls, poets and</u>
<u>readers, that make</u> themselves in God.

At the beginning of his *Theogony*, Hesiod records the speech that the
Muses first spoke to him, when he was awoken to that with which he
could make his soul: 'Field-dwelling shepherds, ignoble disgraces, mere
bellies: we know how to say many false things similar to genuine ones,
but we know, when we wish, how to proclaim true things' (2006: 5).
The relationship between mocking and making is as at least as old as the
beginning of western literature. Poets say, 'the language of the sense' is
twofold. After his experiences with the often misleading spirits that dictate to his wife, luring him 'upon Hodos Chameliontos' (*Au*: 270), and
perhaps suspicious of the spirits that he summons to question in 'The
Tower', Yeats sings of 'mocking Muses' (*YCP*: 221). His theme is the irony
of the Muse and the command to sing, whether spoken by the Muse as
in Hesiod or the poet himself as in Homer. I would argue that for Yeats
the Muses are '<u>personifying spirits that we had best call</u> but Gates and
<u>Gate-keepers,</u> because through <u>their dramatic</u> power they bring <u>our souls</u>
to crisis, to Mask and <u>Image</u>', to 'some articulation of the Image which is
the opposite of all that I am in my daily life, and all that my country is;
yet man or nation can no more make this Mask or Image than the seed
can be made by the soil into which it is cast'. In a footnote to that last
sentence, which generates the same dialectic as his Neoplatonist note to
'The Tower', Yeats acknowledges, 'There is a form of Mask or Image that
comes from life and is fated, but there is a form that is chosen' (*Au*: 272
and 274). As 'mere bellies' that can only become decrepit, it may be that
we make and mock that which mocks and makes us, but pacing the top
of such ironies the 'trivial daily mind' conducts 'fearless immortal Spirit'
(*U*: 109), and another ignoble disgrace is ruined, in a fructifying manner,

at the top, by the crisis of genius. The Muses mock us to make our souls in a crisis that comes when the poet wears the mask of irony.

The ghost of Wordsworth

'Every life', wrote Elémire Zolla, 'bears an invisible interiority that is its substance. The only way to gather this is to sidestep tangible appearances, to take a leap against the current like the salmon, the living symbol of knowledge in the Old Norse Scriptures' (1990: 154; my translation). In 'Sailing to Byzantium', Yeats talks of the 'salmon-falls' as part of 'That' country's fecundity that he would escape (*YCP*: 217). But the image of the salmon swimming upstream, leaping the waterfalls, preludes symbolically the poet's sailing to Byzantium, the city of the Spirit, in that poem, and the climbing of the streams in the succeeding poem. In fact, the published dating that determines the backward arrangement of the first four poems of *The Tower*, makes up a kind of salmon-fall for reader and poet to climb beside. The lush, idealized Irish landscape of 'Sailing to Byzantium', a poem of 1926, but dated 1927 in the collection, is ironized by different versions of the same country that we encounter in the next three poems, each one written after the next, in rage against old age and questioning Galway ghosts ('The Tower': composed 1925; dated 1926), in the time of the Irish civil war ('Meditations in Time of Civil War': composed 1921–2; dated 1923), and officially in 1919 ('Nineteen Hundred and Nineteen'), 'the year in which Ireland's war of independence took on a new ferocity' (Albright 1994: 651), although the poem was actually composed in 1920–1 (see Brown 1999: 317). Such a movement backward through time is 'withershins' (*YCP*: 274) life's current, its arrangement an attempt by the poet 'to sidestep tangible appearances' and to grasp the 'invisible interiority that is its substance'. The very arrangement of the poems attests Yeats to be as antithetical a writer and thinker as Kierkegaard.

Yeats preludes each reference to Plato in 'The Tower', in an antithetical manner, by evoking streams:

> Never had I more
> Excited, passionate, fantastical
> Imagination, nor an ear and eye
> That more expected the impossible –
> No, not in boyhood when with rod and fly,
> Or the humbler worm, I climbed Ben Bulben's back
> And had the livelong summer day to spend.

> (*YCP*: 218)

To my ears and mind, these lines recall the first effusive draft of *The Prelude*, when Wordsworth remembers how he 'Made one long bathing of a summer's day', evoking a favourite stream of his boyhood in order to overcome creative dullness in the face of the projected but abstruse poem, *The Recluse*. Brown also notices 'the ghostly presence of Wordsworth' in *The Tower* (1999: 318; see also Daruwala 1998). I would argue that Yeats's poem, unintentionally or not, conducts the ruthless conversation with Wordsworth to which Coleridge should have risen after 1805. *The Prelude* is the longest of Wordsworth's and Coleridge's conversation poems, dwelling on the middle section of memory (see Abrams 1965), and 'The Tower' takes up the conversation formally by adopting a tripartite structure, like the rondo of Coleridge's 'Frost at Midnight', lying 'coiled with its' tail round its' head' (Coleridge 2001: i. 456). In 'The Tower' Yeats climbs to find the source of the 'stream' (*1850*, xiv. 194) that Wordsworth would trace to the sea in *The Prelude*. The *1805 Prelude*, with which Coleridge should have argued, was only published in 1926 just after Yeats composed 'The Tower', so I quote Wordsworth's revised effusion, embedded within the *1850 Prelude* (in 1915, when living temporarily with Ezra Pound, funnily enough, Yeats was reading this version of *The Prelude* in Dowden's edition of Wordsworth; see *YL*: 590):

> Was it for this
> That one, the fairest of all rivers, loved
> To blend his murmurs with my nurse's song,
> And, from his alder shades and rocky falls,
> And from his fords and shallows, sent a voice
> That flowed along my dreams?
>
> (*1850*, i. 269–74)

The Wordsworth who first asks this question in 1798 was a young man measuring his imaginative powers against his failure ('this') to rise to the task of a long philosophical poem. In 1926 Yeats was on the verge of old age ('this absurdity') and toying with philosophy as a substitute for poetry to tame too fantastical an imagination. The two poems are made out of different predicaments. Although, an Arnoldian might argue, Wordsworth's lines have become a touchstone for all urgent questioning of inadequacy to find 'underlying sources of strength' (Jonathan Wordsworth 1995: 541), a Yeatsian answers that Wordsworth's lines come from the eternal realm of fairy-tale, like 'the fairest of all rivers', to 'blend' their 'murmurs' with

Yeats's lines, and such mixing is 'proof that there is a memory of Nature that reveals events and symbols of distant centuries' (*E&I*: 46):

> For this, didst thou,
> O Derwent! winding among grassy holms
> Where I was looking on, a babe in arms,
> Make ceaseless music that composed my thoughts
> To more than infant softness, giving me
> Amid the fretful dwellings of mankind
> A foretaste, a dim earnest, of the calm
> That Nature breathes among the hills and groves.
>
> (*1850*, i. 274–81)

A comparison based on causality argues that Wordsworth's repeated question, foregrounding the word 'this', prompts the beginning of *The Tower*. Upon this hint Yeats declares, 'That is no country for old men', taking over the 'That' of the first full line of Wordsworth's effusion, 'That one, the fairest of all rivers, loved', which, coming immediately after 'this', seems foregrounded to have demonstrative force as well as conjunctive sense. The beginning of Wordsworth's second question, in turn, provides impetus for the beginning of the second poem of *The Tower*:

> What shall I do with this absurdity –
> O heart, O troubled heart – this caricature,
> Decrepit age that has been tied to me
> As to a dog's tail?

Yeats ends his question, which repeats 'this', with a typographically emphasized half-line when Wordsworth begins his questions half way through lines; the heart as Yeats's troubled addressee usurps the calming river Derwent among man's 'fretful dwellings'; and later in 'The Tower', as we have seen, the elderly Yeats 'shall make' his 'soul', whereas the ceaseless music of Derwent 'composed' the 'thoughts' of baby Wordsworth. The rest of Wordsworth's effusion, in its 1850 version, follows the Derwent as it flows along its natural reflections of Yeats's major emblem in *The Tower* and provides a substantial antetype of the boy fishing 'the livelong summer day':

> When he had left the mountains and received
> On his smooth breast the shadow of those towers
> That yet survive, a shattered monument

> Of feudal sway, the bright blue river passed
> Along the margin of our terrace walk;
> A tempting playmate whom we dearly loved.
> Oh, many a time have I, a five years' child,
> In a small mill-race severed from his stream,
> Made one long bathing of a summer's day;
> Basked in the sun, and plunged and basked again
> Alternate, all a summer's day, or scoured
> The sandy fields, leaping through flowery groves
> Of yellow ragwort; or when rock and hill,
> The woods, and distant Skiddaw's lofty height,
> Were bronzed with deepest radiance, stood alone
> Beneath the sky, as if I had been born
> On Indian plains, and from my mother's hut
> Had run abroad in wantonness, to sport
> A naked savage, in the thunder shower.
>
> (*1850*, i. 282–300)

Wordsworth's lines, like the river whose motion they enact, seem to have become a 'tempting playmate' for Yeats's lines. But is Yeats alluding to Wordsworth, deliberately calling him into play? Or have we happened upon unconscious influence? Yeats is not exploring 'spots of time' (*1805*, xi. 258) in his childhood to find the sources of his creativity; he would have viewed such a project as one cause of Wordsworth's uncreative 'withering' into old age: 'The soul cannot have much knowledge till it has shaken off the habit of time and place' (*M*: 358). But it is tempting to believe that Wordsworth's poems have the same 'renovating virtue' (*1850*, xii. 210) as spots of time in Yeats and Stevens: Wordsworth's lines have seeped up through Yeats's unconsciousness to flood the first pages of *The Tower*, like the calcareous springs that flow from the slopes of Ben Bulben, because they have been 'lov'd like Nature!' (Coleridge 2001: i. 518); these later poets fulfil a covenant intended by Wordsworth 'between nature's formative influence over [Wordsworth], and the influence his poetry has on the minds of his readers' (Newlyn 2000: 127). One river has 'sent a voice' to another. Wordsworth's lines, like the sound of the real river that nurtured his creative imagination, seem to have 'flowed along' the 'dreams' or the composing minds of certain later poets as they make their souls, fulfilling Wordsworth's hopes for his poetry 'Among the second selves' (*OP*: 119).

Then again, Yeats's engagement with Wordsworth in *The Tower* might be as deliberate as Blake's marginalia on 'Poems Referring to the Period of Childhood', the first page of *Poems* (*1815*): 'I see in Wordsworth the Natural Man rising up against the Spiritual Man Continually' (Erdman: 665). As with the conflict of irony and declaration, the interlocking gyres of objectivity and subjectivity can be made to delineate the relation between the two poets and their different modes of calling to each other: the very influence of Wordsworth is that from out of which Yeats would climb in his antithetical manner. 'There is a sympathy in streams, – "one calleth to another"' (1849–50: iii. 251), acknowledges Wordsworth, recalling Psalm 42. When Yeats's poem spirals towards its 'subjective' source, it interlocks with Wordsworth's work that meanders in the opposite direction, to the base of debilitating objectivity, as he refers to his memories. 'Here the thought of Heraclitus dominates all; "Dying each other's life, living each other's death"' (*VB*: 68). Now we have made Yeats engage in an ironic manner with Wordsworth's project that is infected by concerns of our materialist age at the end of the decaying kind. The past and future climbing of the stream in Yeats's poem dramatizes his belief that 'images well up before the mind's eye from a deeper source than conscious or subconscious memory' (*Au*: 183). His backward movement up the stream turns out, ironically, to reach into the future because it is not a tracing of personal history in order to understand the present but a countering of life's current to apprehend man's substantial and immortal interiority. Recognizing the source of a poem as from the future in eternity, Yeats's poem spiritualizes Wordsworth's natural influence.

If Yeats's poems from *The Tower* onwards establish an antithesis to Wordsworth's examination of his memories in *The Prelude*, they also provide us with a way of questioning models of poetic relations that are based on causality, history or memory. 'Deepe calleth unto deepe' (Psalm 42. 7), breaking 'the habit of time and place'. Why should we need to establish the relationship between poets in terms of cause and effect? 'We must admit that there is something to be said for the immense importance of chance', Jung dared to write by the end of his life (1951: xxii). 'The manner in which the *I Ching* tends to look upon reality' may also account for the presence of Wordsworth in 'The Tower'. A manner not confined to the *I Ching*, it certainly provides us with a fresh way of looking at the poem: 'The matter of interest seems to be the configuration formed by chance events in the moment of observation, and not at all the hypothetical reasons that seemingly account for the coincidence' (1951: xxiii). The correspondence between the two poets may have more to do with a poetic version of what Jung calls 'synchronicity' in life, than with influence, allusion or imitation: it is 'Vision' rather than a form of memory (Erdman: 554). Interpretation of this acausal phenomenon of meaningful coincidence, which we have all experienced without perhaps exploring its implications, involves the process of syncretism, often discredited in the modern world. An Aristotelian critic 'carefully sifts, weighs, selects, classifies, isolates', but each of Yeats's poems, like the Tarot pack to which I have already referred and the *I Ching* to which we will turn in my interpretation of Stevens, also requires the reader to paint a picture of its moment that 'encompasses everything down to the minutest nonsensical detail, because all of the ingredients make up the observed moment' (Jung 1951: xxiii). The interlocking gyres are dependent on each other, as deep calls to deep and as a reader brings herself to a poem, but these interrelated relationships are not dependent on causality, although it might appear so from certain phases of the moon.

Whose voice is sent through the generations? Hesiod recounts how the divine, if mocking, muses 'breathed a divine voice into me, so that I might glorify what will be and what was before, and they commanded me to sing of the race of the blessed ones who always are, but always to sing of themselves first and last' (2006: 5). Yeats is not about to write a theogony but he imagines himself as singing 'Of what is past, or passing, or to come' (*YCP*: 218). 'The Tower' takes up what is to come and commands future generations to sing in the manner of Hesiod: 'Let us begin to sing from the Heliconian Muses, who possess the great and holy mountain of Helicon and dance on their soft feet around the violet-dark fountain and the altar of Cronus' mighty son' (2006: 3). Hippocrene, rising on Helicon, calls to Derwent below Skiddaw, and to the streams that Yeats fished, flowing out of Ben Bulben. A conventional tracing of allusion and influence, based on causality, understands that 'the poole of Siloam (which is by interpretation, Sent)' (John 9. 7), whose waters restore to sight the man that was born blind, is invoked by Milton playfully as '*Siloa's* Brook that flow'd | Fast by the Oracle of God' (*PL*, i. 11–12). This confluence blends its murmurs, in turn, with Derwent as it 'sent a voice | That flowed along my dreams'; 'sent', 'by interpretation, Sent' as 'that flow'd' meanders from one poet to another, from right to left over the line, and 'One deep calleth another' (Psalm 42. 9 in BCP 1928). Wordsworth's nurse was also Milton, singing his densely allusive song of the Muse, and the first effusion of *The Prelude*, as it sets out to explore the 'feeding source' (*1850*, xiv. 193) of Wordsworth's creativity, calls to the invocation of *Paradise Lost*, as it sets out to tell the story 'Of Mans First Disobedience' (*PL*, i. 1).

But such conscious and unconscious affluence is essentially 'Formd by the Daughters of Memory', as Hesiod also identifies the Muses, those which Blake sees as responsible for the 'inferior kind of Poetry' of 'Fable or Allegory' but unable to help with works of 'Imagination' (Erdman: 554).

Relying on memory, Milton adapts a classical topos for his Christian purposes and Wordsworth invokes Milton to find the Muse murmuring in the river Derwent. E. R. Curtius asserts, 'For us the Muses are shadowy figures of a tradition that has long since had its day' (1990: 228). But Yeats, like Blake in 'A Vision of The Last Judgment', subverts to regenerate this topos because he believes in 'personifying spirits' (*Au*: 272). In *The Tower*, Yeats would write 'Surrounded by the daughters of Inspiration', and thus to make 'a Representation of what Eternally Exists' involves, initially, irony (Erdman: 554). Since memory is a distraction (see *Hamlet*, I. v. 95–104), he sails from that country of Miltonic imitation and allusion and Wordsworthian allusion and influence to discover another chanceful realm of relations. If 'Sailing to Byzantium' is the anti-Wordsworthian preamble to *The Tower*, the first part of 'The Tower' is the collection's anti-invocation: Yeats 'must bid the Muse go pack' in order to regenerate this vital force within. Defying a model of poetic relations dependent on causality, self and memory, as long as unconsciousness is not regarded as divine, genius joined in crisis to that ahistorical or 'age-long memoried self', Yeats climbs the streams of influence to fish at the internal and eternal fountains of synchronicity. By seeming to bid the Muse go pack, the poet is preparing himself and his readers, ironically, for 'Vision'. He is by no means making a descriptive, allusive and Modernist gesture like Eliot, surrounded by 'the Daughters of Memory', six years earlier, in his erudite examination of another topos, *The Waste Land*. Out of such decrepitude, apparently breaking with the traditional topos of the Muse, Yeats discovers Memory's second self, Vision, Imagination or Inspiration, surrounded by her daughters, the 'Gate-keepers' who 'through their dramatic power . . . bring our souls to crisis' (*Au*: 272).

Yeats's major concern is his legacy. The younger Yeats that climbed the streams is an antetype of his legatees, a relation, which like those of the events in synchronicity, is meaningful but not dependent on causality. In his 'Nationalist Measure' (Vendler 2007: 182), Yeats decides, in the third part of 'The Tower':

> It is time that I wrote my will;
> I choose upstanding men
> That climb the streams until
> The fountain leap, and at dawn
> Drop their cast at the side
> Of dripping stone; I declare
> They shall inherit my pride[.]
>
> (*YCP*: 222)

Remembering W. H. Auden, but not Wordsworth, Bloom considers these lines 'rather inappropriate if not silly. A little irony would have helped, for once, but it does not come' (1970: 351). Wordsworth writes:

> For the delight of a few natural hearts,
> And with yet fonder feeling, for the sake
> Of youthful Poets, who among these Hills
> Will be my second self when I am gone.
>
> (*LB2*: ii. 201)

Of Wordsworth's two or three audiences, the first kind, 'a few natural hearts', is the easiest to classify, because it has been made by *Paradise Lost*: 'still govern thou my Song, | *Urania*, and fit audience find, though few' (*PL*, vii. 30–1), implores Milton. Yeats also wrote 'for a few careful readers and for a few friends' (*VP*: 847):

> I ranted to the knave and fool,
> But outgrew that school,
> Would transform the part,
> Fit audience found, but cannot rule
> My fanatic heart.
>
> (*YCP*: 287–8)

Out of his unruly and fanatic, but not natural heart, in the face of the 'barbarous dissonance' (*PL*, vii. 32) of an ironic crowd, Yeats imagined 'The Fisherman', another antetype of the fishermen in 'The Tower'. Realized in the same trimeter quatrains, this emblem of the poet's future audience, to be differentiated from the well-read 'part' or a few natural friends, is 'A man who does not exist, | A man who is but a dream' (*YCP*: 167). Can such a man, who will be Yeats's 'upstanding men', converse with Wordsworth's other audience, for whom he writes 'with yet fonder feeling', the 'youthful Poets', who become his 'second self' in his absence? In Sonnet 73, 'blacke night' is 'Deaths second selfe that seals up all in rest' (*Q* 1609). Yeats and Stevens, in whom Wordsworth's poems fructify, are his alter ego and his undoing. Wordsworth's allusion to Shakespeare reveals well-founded anxieties about his reception as he makes his epitaphic poems: his greatest poetic heirs, his 'second self', when they have become more than 'youthful Poets', will read him in a disconcertingly antithetical manner; their poems incorporate Wordsworth in a paradoxical way, as if they have not remembered him at all, as if his lines are called to theirs by chance, and not drawn from unconscious wells of past reading. My western mind cannot discredit influence, which is usually understood as unconscious allusion and imitation, my mind cannot let causality pass 'almost unnoticed' like the 'Chinese mind' (Jung 1951: xxii), but I believe that we find promising paths of interpretation when we accept that chance also draws poets together. Such an approach changes the way that we look at poetry fundamentally. Without jettisoning my Aristotelian training as a critic, and aware of the attendant dangers, I would explore rather than restrict 'the practical results' of unruly chance in poetry (Jung 1951: xxiii). Chance, like irony and, ironically, like doubt in science, or intuition and inspiration in art, is an excellent guide to unity of being: it is not the truth but the way.

When the everyday self has been cast off, we are 'reborn' (Raine 1991: 141) at the spiritual source. Yeats chooses this second self, that is not caused by anything but the transformation of the self caught in its causality, to be his upstanding men, the many-in-one and the one-in-many, a non-existent man, made by what sounds like a dangerous bequest:

> Pride, like that of the morn,
> When the headlong light is loose,
> Or that of the fabulous horn,
> Or that of the sudden shower
> When all streams are dry,
> Or that of the hour
> When the swan must fix his eye
> Upon a fading gleam,
> Float out upon a long
> Last reach of glittering stream
> And there sing his last song.

(*YCP*: 223)

Refining a definition of pride, Yeats happens upon an emblem that is of importance in his next collection. The dying swan on the stream will be transformed in later poems to a vital creature taking off amid the 'sudden thunder' (*YCP*: 275) of its beating wings on water. But even at this stage the 'last song' of the swan is in opposition to its drift downstream. Such last songs, in defiance of the stream that flows in the direction of *The Prelude*, are the subject of this book, and we shall see how Stevens cultivates a different style of late singing, although upon the same themes. For Yeats seeks 'Unity of Being', not 'intellectually, critically, and through a multitude of deliberately chosen experiences' but 'emotionally, instinctively, by the rejection of all experience not of the right quality, and by the limitation of its quantity' (*Au*: 354–5). Wordsworth may have begun to sift his memories but he looks on experience for too long, thus damaging his future as a poet. As Wordsworth's antithetical second self, Yeats would remedy the problem, ensuring his own future creativity and that of non-existent future poets:

> I leave both faith and pride
> To young upstanding men
> Climbing the mountain-side,
> That under bursting dawn
> They may drop a fly;
> Being of that metal made
> Till it was broken by
> This sedentary trade.

> (*YCP*: 224)

But the bursting dawn, the beginning of the unborn kind, is preceded by our ironies at the end of the decaying kind. Thus the stream 'spills' (*YCP*: 225) through the grounds of ancestral houses in the next poem of *The Tower* where Yeats conjures our delusions in decrepitude. The first part of 'Meditations in Time of Civil War' refers us back to Homer, the shell in Book V of *The Prelude*, and 'The Song of the Happy Shepherd', which becomes a kind of proem to Yeats's *Collected Works* with its ironic transformation of Hesiod's Muses into 'the many changing things | In dreary dancing past us whirled, | To the cracked tune that Chronos sings', of which 'Words alone are certain good' (*YCP*: 7). In 'Nineteen Hundred and Nineteen', the final poem of the four poem sequence that begins with 'Sailing to Byzantium', the swan returns as a symbol of 'fearless immortal Spirit' taking off from the river of the 'wordsworthian or egotistical sublime' (Keats 2002: 147), as destructive as the lightning that strikes the tower of the everyday self on the Tarot card:

> The swan has leaped into the desolate heaven:
> That image can bring wildness, bring a rage
> To end all things, to end
> What my laborious life imagined, even
> The half-imagined, the half-written page;
> O but we dreamed to mend

> Whatever mischief seemed
> To afflict mankind, but now
> That winds of winter blow
> Learn that we were crack-pated when we dreamed.
>
> (*YCP*: 235)

Whereas Wordsworth would follow the river to the sea, which turns out to be of time and space rather than of eternity as he imagined in his 'Ode', becoming 'empty-witted' in the process, Yeats makes sure, with Blake, that 'Poetry Painting & Music' remain 'the three Powers <in Man> of conversing with Paradise which the flood did not Sweep away' (Erdman: 559).[1] They are a means of climbing the stream in the opposite direction of the river's path to the sea. As Jung understood, 'Everything psychic is pregnant with the future' (1963: 58). Broken by the pursuit of his sedentary trade, Yeats in old age does not write with 'crack-pated' desire to transform the few, or even with fond feeling for the fisherman, but to apprehend the cold dawn rising at the end of the decaying kind. As with all prophetic literature his work, like irony, is used up as the laborious stair is climbed. How does Yeats withstand the wildness necessary for such a project?

'At sudden thunder of the mounting swan'

The Winding Stair (1933) is a sequel to *The Tower*, the heart of the former collection. Central poems pick up the symbol of the stream; they grasp the invisible interiority substantial to a life by finding new ways of moving in the opposite direction to that which flows down. Content to remain caught up in metempsychosis, despite the exhortations of '*My Soul*' to escape the wheel of generation, the final word of '*My Self*' in 'A Dialogue of Self and Soul' reads like a parody of *The Prelude*. '*My Soul*', who knows that 'Only the dead can be forgiven' (*YCP*: 266), would argue that Wordsworth's project also occurs during the first two stages of the period between death and birth. Prematurely Wordsworth has undertaken '*The Vision of the Blood Kindred*' and 'the *Meditation*' that leads to 'the *Dreaming Back*' (see *VB*: 223–5), parts of the purgatorial prelude to reincarnation that I will explore in Chapter 3. Like Wordsworth, Yeats 'was not ready for beatitude' (Raine 1999: 88). But '*My Self*', 'as it moves towards its zenith, is willing to take responsibility for its own salvation' (Albright 1994: 699):

> I am content to follow to its source
> Every event in action or in thought;

> Measure the lot; forgive myself the lot!
> When such as I cast out remorse
> So great a sweetness flows into the breast
> We must laugh and we must sing,
> We are blest by everything,
> Everything we look upon is blest.

(YCP: 267)

'*My Self*' speaks from 'infinite absolute negativity', he sounds like many in the twenty-first century, but at least this ironic attitude is foregrounded in dialogue as AE understood when he read the poem: 'perhaps when you side with the Self it is only a motion to that fusion of opposites which is the end of wisdom' (Finneran 1977: ii. 560). That Yeats seems 'content to live it all again' at the end rather than seek release from the wheel is at once true and an ironist's strategy to deceive us out of selfhood: sympathizing with '*My Self*', we enter the edifice of his canon only to be struck down by lightning, by the time we have clambered up to the battlements.

'What matter if the ditches are impure?' asks '*My Self*' earlier (*YCP*: 266). After crossing the rivers Acheron, Styx and Phlegethon, navigating the ever decreasing 'Malebolge' or evil ditches of the eighth circle of Hell, and lake Cocytus in the ninth, Dante and Virgil descend the body of Satan, at the midpoint reversing their direction, to discover a hidden path above by which they can climb back to the bright world:

> Soon as he reach'd the point, whereat the thigh
> Upon the swelling of the haunches turns,
> My leader there, with pain and struggling hard,
> Turn'd round his head where his feet stood before,
> And grappled at the fell as one who mounts;
> That into Hell methought we turn'd again.
>   'Except that by such stairs as these,' thus spake
> The teacher, panting like a man forespent,
> 'We must depart from evil so extreme:'
> Then at a rocky opening issued forth,
> And placed me on the brink to sit, next join'd
> With wary step my side.

(Cary: 146)

We are at the start of another laborious winding stair. 'Blake understood Dante's Hell to be this world' (Raine 1970: 196). The descent down Satan's or the selfhood's tail that is turned into an ascent, along a stream to Purgatory, is emblematic of Yeats's unconscious, conscious or acausal relationship with Wordsworth:

> There is a place beneath,
> From Belzebub as distant, as extends
> The vaulted tomb; discover'd not by sight,
> But by the sound of brooklet, that descends
> This way along the hollow of a rock,
> Which, as it winds with no precipitous course,
> The wave hath eaten.
>
> (Cary: 147)

'The "brooklet" (*ruscelletto*), which trickles down from Purgatory into Hell, is Lethe, which takes away all memory of sin and evil from the purified soul', Edmund Gardner notes (Cary: 147). Climbing the streams, not of forgetfulness, but of memory, that Wordsworth descends to the sea of time and space, Yeats reverses their function, reaching in his very late poems the time between death and life when the soul can be purged of its memories in preparation for its next incarnation. Again, the relation between Hell and Purgatory, this world and the next, can be conceived in terms of the interlocking gyres:

> By that hidden way
> My guide and I did enter, to return
> To the fair world: and heedless of repose
> We climb'd, he first, I following his steps,
> Till on our view the beautiful lights of Heaven
> Dawn'd through a circular opening in the cave:
> Thus issuing we again beheld the stars.
>
> (Cary: 147)

Desiring to write the body and generating conversation with Wordsworth, Yeats's late poems climb down the ironies of the natural man, but, at the unspeakable midpoint, we find stairs to climb, from which the spiritual man can speak again; as one gyre widens, another moves in the opposite direction, and Yeats's poetry is made out of such conflict, which can be represented by the Shatkona Yantra:

> 'That some stream of lightning
> From the old man in the skies
> Can burn out that suffering
> No right-taught man denies.

> But a coarse old man am I,
> I choose the second-best,
> I forget it all awhile
> Upon a woman's breast.'
> > *Daybreak and a candle-end.*
>
> > > (*YCP*: 358)

Not streak, but 'stream of lightning': Yeats knows that the same self-annihilation occurs at the source of the stream as at the top of the tower. But 'The Wicked Old Man', like the impresario at the end of 'The Circus Animals' Desertion', and '*My Self*', all 'choose the second-best': not laboriously to climb the stairs or streams of the self's accumulated wisdom to find 'Vision', which looks ruinous from below. Instead 'I must lie down where all the ladders start, | In the foul rag-and-bone shop of the heart' (*YCP*: 392). That 'must' must be registered. 'Dante has turned completely round (symbolical of his conversion from sin)' (Cary: 147). Yeats's calling is to speak from this turning point that defines our age and each of us. He speaks out still from the ironies of the self, adopting ironic masks, but the journey has already begun. There are relapses because what occurs all at once inside manifests itself gradually outside; besides, if poems are to have an audience, they must lie down with us to wake us into 'upstanding men' and language is twofold: 'Those masterful images because complete | Grew in pure mind, but out of what began?' (*YCP*: 392). As Kierkegaard understood, irony is essential if you do not write from a position of divine authority. Like most of us, not visionaries, hardly mental travellers, Yeats's ironies at the end are a moving acceptance of his situation, between '*Daybreak and a candle-end*'. Rather than catalogue the foul rag-and-bone shop, like Wordsworth revisiting 'spots of time', Yeats makes poems out of the struggle to get up, to remake himself by purging memory. But the soul, after all, learns from the body; there must be a divine reason for generation. It is the task of a life to integrate everyday self and soul, not simply to jettison selfhood, although at the foot of the tower renovation of the soul just looks like ruination of the self.

The very end of Dante's *Inferno* is also caught up in 'A Dialogue of Self and Soul'. '*My Soul*' plays the role of Virgil, summoning to 'that hidden way' or 'the winding ancient stair' to the stars, the Yeatsian, that is, recalcitrant and ironic, Dante of '*My Self*':

> *My Soul.* I summon to the winding ancient stair;
> Set all your mind upon the steep ascent,

Upon the broken, crumbling battlement,
Upon the breathless starlit air,
Upon the star that marks the hidden pole;
Fix every wandering thought upon
That quarter where all thought is done:
Who can distinguish darkness from the soul?

●　　●　　●　　●　　●　　●　　●　　●

My Self. A living man is blind and drinks his drop.
What matter if the ditches are impure?
What matter if I live it all once more?

(*YCP*: 265–6)

Even at the very end, this ladder gone, when Yeats 'must lie down where all the ladders start', he is ready to 'live it all once more', to climb another ladder, to go back to soul-making school: 'the scope and scale of the great cycle itself is a kind of liberation to the courageous soul' (Raine 1999: 88). Dante and Virgil represent a traditional kind of poetic relationship; the master leads the initiate to complete the work: Dante describes the way out of Hades that we do not find in Book VI of the *Aeneid*. The relationship between Yeats and Wordsworth is made questionable by both poets. One might argue that the later poet attempts to redirect the earlier who may not have looked so fondly on what may be after all an unconscious project. But synchronicity summons poets to the winding stair that ascends out of causality. In Dante we can see that the climbing of the stream is related to the climbing of the tower's spiral stair, up through, but in the opposite direction to, time and space. We require a new model of relations to talk about the poets that tread this stair, one that does not rely on causality. For late Yeats writes in a syncretic manner like Blake. Despite the ironies of the self, which are often the ostensible subject of a poem, Yeats's poems selflessly gather, like magic, diverse sources to attain unity of being, to apprehend the one-in-many and the many-in-one.

'Coole Park and Ballylee, 1931' is the culmination of Yeats's development of the river. The cave with water flowing through it interlocks with the tower on a stream:

Under my window-ledge the waters race,
Otters below and moor-hens on the top,
Run for a mile undimmed in Heaven's face
Then darkening through 'dark' Raftery's 'cellar' drop,

> Run underground, rise in a rocky place
> In Coole demesne, and there to finish up
> Spread to a lake and drop into a hole.
> What's water but the generated soul?

> (*YCP*: 275)

Like Derwent running alongside the terrace at the end of Wordsworth's father's garden, we find here a home on the banks of a spiritual guide or playmate river. If we compare Yeats's natural and symbolic landscape, which draws on the topography of Dante's Hell as well as Porphyry's essay on the cave of the nymphs, with Wordsworth's description of *The Prelude* in Book XIV, which makes a symbol out of his earlier description of the natural river, we find imagination to have been both poets' ultimate theme:

> This faculty hath been the feeding source
> Of our long labour: we have traced the stream
> From the blind cavern whence is faintly heard
> Its natal murmur; followed it to light
> And open day; accompanied its course
> Among the ways of Nature, for a time
> Lost sight of it bewildered and engulphed:
> Then given it greeting as it rose once more
> In strength, reflecting from its placid breast
> The works of man and face of human life;
> And lastly, from its progress have we drawn
> Faith in life endless, the sustaining thought
> Of human Being, Eternity, and God.

> (*1850*, xiv. 193–205)

In the *1805 Prelude*, 'feeding source' is 'moving soul'. Such a poem has a 'moving soul' because it 'becomes a creative self-naming, a finite work that is the incarnation of man's highest aspiring, and that lays claim to permanence because it is not different in kind from "the infinite I AM"' (Jonathan Wordsworth 1984: 328). But it appears to Blake that the 'moving soul' of Wordsworth's work has a tendency to fall asleep, to be carried in the wrong direction. Yeats would grasp the invisible but substantial interior life, the moving soul of eternity, by climbing the stream to its feeding source rather than follow it into riverhood to the sea. Symbolically speaking he is right thus to labour after the source rather than walk to the waters of time and space, where Eternity is hard to find. Yeats writes in the face of a Wordsworthian project that makes it all sound too easy. Redemption for Yeats could never be found revisiting a river first explored on another such walking tour as in 'Tintern Abbey'. Yeats understands the divine or creative imperative to remake himself, again and again, every day. In his poetry he climbs or takes off from the river of a life to find its moving soul, the feeding source of eternity within; he clambers the tower of accumulated human wisdom only to be struck by lightning at the top of the battlements of the ego. Wordsworth's lines flood Yeats's poems for him to climb, out of temporal causality, into the eternal future. The engulphed stream symbolizes a bewildered Wordsworth; Yeats delights in dropping his poems above the holes of underground currents. Ironically, such climbing and casting involves reversals, a lying down in the heart, and the lying of irony put into service to find truth. To declare faith like Wordsworth is not to become a lightning conductor when deep calls to deep, but to build too firmly a tower that must be ruined at the top. Such ironies, which account for Blake's adherence to poetry rather than organized religion, late Yeats discovers for us. When 'all the rant's a mirror of my mood', Yeats is struck by the lightning of a symbol introduced in *The Tower*, a swan taking off from water:

> At sudden thunder of the mounting swan
> I turned about and looked where branches break
> The glittering reaches of the flooded lake.
>
> Another emblem there! That stormy white
> But seems a concentration of the sky;
> And, like the soul, it sails into the sight
> And in the morning's gone, no man knows why;
> And is so lovely that it sets to right
> What knowledge or its lack had set awry,
> So arrogantly pure, a child might think
> It can be murdered with a spot of ink.

(YCP: 275–6)

Yeats does not dwell on Wordsworthian 'spots of time' in his life but he seeks an eternal moment in each day, outside of causality, 'So arrogantly pure, a child might think | It can be murdered with a spot of ink'. Such a moment, symbolized by the mounting swan, is the burden of the last collections as his heart becomes more 'fanatic' or possessed by the divine like a temple:

> There is a Moment in each Day that Satan cannot find
> Nor can his Watch Fiends find it, but the Industrious find
> This Moment & it multiply. & when it once is found
> It renovates every Moment of the Day if rightly placed[.]

(Blake, Milton, plate 35: 283)

Satan is selfhood. The discipline of verse can help the right placing of this moment. Such supernatural self-transcendence energizes the last collection to appear in Yeats's lifetime, *New Poems* (1938). The older the poet gets, the more relentless his look to the eternity of the future in the present:

> Grant me an old man's frenzy,
> Myself must I remake
> Till I am Timon and Lear
> Or that William Blake
> Who beat upon the wall
> Till Truth obeyed his call[.]

(YCP: 347)

In 'What then?' Yeats seeks to understand his psyche in relation to its past and its future, so that a conventional sizing up of a life, a parody almost of *The Prelude*, is undercut by Plato's devastating refrain:

> 'The work is done,' grown old he thought,
> 'According to my boyish plan;
> Let the fools rage, I swerved in naught,
> Something to perfection brought';
> *But louder sang that ghost, 'What then?'*

(YCP: 348)

The tower struck by lightning stands for that 'Something to perfection brought' that must be ruined from the future, a man's work and our civilization's. Plato's refrain should play in anyone's mind who would trace Yeats's relation to other poets. All of our models of imitation, allusion and influence need to be rethought in terms of the magic of synchronicity so that Yeats's relations with other poets, paradoxically, are conceived in terms of 'Looking . . . after' (Q 1604; *Hamlet*, IV. iv. 37): by looking to the future his poems look after, that is, renovate, earlier poets. He makes our tradition vital again so that we apprehend Wordsworth and Milton together as greater than they knew today, speaking from a divine source in the future, their Muses transformed into the daughters of Inspiration. But Yeats's relations to other poets should not be conceived of as perfect: they are ruinous; they are a means of conducting lightning to a body of work and a civilization, in order to make a soul out of an intelligence. We do not trace Yeats's lines simply to Wordsworth, some other power is involved in their relationship, in the lightning strike of revelation. Yeats's poems renovate Wordsworth's project, waylaid in *The Prelude*, his way of looking on nature, so that they influence in reverse, just as Kierkegaard's concept of repetition revolutionizes Plato's recollection of forms (see Kierkegaard 1983: 324), and Blake's forward looking 'Vision or Imagination' is not backward looking 'Fable or Allegory' (Erdman: 554). Rather than construct another fable based on memory and a limited understanding of the unconscious, like Bloom's Freudian anxiety of influence, when thinking of Yeats's relations to other poets, we should keep in mind the three doctrines, which are 'the foundations of nearly all magical practices', including poetry:

(1) That the borders of our mind are ever shifting, and that many minds can flow into one another, as it were, and create or reveal a single mind, a single energy.
(2) That the borders of our memories are as shifting, and that our memories are a part of one great memory, the memory of Nature herself.
(3) That this great mind and great memory can be evoked by symbols. (*E&I*: 28)

I am not a Jungian critic but Yeats draws me dangerously close to the territory of archetypal criticism; as Raine says of her relationship to her 'master' Blake, it is 'inevitable' that a follower of Yeats 'must be, if not a follower of Jung, at all events a fellow traveller': Yeats, Blake and Jung 'draw upon, and themselves represent, the mainstream and fulfillment of the Protestant tradition of the "Kingdom within"' (Raine 1992: 167–8). But 'Blake goes as far beyond Jung as Dante travelled beyond Virgil, his first guide' (Raine 1991: 3). One modern ironist remarks dryly of Northrop Frye's cyclical theory of history in *Anatomy of Criticism* that 'in 1957 we were evidently somewhere in the ironic phase with signs of an impending return to the mythic'. He argues that 'Frye's work emphasizes . . . the utopian root of literature [or 'collective utopian dreaming'] because it is marked by a deep fear of the actual social world, a distaste for history itself' (Eagleton 2008: 80 and 81). 'Certain critics who have written hand-books of modern criticism', demurs James Baird, naming no names, 'may have disavowed concerns with the basic experience ['the vision' that "underlies" art]. But the unanswerable questions remain'. There is no escaping the 'problem of the anagogic' (Baird 1992: 40–1).

Frye answers another major criticism: 'As for the danger of poetry becoming a "substitute" for religion, that again is merely bad metaphor: if both poetry and religion are functioning properly, their interpenetra-tion will take care of itself' (Frye 1992: 37). True enough, but I agree with Eagleton that Frye's approach 'combines an extreme aestheticism with an efficiently classifying "scientificity", and so maintains literature as an imaginary alternative to modern society while rendering criticism respectable in that society's terms' (2008: 81): the decline of archetypal criticism 'is directly related to the weaknesses of its conception of his-tory, its willingness, as in Frye, to attend to change in literary forms and modes while failing to attend to larger historical forces outside the "con-ceptual universe" of literature' (Davis and Schleifer 1998: 397). Yeats foresees in 'The Black Tower' that poetry and its interpretation have a more important part to play during our turning point in history than the critical debate just outlined. Unlike Frye and Eagleton, but like Blake, Yeats's major concern is to awaken each reader to 'age-long memoried self' or 'fearless immortal Spirit' because he sees that the future of our civilization depends upon such inner apprehension. This process is less scientific and more urgent, historically speaking, than the Aristotelian Frye and others make out. Yeats and Stevens bring our tradition to a point where we can recognize its 'moving soul' and criticism today must learn to climb to that eternal 'feeding source' to consult with that which 'rolls' through our world and 'the mind of man' (*LB1*: 207).

Yeats's relation to Wordsworth makes good his insight that 'Confusion fell upon our thought' (*YCP*: 400) in the middle nineteenth century. In *Last Poems*, the posthumous collection whose texts and arrangement have been much disputed, poems like 'Under Ben Bulben', to be differ-entiated from Yeats's work in the ironic mode, are written for the sake of non-existent future poets, at the confused end of the decaying kind, apprehending creatively the beginning of the unborn kind:

> Poet and sculptor, do the work,
> Nor let the modish painter shirk
> What his great forefathers did,

> Bring the soul of man to God,
> Make him fill the cradles right.
>
> (*YCP*: 399)

Having toiled up the stream, Yeats is not being ironic at all here. Ancient Egyptian art, the Parthenon and Michelangelo's frescoes on the Sistine ceiling are:

> Proof that there's a purpose set
> Before the secret working mind:
> Profane perfection of mankind.
>
> (*YCP*: 399)

Like Kierkegaard, Yeats publishes 'directly religious' (Kierkegaard 1998: 7) work alongside aesthetic or ironic works. Irony is one way of waking the everyday self so that 'We say God and the imagination are one'. Such declaration is another. One mode helps the other in their unsettling dialectic, allowing the poet to plant spiritual trees in the ear as well as prune their enthusiastic, wild shoots so that they produce fruit, 'Till body up to spirit work, in bounds | Proportiond to each kind' (*PL*, v. 478–9). The first epigraph to 'The Ways of Ascent', Chapter III of Harold Bayley's *The Lost Language of Symbolism* '(a book Yeats knew)' (Raine 1986: 178) is by Sir Walter Raleigh:

> My soul, like quiet palmer,
>   Travelleth towards the land of heaven;
> Over the silver mountains,
> Where spring the nectar fountains.
>
> (Bayley 1912: i. 32)

'One might indefinitely multiply the symbols under which Allegory has veiled the Quest of the Ideal', comments Bayley before he reproduces designs of 'the Ladder of Perfection, the time-honoured *Scala Perfectionis* of Mysticism': '" Our teaching," says Plotinus, "reaches only so far as to indicate the way in which the Soul should go, but the Vision itself must be the Soul's own achievement"' (1912: i. 32). Figure 1047 of Bayley's book shows the emblem of 'the Dragon or Great Serpent' within or upon the tower (1912: ii. 142–3): we have been playing in this chapter a game of snakes and ladders or *Paramapada Sopanam*, which can be conceived as a version of the cabbalistic Tree of Life (see *Au*: 375).

Yeats and his generation were 'crack-pated' when they 'dreamed', especially at our turning point of history. Great poets have nothing to do with mending localized mischief, their poems do not achieve anything in this world, but they can help each to turn himself about on the Great Dragon's tail to ascend the Steps to the Highest Place. Yeats's ordering of his last poems has been reinstated in new editions of the *Collected Poems*. In the new penultimate poem of his last collection, the speaker, looking over his past work, becomes emblem for his reader: 'Now that my ladder's gone, | I must lie down where all the ladders start, | In the foul rag-and-bone shop of the heart' (*YCP*: 392; Finneran 1997: 356). That reader may be surprised to find the distracted, ageing poet in the very last poem, 'Politics', longing for the 'arms' (*YCP*: 393 and Finneran 1997: 356) of the very world from which he would embark in 'Sailing to Byzantium', which marks the beginning of his late phase. Yeats's point seems to be that his life and poetry can guide, but we each have to make our soul in this world of generation. At the end of the *Collected Poems*, the reader finds herself at the bottom of her soul-making ladder. It is more important to know yourself than to know Yeats. An honoured poet, but not empty-witted, even Yeats embodies this truth at the end of his life. Like all prophetic works, Yeats's *Collected Poems*, is made in such a way as to be used up again and again as it puts each new reader on the right path of revelation, conjoining self and Self, from without, coiled with its tail round its head, from within, asymptotic in its passing.

If there is any relation of Wordsworth to Yeats it must be conceived of in terms of Yeats's own legacy. The 'intended result' of Yeats's poetry is 'a return to that "most blessed", prelapsarian or precarnate state of wholeness which was "the primal sphere" of our beginning and which remains the longed-for "primal sphere" of our end' (Olney 1975: 49). Irony is involved in such a project because his poems have been written and are to be read in a world of seeming as we discover the way of truth (see Olney 1975: 47). The soul enters generation, this world of irony, for its own reasons. The labour of its recovery is also Yeats's poetic project, and he was careful to make poems that survive long enough to be disposed of by each new reader. Like Kierkegaard, Yeats does not write from a position of achieved wisdom, but our journey is after all around a point: 'What we call development or progress is going round and round a central point in order to get gradually closer to it' (Olney 1975: 45). Yeats's relation to Wordsworth turns around causality to establish this asymptotic movement. Irony is involved, as his work attempts to move himself,

Wordsworth and his readers from the way of seeming to the way of truth. Such a reading moves from the fable or allegory of influence, and its spots of time in life and literature, to anagogy that looks to eternity in the future: that chance moment in each industrious day that renovates all the others. Then we understand that irony is causality, but revelation is synchronicity. Both are needed: everyday self and 'fearless immortal Spirit' should be integrated. The symbol of the tower, with its outer and inner meanings, denotes this assimilation, as self serves spirit.

2
Stevens from *Transport to Summer* to the Last Poems

Irony in Stevens

'God Is Good. It Is a Beautiful Night' begins Stevens's *Transport to Summer* (1947): 'Look round, brown moon, brown bird, as you rise to fly'. This prayer that supplicates for vigilance, luring a harvest moon, becomes in retrospect a proem that announces a late phase, functioning like Yeats's 'Sailing to Byzantium' in his *Collected Poems*: 'The venerable song falls from your fiery wings. | The song of the great space of your age pierces | The fresh night' (*SCP*: 285). Stevens's future re-readers are transported momentarily out of his *Collected Poems* (1954) to his very last poem, uncollected at his death, in which 'The bird's fire-fangled feathers dangle down' (*OP*: 141) from the palm where it sings a foreign song. 'Now, again', in the brown moon's light of 'God Is Good', 'the head is speaking. It reads the book. | It becomes the scholar again, seeking celestial | Rendezvous' (*SCP*: 285). The scholar, the Stevensian equivalent of Yeats's fisherman, finds celestial rendezvous that is also down-to-earth as '*One of the countrymen*' in the last poem of Stevens's next collection of poems, *The Auroras of Autumn* (1950). '*The angel* 'of reality', in 'Angel Surrounded by Paysans', 'standing in the door', speaks to the countrymen as one of them and as 'the necessary angel of earth':

> Since, in my sight, you see the earth again,
>
> Cleared of its stiff and stubborn, man-locked set,
> And, in my hearing, you hear its tragic drone

Rise liquidly in liquid lingerings,
Like watery words awash; like meanings said

By repetitions of half-meanings.

(*SCP*: 496–7)

Stevens does not so much mock as evade Plotinus' thought in this poem, in order, like Yeats, to return upon it, or something like it. To see the earth again in the sight of the necessary angel, 'Cleared', not of man, but 'of its stiff and stubborn, man-locked set', is to apprehend that man 'Made lock, stock and barrel | Out of his bitter soul' and 'That, being dead, we rise, | Dream and so create | Translunar Paradise' (*YCP*: 223). Since we are already dead, or 'man-locked', the angel of this reality can help us dream or hear our and the earth's intertwined and 'tragic drone | Rise liquidly in liquid lingerings': 'Translunar Paradise' is created 'By repetitions of half-meanings', by the poem's evasions, interpretation of which returns the scholar-countryman, thus cleared, to an apprehension that 'poems, although makings' of Ariel's 'self, | Were no less makings of the sun' (*SCP*: 532):

> Let every soul recall, then, at the outset the truth that the soul is the author of all living things, that it has breathed the life into them all, whatever is nourished by earth and sea, all the creatures of the air, the divine stars in the sky; it is the maker of the sun; itself formed and ordered this vast heaven and conducts all that rhythmic motion – and it is a principle distinct from all these to which it gives law and movement and life, and it must of necessity be more honourable than they, for they gather or dissolve as soul brings them life or abandons them, but soul, since it never can abandon itself, is of eternal being. (*YCP*: 533)

Stevens's later poetry lets every soul recall the truth out of that which gathers or dissolves; like Heidegger's later work, it concerns itself with the evasions of language in relation to being. Both philosopher and poet come to an understanding of truth as that which loves to conceal itself: both are interested in 'a mode of being-manifest, i.e. of *unhiddenness*, which in itself is simultaneously, and indeed essentially, *hiddenness*; a truth to whose essence there belongs un-truth' (Heidegger 2002a: 227), and in 'Deconcealment as the Fundamental Occurrence of the Ex-istence of Man' (Heidegger 2002a: 53), which sounds even more exotic than one of Stevens's quasi-philosophical titles for his poems, Heidegger meditates on the work of art in its 'setting up of a world' and its 'setting forth of earth':

> The world is the self-opening openness of the broad paths of simple and essential decisions in the destiny of a historical people. The earth is the unforced coming forth of the continually self-closing, and in that way, self-sheltering. World and earth are essentially different and yet never separated from one another. (2002: 26)

Reading late Stevens, we understand that language is 'the relation of all relations', maintaining, proffering and enriching world and earth, order and wildness, energy and subtlety. Brooding upon, 'By repetitions of half-meanings', the relation that keeps and holds these relations while holding 'itself – Saying – in reserve' (Heidegger 1971: 107), his often evasive and ironic poems keep company with truth as 'Saying'; they hide that which loves to hide, because its continued concealment makes it continuously unconcealable, not merely correct:

> In setting up world and setting forth earth the work instigates this strife. But this does not happen so that the work can simultaneously terminate and settle the conflict in an insipid agreement, but rather so that the strife remains a strife. . . . It is because the strife reaches its peak in the simplicity of intimacy that the unity of the work happens in the fighting of the fight. The fighting of the fight is the continually self-surpassing gathering of the agitation of the work. The repose of the work that rests in itself thus has its essence in the intimacy of the struggle. (Heidegger 2002: 27)

Heidegger's emphasis on strife sounds more like Yeats's late project but Stevens's choice 'to include the things | That in each other are included, the whole, | The complicate, the amassing harmony' (*SCP*: 403) is not a choice of 'insipid agreement': the 'harmony' is 'complicate', or folded together and intricate, and 'amassing', or that which heaps up simply; it is an arrangement at once complex and simple, because such repose 'has its essence in the intimacy of the struggle'. This choice of, not between, world and earth is made by 'the Canon Aspirin' in the last poem of *Transport to Summer*, 'Notes toward a Supreme Fiction': such repose, within a fable within a long poem within a collection within a *Collected Poems*, is made out of 'the continually self-surpassing gathering of the agitation of the work'.

Largely oblivious of each other, Stevens, Yeats and Heidegger were all crying in Plato's teeth at about the same time in order to learn a way of apprehending that which Stevens called 'being' and Yeats, 'fearless immortal spirit'. Both Yeats and Heidegger claimed boldly to stand at the end of long traditions, Heidegger professing that 'With Plato's thought western philosophy takes off on an erroneous and fateful course' (2004: 12), which he would now interrogate and reorient, and Yeats returning upon the story that Homer began, by composing on his deathbed its new episode, 'The Black Tower'. Stevens's work also wonders about evading our metaphysical fate because he would have us listen again to the 'tragic drone' of earth in our world, to return to Heidegger's dichotomy. Separated world and earth evade thinking with Plato, Stevens's work foregrounds the means of evasion, to let earth rise again in 'liquid lingerings', which are to be thought of in relation to our world, that is, 'Like watery words awash; like meanings said | By repetitions of half-meanings'. In our complex world, earth evades us in our language, but language instigates our intimacy: it is of world and earth; complicate and amassing, its drone is of the man-locked earth, but we hear it rise again, if we listen to the strife of this tragedy.

While Yeats values mockery as a means of awakening a mocking age, Stevens is also ironic because his poems exploit the evasions of language to come upon the truth, a path of thinking that marks the end of a certain metaphysical tradition. In *The Never-Resting Mind*, Anthony Whiting has outlined Stevens's 'romantic irony' in relation to Hegel, Schlegel and Kierkegaard, eventually arguing 'that individual creative activity is inseparable from but not identical with the overall process of nature' in late Stevens (1996: 183). I believe that we should approach Stevens with the same care as Heidegger when he explores the relation itself between world and earth. That dynamic bond impels Heidegger to carry out his 'discussion' of the 'site that gathers Georg Trakl's poetic Saying into his poetic work' in relation to 'clarification' of individual poems:

> Every great poet creates his poetry out of one single poetic statement only. . . . The poet's statement remains unspoken ['Das Gedicht eines Dicthers bleibt ungesprochen']. None of his individual poems, nor their totality, says it all. Nonetheless, every poem speaks from the whole of the one single statement, and in each instance says that statement. (1971: 160; 2007: 37)

A sceptic like Theseus in *A Midsummer-Night's Dream* might ask about the validity of a statement that remains unspoken and doubt the possibility of Heidegger's project of trying 'to point to the site of the unspoken statement'; 'in den Ort des ungesprochenen Gedichtes zu weisen' (1971: 161; 2007: 39). But Stevens appropriates Theseus' famous speech of disbelief that undermines itself in so many ways (*F*; *A Midsummer-Night's Dream*, V. i. 2–22) in order to formulate the response of poetry: 'One poem proves another and the whole, | For the clairvoyant men that need no proof: | The lover, the believer and the poet' (*SCP*: 441). The relationship of site and poems unfolds like that of world and earth; 'It was not a choice || Between, but of' (*SCP*: 403):

> From the site of the statement there rises the wave that in each instance moves his Saying as poetic saying. But that wave, far from leaving the site behind, in its rise causes all the movement of Saying to flow back to its ever more hidden source ['Die Woge verläßt jedoch den Ort des Gedichtes so wenig, daß ihr Entquellen vielmehr alles Bewegen der Sage in den stets verhüllteren Ursprung zurückfließen läßt']. The site of the poetic statement, source of the movement-giving wave, holds within it the hidden nature of what, from a metaphysical-aesthetic point of view, may at first appear to be rhythm. (Heidegger 1971: 160; Heidegger 2007: 38)

This very description, far from leaving Plotinus behind, flows back to his ever more hidden source, the soul, which 'conducts all that rhythmic motion' of earth, sea and heaven, while it is of necessity 'distinct' and 'of eternal being'. Such a wave rises and flows back on that which Stevens calls 'liquid lingerings', that which is given motion by the repetition of 'like', a repetition that rises out of the sound of 'liquidly in liquid': 'Like watery words awash; like meanings said | By repetitions of half-meanings'. We climb or rather we are washed to a source that is discerned at the end according to the principle of synchronicity: 'The site, the gathering power [Der Ort, das Versammelnde'], gathers in and preserves all it has gathered, not like an encapsulating shell ['eine abschließende Kapsel'] but rather by penetrating with its light all it has gathered, and only thus releasing it into its own nature' (Heidegger 1971: 159–60; Heidegger 2007: 37). Heidegger warns:

> Only a poetic dialogue with a poet's poetic statement is a true dialogue – the poetic conversation between poets. But it is also possible, and at times indeed necessary, that there be a dialogue between *thinking* and poetry, for this reason: because a distinctive, though in each case different, relation to language is proper to both. (1971: 160–1)

The theme of this book is 'the poetic conversation between poets': 'das dichterische Gespräch zwischen Dichtern' (2007: 38). I am interested in that which makes such *Gespräch, dichterische*; such conversation, poetic: dissatisfied with models of influence that rely on causality, I see that we are often dealing with meaningful coincidence when we notice correspondences between late Stevens and earlier poems, perhaps even more so than in Yeats, and such literary synchronicity points to a site beyond the familiar causal realm of 'literary influence' (Heaney 1980: 62). Stevens's work also establishes a dialogue between thinking and poetry which calls forth 'the *nature* of language, so that mortals may learn again to live within language' (Heidegger 1971: 161). With that in mind this chapter immerses itself in the 'liquid lingerings' of Stevens's late poetry, riding Heidegger's wave, and eventually focusing on a cluster of poems that are 'Brooding sounds of river noises' (*SCP*: 444), 'das *Wesen* der Sprache hervorzurufen' (Heidegger 2007: 38), to call forth the being of language: the 'moving soul' of a poet's 'long labour' (*1805*, xiii. 171 and 172).

Heidegger explicates like the moon-scholar in 'God Is Good', he seeks 'celestial | Rendezvous', a conversation between poets, which Stevens represents as the more earthy meeting of the countryman and the angel at the end of *The Auroras of Autumn*. We find this non-exclusive choice of revelation and evasion made from one poem to the other, but not necessarily in time. In Stevens's *Collected Poems*, 'Notes toward a Supreme Fiction', the last poem of *Transport to Summer*, comes immediately before 'The Auroras of Autumn', the first poem of its collection. The transition of these poems marks a crucial turn in Stevens's late phase. In the middle part of 'Notes', in Canto IX of 'It Must Change', we find Stevens formulating the questions of of:

> The poem goes from the poet's gibberish to
> The gibberish of the vulgate and back again.
> Does it move to and fro or is it of both
>
> At once? Is it a luminous flittering
> Or the concentration of a cloudy day?
> Is there a poem that never reaches words
>
> And one that chaffers the time away?
> Is the poem both peculiar and general?
> There's a meditation there, in which there seems

> To be an evasion, a thing not apprehended or
> Not apprehended well. Does the poet
> Evade us, as in a senseless element?

> (*SCP*: 396)

Some critics have interpreted this canto as Stevens's negotiation of 'the two conflicting traditions in modern American poetry, the Emersonian and the Symbolist' (Fredman 1990 126; see also Kermode 2002: 186, Bloom 1977: 199–200, and Gelpi 1987: 78), but the most perceptive readers become self-conscious as they construe their commentaries (see Cook 1988: 243). The coherence of this poem is not that of a discussion that moves in a propositional or interrogative drive from proof to proof towards lucidity. If it is at all clear, the familiar tropes of lucidity are suggestively adjusted. Are we right to talk in terms of it having different speakers? The questions and statements, which constitute the movement of the poem, cannot be simply reconstituted as an expression of Stevens's own inner dialogue. The poem itself 'goes from' 'clarification' (of the 'poet's gibberish') to 'discussion' (of the 'gibberish of the vulgate') and back again. As a poem it derives its light only from one single poetic statement, which is always dark itself, nonetheless the poem also attempts a discussion of that site, which must pass through precursory clarification of the individual poem: is it, then, 'a luminous flittering | Or the concentration of a cloudy day?' How does one apprehend well the 'evasion' in this meditation? Dependent on the poet's unspoken statement and its future readers, relating the orator to his listeners, this poem attempts a dialogue with interpretation: it considers the relation between thinking and poetry by riding the wave of explication that implicates individual poems in that which loves to conceal itself, its concealment in poems a part of its unspoken unconcealment:

> Evade, this hot, dependent orator,
> The spokesman at our bluntest barriers,
> Exponent by a form of speech, the speaker

> Of a speech only a little of the tongue?
> It is the gibberish of the vulgate that he seeks.
> He tries by a peculiar speech to speak

> The peculiar potency of the general,
> To compound the imagination's Latin with
> The lingua franca et jocundissima.

> (*SCP*: 397)

In reply to Bernard Heringman's questions about his work, Stevens denied influence (especially that of Wordsworth and Coleridge) and warned: 'I do not think that a thesis should be based on questions and answers like an interview. On the contrary, I believe in pure explication de texte. This may in fact be my principal form of piety' (*SL*: 793). If questions and answers are a means of arriving at clear conceptions about things, to step back into 'pure explication de texte' is to give oneself over to the evasive movement of language. Canto IX of 'It Must Change' enacts such a movement from the interrogative to language at work or at play in the poem: 'To compound the imagination's Latin with | The lingua franca et jocundissima', its jocular Latinate neologism heralding the arrival of thought that evades our approach. Such is the ostensible subject of the poem: 'a meditation' in which there is 'an evasion'. In her commentary, Eleanor Cook argues, 'It is not so much that [Stevens] *locates* his poetry in a space, a betweenness. Rather, he plays with that space itself, seeking a figure for it'. For her the subject of Canto IX is 'translation', which is 'always a crossing, more or less conscious, from one meaning to another' (Cook 1988: 244).

Stevens delighted in pouring over *A Latin Dictionary* by Lewis and Short, even giving a copy to Robert Frost (see *SL*: 275), and he is often the cause of our doing so too, making a certain kind of scholar out of his readers. But this poem is the occasion of a poet giving himself over to that which cannot be described, conceptualized or traced to an etymon or literary source, but is only revealed in process, in the form of the poem as the demand of its emergent project is undertaken. The 'piety' of Stevens's 'pure explication de texte' is exhibited in the exigency of its production, not isolated by any grand conception or definition. Although we can define piety as at once a filial relation when one is faithful to the duties owed to parents and an habitual reverence and obedience to God, in the context of poetry, it describes, not only relations between poets through the generations, but a movement of self-sacrifice 'exalted by an underpresence' (*1805*, xiii. 71). Regardless of the piety of 'literary influence', 'Every great poet creates his poetry out of one single poetic statement only. The measure of his greatness is the extent to which he becomes so committed to that singleness that he is able to keep his poetic Saying wholly within it' (Heidegger 1971: 160). Only a poet's explications of that 'poetic statement' make it seem peculiar to him: it is 'the one life within us and abroad', which evades a certain kind of questioning, but 'Which meets all motion and becomes its soul, | A light in sound, a sound-like power in light, | Rhythm in all thought, and joyance every where' (Coleridge 2001: i. 233). Such faithfulness to that which is forever in the future, makes poets full of meaningful coincidence, as they write to the rhythm of liquid lingerings. Their peculiar commitment to this singleness, which evades, makes for literary synchronicity: the more devoted their poems are to this soul, or site of the future in eternity, the more they correspond with other acts of such devotion, because they all rise upon waves that flow to the same source. Such is the 'moving soul', beyond causes, of literature with which interpretation should learn to converse.

From our world Stevens addresses earth at the end of 'Notes', to find the 'repining restlesnesse', which remains in the repose of the work, keeping us 'rich and wearie' (Herbert 1968: 154):

> Fat girl, terrestrial, my summer, my night,
> How is it I find you in difference, see you there
> In a moving contour, a change not quite completed?
>
> You are familiar yet an aberration.
> Civil, madam, I am, but underneath
> A tree, this unprovoked sensation requires
>
> That I should name you flatly, waste no words,
> Check your evasions, hold you to yourself.
> Even so when I think of you as strong or tired,
>
> Bent over work, anxious, content, alone,
> You remain the more than natural figure. You
> Become the soft-footed phantom, the irrational
>
> Distortion, however fragrant, however dear.
> That's it: the more than rational distortion,
> The fiction that results from feeling. Yes, that.
>
> They will get it straight one day at the Sorbonne.
> We shall return at twilight from the lecture
> Pleased that the irrational is rational,
>
> Until flicked by feeling, in a gildered street,
> I call you by name, my green, my fluent mundo.
> You will have stopped revolving except in crystal.

(*SCP*: 406–7)

In this canto the intimacy of the struggle of imagination or world with reality or earth is slightly erotic and grotesque at first. The familiar fat girl is 'the unforced coming forth of the continually self-closing', 'my summer, my night', who arouses the 'Civil' speaker underneath or as 'A tree', with 'this unprovoked sensation', and then leaves within the etymologies of 'aberration' and 'evasions'. As an apostrophe the poem makes this situation: Stevens is invoking the muse, ironically, at the very end of his long poem. But his words are wasted as they slide alliteratively from each other to gain even more consonantal weight, 'fat' becoming 'that' and then 'flatly'. The speaker's desired embrace, to 'Check your evasions', merely sets forth a self-closing, since language can only 'hold you to yourself', the fat girl becoming more ethereal as the poet's words become fatter. There is another attempt to catch the girl, in her supernatural emanation, in the fifth stanza, with its pincer-like epanaleptic repetition of 'that', which is undermined by its echo of fat. I also detect a gentle irony in the last two stanzas as we return from a lecture in Paris, 'Pleased' with this aperçu 'that the irrational is rational'. The street is 'gildered', gilded as if painted by the gilder twilight, but also laid with gilders or snares, like the poem. Stevens will invoke his muse in the future as a daughter of inspiration, not memory: if she is of the earth, then that globe crystallizes itself into a ball in which one foresees eternity. That which gives pleasure changes our notions of the abstract so that we can begin to apprehend being as that before us, which withdraws and returns in its revolving.

   That Stevens chose to keep 'Notes' as the final poem of *Transport to Summer*, despite the fact that it was composed in the spring of 1942 before nearly all of its other poems, when that collection became part of the *Collected Poems*, means that its readers reach the final cantos often without knowing that they are at an anachronistic point of revolving repose in the book. I imagine that Stevens was pleased with this arrangement because it makes the poem that comes immediately afterwards all the more unexpected. When readers turn to 'The Auroras of Autumn', 'The denouement has to be postponed . . .' (*SCP*: 416). Having left the Sorbonne, presumably with his notes from the lecture on a supreme fiction, the scholar reappears in the next poem as he arrives home, at the crucial turning point of Stevens's soul-making journey within the *Collected Poems*:

> This is nothing until in a single man contained,
> Nothing until this named thing nameless is
> And is destroyed. He opens the door of his house
>
> On flames. The scholar of one candle sees
> An Arctic effulgence flaring on the frame
> Of everything he is. And he feels afraid.

(SCP: 416–17)

The 'This' is 'a theatre floating through the clouds, | Itself a cloud, although of misted rock | And mountains running like water, wave on wave, | Through waves of light' (*SCP*: 416). Finding rhythm in all thought, let every soul recall that the soul is author of the fluent mundo that cannot be caught by naming. Towards the source of this wave that withdraws, the self of the scholar is consumed by flames. 'The scholar of one candle' describes Milton's 'Il Penseroso' unsphered, moved out of his tower into an American cabin on the beach:

> Or let my Lamp at midnight hour,
> Be seen in som high lonely Towr,
> Where I may oft out-watch the *Bear*,
> With thrice great *Hermes*, or unsphear
> The spirit of *Plato* to unfold
> What Worlds, or what vast Regions hold
> The immortal mind that hath forsook
> Her mansion in this fleshly nook:
> And of those *Damons* that are found
> In fire, air, flood, or under ground,
> Whose power hath a true consent
> With Planet, or with Element.

> (*1645*: i. 40–1)

Stevens's concerns in his late poems are those of a Neoplatonist scholar caught in the evasions of language. Written with words from 'this fleshly nook', his poems nonetheless contain 'pure explication de texte' 'to unfold | What Worlds . . . hold | The immortal mind'. In the next canto of 'Auroras' we find an apocalyptic 'imagination that sits enthroned', 'the just and the unjust', with 'crown and diamond cabbala', and as destructive of the scholar's self as the lightning that strikes the tower of that self's accumulated wisdom in the Tarot pack, which Yeats connects with the swan taking off in sudden thunder from a flooded lake:

> It leaps through us, through all our heavens leaps,
> Extinguishing our planets, one by one,
> Leaving, of where we were and looked, of where
>
> We knew each other and of each other thought,
> A shivering residue, chilled and foregone,
> Except for that crown and mystical cabala.

> (*SCP*: 417)

The poetry is urgent and questioning at first but I detect no irony as the canto addresses the relation itself between evasion and revelation. Stevens's 'mystical cabala' is an unwritten tradition of esoteric doctrine; like the oral tradition handed down from Moses or the poet's unspoken statement, it unreasonably folds into itself on waves of explication. An anagogical reading of even the Vulgate would detect its 'extinguishings' (*SCP*: 417) in translation but it is beyond the dead leaves of the book: such tradition comes to us from eternity in the future. We might say that Stevens's figure of enthroned imagination conjoins Old Testament with New except 'The Last Judgment is not Fable or Allegory but Vision . . . a Representation of what Eternally Exists' (Erdman: 554). In vision or celestial rendezvous, man makes up the whole: 'whenever any Individual Rejects Error & Embraces Truth a Last Judgment passes upon that Individual' (Erdman: 562). Appropriately, Stevens meditates on chance: 'But it dare not leap by chance in its own dark. | It must change from destiny to slight caprice', etymologically unsurprising since it is a January 'Goat-leaper':

> And thus its jetted tragedy, its stele
>
> And shape and mournful making move to find
> What must unmake it and, at last, what can,
> Say, a flippant communication under the moon.

> (*SCP*: 417–18)

Charles Altieri argues that this canto of the poem proposes a move from cumbersome theatrics to the glossy consolations of the nonchalant ironist. It all depends on how one reads the word 'flippant', although I would argue that Altieri misreads this crucial section of the poem because he does not always relate the evasions of language to the internal alterations of thinking. Altieri discusses 'The Auroras of Autumn' in order to work out why 'Angel Surrounded by Paysans' should be at the other end of its collection, nicely sifting, in the course of his superb essay, recent criticism on the relation between this poem and the still life by Pierre Tal-Coat that Stevens purchased in 1949 (2008: 151–70). He argues that later Stevens came to see the enchantments of Romanticism as having joined with scepticism itself since its aesthetic attitudes insisted on a distance between the world and the intelligence at work. Stevens's poetry might redress this situation by attempting to engage readers' dispositions by shaping paths of thinking, so that we begin to notice how alterations within thought might present themselves, altering our perception of our place in the world. Thus the longest poem of *The Auroras of Autumn*, 'An Ordinary Evening in New Haven' is made out of variations on its first line, 'The eye's plain version is a thing apart' (*SCP*: 465). As Stevens grew older he was occupied in working out how his poems could become part of the flux of the world. With this in mind, Altieri insists on the playfulness of 'Angel Surrounded by Paysans', that it at once emphasizes and naturalizes as poetry a metaphysical dimension to the earth in its becoming, the irrepressible imagination transforming what could become lugubrious and pious. I see that that poem's capacity to insist on a series of transformations that dramatize the imagination's inexhaustible powers makes its 'communication' also 'flippant' if that word is given back its twofold meaning. Flippant is defined by the *OED* as 'Of the tongue: "Nimble", voluble' and 'Of conversation or discourse: Fluent, sparkling', before it was obscured by decorous eighteenth-century derogatory applications. Returning to Canto VII of 'The Auroras of Autumn', what seems unbecoming superficially, turns out to be the necessary levity, not of irony, but of vision: then we apprehend the 'fluent mundo', 'revolving . . . in crystal'; 'a new heaven' that makes us hear 'a new earth' (Revelation 21. 1) 'Rise liquidly in liquid lingerings'.

To find the kind of words inscribed on the imagination's stele that vanishes into unwritten cabala, 'That scholar hungriest for that book' (*SCP*: 178) might well turn, with a Stevensian kind of unsolemn piety, to *The Egyptian Book of the Dead*, type of the artefact that speaks of what can no longer be spoken: 'Homage to thee, O Rā, when thou risest [and to thee], O Temu, in thy risings of beauty. Thou risest, thou risest, thou shinest, thou shinest at dawn of day . . . thy divine boat advanceth in peace . . . Rā liveth, and the serpent-fiend Nak is dead'. 'Thou hast come with thy diadems, and thou hast made heaven and earth bright with thy rays of pure emerald light' (Budge 2008: 7, 8, 9, and 12): 'its polar green, | The colour of . . . solitude' (*SCP*: 413). At the syncretic climax to 'The Auroras of Autumn' Stevens illustrates the mystical and nocturnal version, 'in the recesses of thy nature' (*1805*, xiii. 195), of the rendezvous in green with the 'Fat girl, terrestrial' underneath a tree at the end of 'Notes'. That which appears to us as 'a flippant communication', becomes, 'flicked by feeling', an unmaking and a making, at once evading and revealing moon and countryman or world and earth: such celestial rendezvous on earth we discover at the end of *The Auroras of Autumn* in 'Angel Surrounded by Paysans'. Now turning, like Wordsworth's river, to 'measure back his course' (*1850*, ix. 5) for a spell, we will journey to Stevens's very late poems, some of which were collected in 'The Rock', some published posthumously, to disclose the poet brooding 'that which arranged' 'the intensest rendezvous' with 'the Interior Paramour' (*SCP*: 524).

'Brooding sounds of river noises'

We can consider Stevens's equivocal relations with Milton, Wordsworth and other poets through the 'general and gregarious' (Keats 2002: 90) 'generations of the bird' (*SCP*: 304) by following a constellation of poems spread across the *Collected Poems* and beyond that are made out of the topos of brooding dove and water. In terms of their arrangement in the book, the first is 'Somnambulisma', which tells an old story:

> On an old shore, the vulgar ocean rolls
> Noiselessly, noiselessly, resembling a thin bird,
> That thinks of settling, yet never settles, on a nest.
>
> (*SCP*: 304)

Like the repetition of 'noiselessly', which undercuts its meaning, the onomatopoeia capturing the noise of waves on shale, Stevens's observation unsuccessfully evades two foundations of our poetic tradition. Bird and sea are made out of Milton's renovation of the opening of Genesis as he invokes the 'Spirit' that

> from the first
> Wast present, and with mighty wings outspread
> Dove-like satst brooding on the vast Abyss
> And mad'st it pregnant[.]
>
> (*PL*, i. 19–22)

Stevens's 'vulgar' makes one sense of his poem to be later poets' relations to different versions of Genesis, before and after the Vulgate; at the end of the vulgar era, 'To compound the imagination's Latin with | The lingua franca et jocundissima'. As Alastair Fowler notes, Milton's 'brooding' renders 'the Hebrew word that [KJV] Genesis 1:2 translates "moved" but St Basil and others give as *incubabat* (brooded)' (1998: 60): Stevens's lines, which make the ocean at the shore, rather than at its deep, resemble a bird, seem to dramatize the movement between different translations of the Hebrew word: the poem is 'a luminous flittering' and 'the concentration' of brooding that quite literally 'mooved'. Its concern with liminality captures too Milton's 'Mixed metaphor implying the Hermetic doctrine that God is both masculine and feminine, and indicating a vitalistic tradition' (Fowler 1998: 60):

> In the beginning God created the Heaven, and the Earth. And the earth was without forme, and voyd, and darkenesse was upon the face of the deepe: and the Spirit of God mooved upon the face of the waters. (Genesis 1. 1–2)

'It is the gibberish of the vulgate that he seeks' even if Stevens's American English is more vulgar than the English fixed in the KJV. Milton, 'separately dwelling' with St Basil, makes a bird out of the spirit of God, pouring forth with the word 'brooding' all 'the gawky beaks, the personalia' (*SCP*: 304) of later brooding poets, which are not to be found in the Vulgate:

> In principio creavit Deus caelum et terram
> terra autem erat inanis et vacua
> et tenebrae super faciem abyssi
> et spiritus Dei ferebatur super aquas.
>
> (Genesis 1: 1–2)

Stevens's poem like the vulgar sea of the generations in time and space, full of Milton and other poets, rolls on the old shore of the Vulgate, 'Noiselessly, noiselessly', it 'thinks of settling, yet never settles'. It invokes Milton's bird that seems to hover and brood and give birth all at once but returns to our reading of the Vulgate where 'The wings keep spreading and yet are never wings', 'et spiritus Dei ferebatur super aquas':

> Without this bird that never settles, without
> Its generations that follow in their universe,
> The ocean, falling and falling on the hollow shore,
>
> Would be a geography of the dead: not of that land
> To which they may have gone, but of the place in which
> They lived, in which they lacked a pervasive being,
>
> In which no scholar, separately dwelling,
> Poured forth the fine fins, the gawky beaks, the personalia,
> Which, as a man feeling everything, were his.
>
> (*SCP*: 304)

From 'a geography of the dead' that is also Pennsylvania, emerge the 'generations of the bird' in 'A Completely New Set of Objects':

> From a Schuylkill in mid-earth there came emerging
> Flotillas, willed and wanted, bearing in them
>
> Shadows of friends, of those he knew, each bringing
> From the water in which he believed and out of desire
>
> Things made by mid-terrestrial, mid-human
> Makers without knowing, or intending, uses.

The shapes that 'These figures verdant with time's buried verdure' carry are 'of such alleviation, | That the beholder knew their subtle purpose, | knew well the shapes were the exactest shaping | Of a vast people old in meditation . . .' (*SCP*: 352–3): some of these shapes are poems. We might argue that the beholder is the scholar who has 'learned | To look on' verdant Wordsworth, 'hearing oftentimes' Milton (*LB1*: 206), to know their subtle purpose as poets who are greater than they knew, a greatness revealed in their relationships today as they come 'emerging' out of tradition or the continual renewal of divine revelation in time.

In 'Thinking of a Relation between the Images of Metaphors' the beholder-scholar is imagined as the fisherman, as in Yeats, emblem of the poet's second self or ideal audience of future poets, to be distinguished from the 'fit audience . . . though few' (*PL*, vii. 31):

> The wood-doves are singing along the Perkiomen.
> The bass lie deep, still afraid of the Indians.
>
> In the one ear of the fisherman, who is all
> One ear, the wood-doves are singing a single song.

> (*SCP*: 356)

As Wordsworth finds Milton's 'murmur' (*1673*: i. 59) intertwined with murmuring in the KJV (see, for example, Matthew 20. 11) by making the Derwent murmur in his effusive very first draft of *The Prelude*, Stevens finds Wordsworth and Milton and 'a vast people old in meditation', in his native American rivers of Pennsylvania. I am even tempted to mention Wordsworth's description of his younger self in later revisions of the first effusion as 'A naked savage', 'alone | Beneath the sky, as if I had been born | On Indian plains' (*1850*, i. 300 and 296–8). Stevens's poems can also make interpretation want to tell fables of itself: as fishermen readers seek the single song, and climb the streams to the realm of syn-chronicity, so the Latinate 'single' emerges in an acausal manner out of the Old English 'singing'. But the poem evokes the fisherman to tell the fable of the poems that evade interpretation:

> The bass keep looking ahead, upstream, in one
> Direction, shrinking from the spit and splash
>
> Of waterish spears. The fisherman is all
> One eye, in which the dove resembles the dove.

> (*SCP*: 356)

Yeats wished to write just one poem for his elusive Irish fisherman while Stevens's poems evade in 'liquid lingerings' his Native American fisherman. But both poets face resolutely upstream rather than trace a river to the sea like Wordsworth. Such an allegorical or inferior reading supposes that Stevens's poems are intended to be the bass that shrink from our interpretive spears; we will not quite catch Stevens between the Vulgate and Milton: 'Yet coo becomes rou-coo, rou-coo. How close || To the unstated theme each variation comes . . .' (*SCP*: 356–7). The fisherman also emblematizes Stevens's commitment, in the 'liquid lin-gerings' of 'pure explication de texte' situated within his poems, to that single unspoken statement as it recedes on the crest of its wave. Out of his unholy trinity of dove, bass and fisherman there 'might' come a hatching of the dove or 'disclosure' (*SCP*: 357) as 'any right clarification [of individual poems] itself already presupposes discussion' of the site 'of one single poetic statement'.

An early poem, from *Harmonium*, 'Depression before Spring', con-trasts the harshness of cock-crow with the softer cooing of the dove which does not come yet:

> But ki-ki-ri-ki
> Brings no rou-cou
> No rou-cou-cou.
>
> But no queen comes
> In slipper green.

> (*SCP*: 63)

We shall turn our attentions to the cry of cock-crow in Chapter 4. Younger Stevens equates the 'rou-cou' of the dove with a queen 'In slipper green' a colour addressed at the end of 'Notes' as 'my green, my fluent mundo', and later etherealized as celestial and 'pure emerald light' in the 'gusts of great enkindlings', the 'polar green, | The colour of ice and fire in solitude' (*SCP*: 413) of 'The Auroras of Autumn'. In *Transport to Summer* Stevens has still not found the word for the dove's roucoulement: 'The dove in the belly builds his nest and coos, || Selah, tempestuous bird' (*SCP*: 366); out of the Psalmist's musical direction, Stevens finds an evening service of benediction to salute a new kind of Host: ' – oh, brave salut! | Deep dove, placate you in your hiddenness' (*SCP*: 367). The cooing dove becomes involved with the poem's capacity to foreground a metaphysical dimension to the earth in its becoming: 'How is it that | The rivers shine and hold their mirrors up, | Like excellence collecting excellence?' (*SCP*: 366–7), Stevens almost asks of the bird. But the dove's evasiveness in the belly allows the poet to escape what might become lugubrious and pious. In the first section of 'Notes', 'Life's nonsense pierces us with strange relation': 'By day | The wood-dove used to chant his hoobla-hoo || And still the grossest iridescence of ocean | Howls hoo and rises and howls hoo and falls' (*SCP*: 383). In very late Stevens we shall hear the dove howl again.

By *The Auroras of Autumn*, after the bird has disappeared into the belly or imagination of the speaker, Stevens finds the word to describe the sound of the dove. The dove and its cooing vanish just as Stevens's poems start 'brooding', in the same way that the cherub of Blake's 'Introduction' to *Songs of Innocence* vanishes into the book that he requests. Out of such brooding and at the centre of the constellation of poems that we are tracing, 'Metaphor as Degeneration' schemes a doubtful and elegiac scenario, a delineation of two brooders that begins with a supposition:

> If there is a man white as marble
> Sits in a wood, in the greenest part,
> Brooding sounds of the images of death,
> So there is a man in black space
>
> Sits in nothing that we know,
> Brooding sounds of river noises[.]
>
> (*SCP*: 444)

'If' heralds the protasis of a conditional sentence, so that as we read we are also waiting for the apodosis. The poem, like much of late Stevens, exploits and experiments with this conditional movement. The first impression is that the poem all too easily satisfies the reader's desire for symmetrical resolution: 'If there is a man white as marble . . . || So there is a man in black space'. The second clause recompenses the first as if in a game of chess. One piece is exchanged for another. On closer inspection these figures are barely counterparts. One man is white but the other is colourless since he sits in black space and the respective movements of each man later on similarly disrupt any simple black and white chiasmal relation. Our dialogue with the poem thus moves between its 'clarification' and a 'discussion' of the dark site that gathers Stevens's 'poetic Saying into his poetic work'.

'If', that is, on the condition it is certain that 'I stand heere, I saw him' (*F*; *Macbeth*, III. iv. 75): the first 'If' of 'Metaphor as Degeneration' conceals the 'It' so important to the poem:

> It is certain that the river
>
> Is not Swatara. The swarthy water
> That flows round the earth and through the skies,
> Twisting among the universal spaces,
>
> Is not Swatara. It is being.

> (*SCP*: 444)

We cannot know what 'It' is. The poem emphasizes the meaningless-ness of this pronoun when it is reiterated in the last line. When 'It is being' are we referred to the river that 'Is not Swatara' or this other even more elusive 'It'? The poem prompts us to ask such questions, to search for definitions, in our attempt to locate the site of the poet's 'unspoken statement': 'That is the flock-flecked river, the water, | The blown-sheen – or is it air?' Where and what exactly is or was 'That'? The poem possesses '*Negative Capability*' because in it 'it' undermines 'that', like 'this', an empiricist expression because it pledges the sufficiency of what can be observed, with no 'irritable reaching after' meaning (Altieri 2008; Keats 2002: 41–2). As we try and imagine the figures in the first stanza we will ask, 'what do they represent?' as Keats does of those on the Grecian urn. Any such exegetical quest should take note of the explication de texte within Stevens's poem, when the speaker interprets for us 'these images' and the river in its third and sixth stanzas and questions the title of the poem in line 19. Stevens supposes a scene, which he knows we cannot help but imagine, and yet 'Metaphor as Degeneration' seems designed to foil and pre-empt our attempts to visualize and interpret what is going on: figures suddenly vanish (or become transmuted into 'black violets' and covered by 'memorial mosses'), the river evaporates from our more familiar sense of geography, and the beginnings of explication are included within the poem as it foregrounds, to evade, interpretation. The poem resists 'clarification' even as it invites 'discussion'; it continually undermines what it insists. It questions the 'imagination' at work as a power that evades the poet's control or the reader's suppositions, to be included with death in being.

Poussin paints 'Et in arcadia ego' as inscribed on the tomb in his paintings of that name, alluding to Virgil's fifth eclogue, and a subject upon which the melancholy Jaques might have brooded, watching a dying stag, 'as he lay along | Under an oake, whose anticke roote peepes out | Upon the brooke that brawles along this wood' (*F*; *As You Like It*, II. i. 30–2), his position recommended by Coleridge in 'The Nightingale'. In Theocritus' seventh idyll the speaker journeys with friends to a harvest-feast held by grandsons of 'that very Chalcon whose sturdy knee planted once against the rock both made Burina fount to gush forth at his feet and caused elm and aspen to weave above it a waving canopy of green leaves and about it a precinct of shade' (Edmonds 1928: 93). The founder of bucolic poetry describes the creation of a *locus amoenus* within a fictional genealogy of a fictional future host. Theocritus was the first to create a 'fictional world', not as an image of reality but as an alternative to it, and such a world is mediated by form: 'textuality highlights the strange authority of [fictional beings'] appearance, the fact that the agency in this encounter seems to lie with them. It is they that seek us out' (Payne 2007: 92). 'Metaphor as Degeneration' shows itself aware of its literary genealogy when it describes 'these images' as 'these reverberations', but the poem looks forward to the imaginative process of creating and holding conversation within a *locus amoenus* today.

Stevens's use of the superlative, 'greenest', to describe the conventional setting of the poem founds its opening 'If' upon 'Once upon a time': upon stories that readers have been quite willing to believe temporarily, since before the time of Theocritus' alternative worlds, when that mythical Chalcon was alive, 'in old time' (*1805*, x. 1020). The exegesis within 'Metaphor as Degeneration' makes us reconsider our pact with that initial 'If', in order to examine our willingness to be beguiled. The dynamic between the dark story and its interpretation is most important as Stevens foregrounds our encounter with his fictional beings or non-beings. The silent forms of 'Metaphor as Degeneration' 'tease us out of thought | As doth eternity', resisting imagination and interpretation; they seek us out, as death eventually will, in their 'Cold Pastoral' (Keats 1820: 116), but Stevens's poem also seeks out such pastoral characters as those in Theocritus' idylls, thus placing the reader, Stevens's familiar 'scholar', within the poem. Keats's urgent questioning of the Grecian urn betrays his horror that we can never manifest ourselves to its figures. Is there a possibility of communication between literary beings and readers in Stevens's poem as it explores the imagination at work in relation to language? If Stevens's fictional beings seek us out, we are already there to meet them, our response anticipated by the explication de texte within the poem. Ironically, we find ourselves within such evasions, the poem is 'The spokesman at our bluntest barriers'.

No narrative is simple no matter how sparse: the most pared down parable becomes with time a dark saying overburdened with meaning. The explanations of the poem within the poem rely on metaphysical locution familiar from Plato onwards. But terms like 'being', 'imagination', 'space' and 'universal' can mesmerize interpretation. Ironically, the poem itself is 'Twisting among the universal spaces', as it invites to confound clarification, at once promising and withdrawing epistemological certainty. The poem forestalls acts of supposition in our reading, whether we are imagining the figure or conjecturing what it represents. Like Milton's use of the mixed metaphor of hovering, brooding, pregnant spirit, 'Metaphor as Degeneration' ambushes our conceptualizing, to trick us out of supposing its theme. Ironically, we are to stop relying on metaphors while thinking about its metaphors. We are as committed to terms like 'being' and 'imagination' as we are to stories and opaque parables but the poem points to a path of thinking out of metaphysics by suggesting the necessary evasiveness of 'being' and the waywardness of words as they echo others. It is a poem capable itself of brooding a new kind of brooding as it discloses the relationship itself between 'clarification' of an instance and 'discussion' of an eternal source.

The ghost of Wordsworth

Brooding in 'Metaphor as Degeneration' occurs at the site that has or is 'the gathering power' as it penetrates 'with its light all it has gathered . . . only thus releasing it into its own nature'. Milton's scholarship discloses such incubation in Genesis; enriched by *Paradise Lost*, Wordsworth turns to nature to discover such creative power in the mind of man. That he thus helped to make his and subsequent generations 'of the bird' is made explicit in his explication of his own line, 'Over his own sweet voice the Stock-dove *broods*' (Wordsworth's italics, as quoted in his 1815 'Preface'):

> The Stock-dove is said to *coo*, a sound well imitating the note of the bird; but, by the intervention of the metaphor *broods*, the affections are called in by the imagination to assist in marking the manner

in which the Bird reiterates and prolongs her soft note, as if herself delighting to listen to it, and participating of a still and quiet satisfaction, like that which may be supposed inseparable from the continuous process of incubation. (*1815*: i. xxiii)

The supposed clarification of 'Metaphor as Degeneration', when Stevens glosses in the third stanza the first two stanzas of his poem and 'others' that also reverberate 'these images', brings explication into the poem by developing a manner of self-exegesis that is only prefatorial in Wordsworth. Stevens links Wordsworth's rather uncomplicated description of the action of the 'imagination' calling in the 'affections' to assist it 'in marking the manner', to the actual 'continuous process of incubation' suggested by the bird delighting in her cooing, as she prolongs 'her soft note'. Stevens's poem broods on 'the intervention' of metaphor as disclosure and as degeneration after a continuous process of incubation, understanding that the very metaphor *broods* describes and undermines straightforward notions of the imagination at work, choosing such words. Stevens's 'make certain' is ironic; such explication of 'these images' seems a better parody of Wordsworth glossing his own poems in his prefaces than actual interpretation of 'Metaphor as Degeneration'. Wordsworth's 'imagination' operates in an assured manner with his helpers the affections, Stevens's poem returns upon its brooding figures to brood on language itself as it operates evasively within the poem.

The second figure in 'Metaphor as Degeneration' is 'Brooding sounds of river noises'; not just river noises, but sounds of river noises: the noises of rivers in literature. This constellation of Stevens poems that we are tracing comes at the end of a distinct tradition of poems organized around the structuring principle of a river. The most important precursor is Wordsworth's *The Prelude*, which is, in turn,

clearly influenced by lines from [Cowper's] *The Task*. The Derwent at the opening of *1799* links *The Prelude* back via *Tintern Abbey* and the Wye to Coleridge and the Otter, Bowles and the Itchen, Warton and the Loden, Akenside and 'Wensbeck's limpid stream'; but as well as these nostalgic revisited rivers there is in the background Coleridge's scheme for *The Brook*, forerunner to *The Recluse*, in which the river was designed specifically to give the cohesion lacking in Cowper. (Jonathan Wordsworth 1984: 333)

One might say that all of these poets and rivers flow into Stevens and the Swatara, a Pennsylvanian creek that joins the Susquehanna.

Mary Jacobus identifies 'the topographical elegy, or "revisit" poem' (1976: 113), popular in the eighteenth century, at once culminating and transformed forever in 'Wordsworth's potent intertwining of elegy and landscape' in 'Tintern Abbey'. With its 'repeated out-in-out process, in which the mind confronts nature and their interplay constitutes the poem' (Abrams 1965: 528), 'Tintern Abbey' is itself an important example of what M. H. Abrams terms the 'Greater Romantic Lyric', developed by both Wordsworth and Coleridge. Jacobus sees also that 'Wordsworth's Wye is in origin a poet's river' (1976: 116) and further argues that the 'undercurrent of elegy' in this poem 'is ultimately a Miltonic legacy' (1976: 112). I am interested in how Stevens's poems productively disrupt such critical classifications and how they call into question the very idea of poetic influence that the poems' shared motif suggests. Heaney says of Wordsworth's Derwent, 'The river flows into dreams and composes' (Heaney 1980: 70), thus changing the tradition of the topographical lyric; Stevens's poems brood upon 'this undulant river' (*SCP*: 444) of being, rising and flowing back on the wave of rhythm, as the moving site or acausal soul that gathers poems and poets, thus changing our notions of poetic influence. Great poets speak from the same source, and strength of commitment to that site makes each distinctive. Such poets appear to correspond across the generations because each shares his unspoken statement that comes to us from eternity in the future, but his devotion to that site in his work releases him into his own nature: such are the disclosures of brooding.

The summit of the 'Greater Romantic Lyric' is just above the mist-line of Snowdon, at the climax of *The Prelude*, in Wordsworth's account of a spot of time, which seems to fructify also in Stevens. Although, as with Yeats's relation to the beginning of *The Prelude*, it is productively impossible to determine whether Stevens consciously alludes to or is influenced by Wordsworth in his river poems. It may be that 'Metaphor as Degeneration' is at work on the border of such an ambiguous relationship to reconfigure tradition. De Selincourt's 1926 edition of *The Prelude* revealed the failure of Wordsworth's commitment 'to keep his poetic Saying wholly within' the 'singleness' of his unspoken 'poetic statement', by publishing for the first time the earlier 1805 version of the poem alongside the familiar 1850 text. We can assume that the younger Stevens had read the 1850 text; we do not know if he consulted the 1805 version of the poem after it was published. But, even from a Wordsworthian perspective, it may not matter. It is tempting to say that Stevens's poems fulfil, as Wordsworth's revisions and future work do not, Wordsworth's 'hope that his own work, "*Proceeding from the depth of untaught things*, | Enduring and creative" may "become | A power like one of Nature's"' (Jonathan Wordsworth 1984: 327, quoting with emphasis from *1805*, xii. 310–12).

The humbling 'influx' 'vouchsafed' (1805, xii. 308 and 307) to Wordsworth also grants 'the intensest rendezvous' between poets, out of which Stevens broods his beautiful 'Final Soliloquy of the Interior Paramour': it is 'A light, a power, the miraculous influence' (*SCP*: 524); 'A presence that disturbs' the everyday self, 'A motion and a spirit' (*LB1*: 207) that disrupts causality to gather poets, and so it appears to us as if their later work even influences that which has come before. Such correspondence is not dependent on poets' individual memories; 'that which arranged the rendezvous', 'that age-long memoried self', penetrating with its light all it has gathered, hatches poetic identities, by making their work greater than they knew. From the perspective of our world we discern influence as if it flows from the past when in reality it acts on earth the future in eternity. In Yeats, symbols and the discipline of old forms help him to generate such action; in Stevens, such reality is caught in the evasive movement of language itself. As Stevens intimated, in his reply to Heringman's questions about Wordsworth and Coleridge, his greatest poems are not 'Formd by the Daughters of Memory': he writes 'Surrounded by the daughters of Inspiration'. His labour to let his idiom speak the one life that withdraws makes his poetry distinctive; that evasive power also gives his poems affinities with the work of other poets so committed, making the question of whether or not he had read their poems, irrelevant. In distinctive ways, great poets speak from the same source; their work gives 'Expression ever varying' (*1849–50*: vi. 15) to the same 'moving soul' that is within us and abroad. Thus Wordsworth's 'animating faith' (*1850*, xiii. 300):

> That poets, even as Prophets, each with each
> Connected in a mighty scheme of truth,
> Have each for his peculiar dower, a sense
> By which he is enabled to perceive
> Something unseen before[.]
>
> (*1805*, xii. 301–5)

It is not so much 'Something unseen before' that Stevens is 'enabled to perceive' but the evasive process itself of such perception as it unfolds in language.

At the climax of *The Prelude*, Wordsworth relates how, in 1793, on one of his walking 'excursions' 'with a youthful Friend', they 'Rouz'd up the

Shepherd, who by ancient right | Of office is the Stranger's usual guide', in the middle of a 'glaring' night, 'to see the sun | Rise from the top of Snowdon' (*1805*, xiii. 1–9):

> With forehead bent
> Earthward, as if in opposition set
> Against an enemy, I panted up
> With eager pace, and no less eager thoughts.
> Thus might we wear perhaps an hour away,
> Ascending at loose distance each from each,
> And I, as chanced, the foremost of the Band;
> When at my feet the ground appear'd to brighten,
> And with a step or two seem'd brighter still;
> Nor had I time to ask the cause of this,
> For instantly a Light upon the turf
> Fell like a flash: I looked about, and lo!
> The Moon stood naked in the Heavens, at height
> Immense above my head, and on the shore
> I found myself of a huge sea of mist,
> Which, meek and silent, rested at my feet[.]

> (*1805*, xiii. 29–44)

With gentle and affectionate mockery, Wordsworth puts his younger self on a natural version of 'the time-honoured *Scala Perfectionis* of mysticism' (Bayley 1912: i. 32), which Curtius would call a topos, Jung, an archetype. Certainly the landscape exists both outside and inside the poet as Wordsworth will recount the meditation on the scene within his memory, and his poetry also recalls, among other things, the first canto of Dante's *Comedy*. Omitting the traditional topics of exordium, Dante nonetheless announces the major image of his poem by having the pilgrim climb a mountain out of the dark wood at the very beginning of the *Inferno*. As at the very end of Wordsworth's poem, we join a younger self on the ladder of creation, which is also the chain of being:

> But when a mountain's foot I reach'd, where closed
> The valley that had pierced my heart with dread,
> I look'd aloft, and saw his shoulders broad
> Already vested with that planet's beam,
> Who leads all wanderers safe through every way.
>   Then was a little respite to the fear,
> That in my heart's recesses deep had lain

All of that night, so pitifully past:
And as a man, with difficult short breath,
Foresprent with toiling, 'scaped from sea to shore,
Turns to the perilous wide waste, and stands
At gaze; e'en so my spirit, that yet fail'd,
Struggling with terror, turn'd to view the straits
That none hath past and lived.

(Cary: 1–2)

The anxious beginning in a forbidding setting, the promise of 'that planet's beam', the turn to look at the view half-way up, wood or mist below now appearing as a sea lapping the shore of the mountain, all conspire to bring together the beginning of the *Comedy* and the end of *The Prelude*. By ending in this way Wordsworth is indicating that this poem marks just the first steps of a longer project, a preliminary ascent, that is, like the pilgrim's, unexpectedly interrupted:

My weary frame
After short pause recomforted, again
I journey'd on over that lonely steep,
The hinder foot still firmer. Scarce the ascent
Began, when, lo! a panther, nimble, light,
And cover'd with a speckled skin, appear'd;
Nor, when it saw me, vanish'd; rather strove
To check my onward going; that oft-times,
With purpose to retrace my steps, I turn'd.

(Cary: 2)

'Ed ecco' (*Inferno*, i. 31); 'and lo!': Wordsworth's interjection of surprise is near to Cary's translation of Dante. The drama of the pilgrim's shock encounter with the snow leopard or lynx ('taxonomy has been the central crux in explicating the first of the beasts' [Lansing 2010: 87]) after his rest is intensified in *The Prelude* because Wordsworth's moon simultaneously causes his younger self to turn and reveals the natural landscape to him below. Yeats on the ruined battlements of his tower makes such a figure: each poet is struck by visionary lightning; Wordsworth by moonlight that 'Fell like a flash', fulfilling imaginatively the storm half-threatened by the sky (*1805*, xiii. 12–13); Dante's path cut by a light and quick ounce; and each scene is reminiscent of the tower struck by lightning in the Tarot pack. In each case the visionary strike surprises the poet's younger self into recognizing or unwittingly enacting the form and theme of his future poem: the pilgrim's turning backwards on the mountain, in face of the ounce, at such numerologically significant lines, symbolizes the concatenated form of *terza rima*, taking steps back in rhyme as its stanzas progress, which Dante now uses to write about the chain of being:

> e non mi si partia dinanzi al volto,
> anzi 'mpediva tanto il mio cammino
> ch'i' fui per ritornar più volte vòlto.
>
> (*Inferno*, i. 34–6)

In Canto XXV of 'An Ordinary Evening in New Haven', 'Life fixed him, wandering on the stair of glass, | With its attentive eyes' as 'A hatching that stared and demanded an answering look' (*SCP*: 483–4). Stevens's pun on wandering and conflation of stair and stare catches Dante's juxtaposition of 'al volto' and 'volte vòlto'. Each poem is 'at several turns turned to go back' (*Inferno*, i. 36) as their poets seek the truth that at once makes and evades the concatenations of language. The stair or stare of glass is also 'a glasse' through which we see 'darkly' (1 Corinthians 13. 12); on reflection, it seems to Wordsworth that the landscape revealed suddenly by the moon on the mountain reflects not a face but 'a mighty mind' that broods, which we can relate to 'A hatching' in Stevens: 'a man in black space'. The matter of Stevens's work is the evasiveness of Wordsworth's theme of imagination: his work broods upon the moving of this 'moving soul' in language.

Dante structures his whole poem explicitly on the ways of ascent, drawing with deliberation on classical and biblical sources. Turning from the first canto of the *Comedy* to the end of *The Prelude*, one begins to wonder about Wordsworth's 'Shepherd' countering Virgil's appearance on the mountain in Dante, and one discerns a complex of allusions to Milton and many others. But Wordsworth balances knowledge of the Bible and classical and vernacular literature with a naturalistic description because he would have his poem proceed also from the depth of untaught things to become a power like one of nature's: he understands that the knowledge contained in tradition can also well from within if one looks on nature with right regard. Yeats, on the other hand, constructs poems that seem realistic enough but whose naturalism is designed merely to conceal an underlying symbolic structure made out of the same range of sources from which Dante draws, and which Yeats understands as the ever-varying expression of anima mundi (see de Man 1984: 143). Stevens's poems explicate the furtive ways in which language mediates the relationship between earthy reality and imaginative worlds to come upon the truth that always withdraws. All four poets reconfigure the ways of ascent as they labour to make a soul. Their commitment to that unspoken statement makes them at once distinctive and correspondent. By committing themselves to vision they are gathered by it, a movement that occurs within verse, disrupting an outsider's causal understanding of influence.

Struck by moonlight after midnight, Wordsworth is frightened out of his younger self and afforded a fearful, almost Gothic, vision of the 'Goddess': like that of Isis revealed to Apuleius' ass, she appears a full moon 'as though she leaped out of the Sea' at 'the most secret time, when the goddesse Ceres had most puissance and force, considering that all humane things be governed by her providence' (Apuleius 1922: 217). Various watermarks that 'represent the ascent of the soul by means of the Ladder of Perfection' (Bayley 1912: i. 32) show a moon or a dove at the summit. The undercurrent of tradition upon which poets draw is to be found both without and within, and Wordsworth finds an emblem for this hidden wisdom, or divine revelation in time, in the landscape before him:

> Meanwhile, the Moon look'd down upon this shew
> In single glory, and we stood, the mist
> Touching our very feet; and from the shore
> At distance not the third part of a mile
> Was a blue chasm; a fracture in the vapour,
> A deep and gloomy breathing-place through which
> Mounted the roar of waters, torrents, streams
> Innumerable, roaring with one voice.
>
> (*1805*, xiii. 52–9)

Out of Wordsworth's sea of mist mounts the roar of Stevens's 'undulant river' that 'becomes the landless, waterless ocean' (*SCP*: 444) in the likewise nocturnal landscape of 'Metaphor as Degeneration'. As in Apuleius, Wordsworth's vision prompts meditation, but this time bringing divinity within the poet and his works to become 'the moving soul | Of our long labour' (*1805*, xiii. 171–2); she seeks us out as we make ourselves manifest to her: 'Deepe calleth unto deepe at the noyse of thy water-spouts: all thy waves, and thy billowes are gone over me'

(Psalm 42. 7). Wordsworth's brooding upon these river noises is part of his memory:

> A meditation rose in me that night
> Upon the lonely Mountain when the scene
> Had pass'd away, and it appear'd to me
> The perfect image of a mighty Mind,
> Of one that feeds upon infinity,
> That is exalted by an underpresence,
> The sense of God, or whatsoe'er is dim
> Or vast in its own being[.]

(1805, xiii. 66–73)

In this 1805 version, 'The perfect image of a mighty Mind' is the landscape at the poet's feet 'That is exalted by an underpresence', the roar of waters, 'welling up from within to speak of inner vastness and infinite possibilities' (Jonathan Wordsworth, 1984: 331). In later revisions 'the scene' becomes 'That vision' or 'marvel', considered not simply as 'image', but as 'type' or 'emblem' (see *1805*: 474–5), collecting and giving back meaning like Yeats's tower and Stevens's river. By 1850 the emblem is clearly the moon, which broods on the torrent of waters from above, Wordsworth drawing on Milton more explicitly in his revisions:

> There I beheld the emblem of a mind
> That feeds upon infinity, that broods
> Over the dark abyss, intent to hear
> Its voices issuing forth to silent light
> In one continuous stream[.]

(1850, xiv. 70–4)

The river noises are 'now caught by an external listener waiting to be sustained by recognitions of a power beyond the self', and, as Jonathan Wordsworth points out, 'It is a very big change' (1984: 331). 'Metaphor as Degeneration' seems to meditate on this aporia between versions of *The Prelude*, transforming Wordsworth's ambiguous moonlit landscape in Snowdonia, to re-engage with the earlier poet's struggle with the transcendental as he allegorizes this nightscape. 'Nor had I time to ask the cause of this': the confluence of the two poems is as chanceful as the very vision that is afforded Wordsworth, 'as chanced', ahead of the others. That night's meditation, revised by Wordsworth, is also Stevens's commitment to keep his work of that acausal, 'mighty Mind'; 'in the universe | Of that single mind': 'Distant, yet close enough to wake | The chords above your bed to-night' (*OP*: 132).

Milton only uses the word 'brooding' twice in *Paradise Lost*, the second time when Raphael tells Adam of the creation of the world (*PL*, vii. 235). In his invocation he is 'taking an established tradition of the Spirit of God brooding over the waters at the creation and associating it with the poet brooding over his material in the process of creation' (Daiches 1960: 67); despite Milton's judgement in *De Doctrina* that 'invocation of the Holy Spirit' is 'unbiblical', 'Now, at least, the Logos or the Holy Spirit is addressed' (Fowler 1998: 59). This analogy between creation and poetic making becomes the central preoccupation of *The Prelude*. Stevens's poems incorporate explication because they are 'intent to hear | Its voices issuing forth to silent light'. Each intends to listen to itself and, 'as chanced', to others. Such brooding makes Stevens's 'imagination' closer to Milton's 'Spirit' or Wordsworth's 'mighty mind', at work gathering poems and withdrawing meaning from their images even as it generates 'these images': together his poems explicate the relation of imagination to the evasive operation of language itself. In the poem immediately before 'Metaphor as Degeneration' in *The Auroras of Autumn*, 'A Primitive Like an Orb', it is claimed, 'We do not prove the existence of the poem. | It is something seen and known in lesser poems' (*SCP*: 440). The poem that comes after 'Metaphor as Degeneration', 'The Woman in Sunshine' transmutes 'It is being', returning upon it: 'It is not that there is any image in the air | Nor the beginning nor end of a form: || It is empty' (*SCP*: 445). The poet's unspoken statement, 'the poem', not proven, but seen and known in lesser poems, is 'like an empty vessel | That yet may be drawn from | Without ever needing to be filled' (Waley 1934: 146), from which 'rises the wave that in each instance moves his Saying as poetic saying', its rise flowing back to its ever more hidden source in the 'liquid lingerings' of language that so fascinate Stevens: 'in lesser poems', 'Deepe calleth unto deepe' to flow back to itself; 'in the most furtive fiction' of earth, Stevens does not rest from his task 'to open the immortal Eyes | Of Man inwards into the Worlds of Thought: into Eternity | Ever expanding in the Bosom of God, the Human Imagination'.

'The River of Rivers'

In Section XXIV of 'The Man with the Blue Guitar' Stevens talks of:

> A poem like a missal found
> In the mud, a missal for that young man,

> That scholar hungriest for that book,
> The very book, or, less, a page
>
> Or, at the least, a phrase, that phrase,
> A hawk of life, that latined phrase:
>
> To know; a missal for brooding-sight.
> To meet that hawk's eye and to flinch
>
> Not at the eye but at the joy of it.
> I play. But this is what I think.
>
> (*SCP*: 177–8)

The 'brooding-sight' of the hungry scholar functions with 'the one ear of the fisherman' on that other Pennsylvanian creek of Stevens's *Collected Poems*, the Perkiomen, tributary of the Schuylkill River, in 'Thinking of a Relation between the Images of Metaphors'. Attempts to locate the hawk's eye take us to the realm of Stevens's 'jocundissima'. A bird of prey might disturb the wood-doves but a hawk might be a latined phrase in a missal or mass-book. In an outrageous pun a hawk might be a bird of prayer, symbolizing the 'piety' of 'pure explication de texte' as its opposite, the brooding dove, symbolizes the Spirit of God. A missal also recalls missile, like the 'waterish spears' aimed at the fish in the later poem. But we should be wary of allegorizing Stevens so neatly. We come upon him again wondering how to 'State the disclosure' (*SCP*: 357); to make us 'flinch' with joy when 'In that one eye the dove | Might spring to sight and yet remain a dove' (*SCP*: 357): 'one eye' looks out of the 'hawk's eye' in 'The Man with the Blue Guitar' and one has the uncanny impression that in both cases it is the poem that is watching or reading us, which is Stevens's 'unstated theme'.

Beyond 'Metaphor as Degeneration', three other river poems present themselves as missals for brooding-sight in *The Auroras of Autumn*. In 'This Solitude of Cataracts', 'He never felt twice the same about the flecked river, | Which kept flowing and never the same way twice, flowing | Through many places, as if it stood still in one' (*SCP*: 424). According to Arius Didymus, as recorded in Eusebius' *Preparation for the Gospel*, Cleanthes argues that Heraclitus, 'wishing to show that souls being nourished by exhalations are always intelligent . . . compares them to rivers, saying, On those stepping into rivers staying the same other and other waters flow' (Graham 2010: 183). Graham's translation attempts to capture the syntactical ambiguity of the fragment of Heraclitus as does Stevens's allusion to Heraclitus' 'hawk of life' found buried in others' books: '"the same" is sandwiched between "rivers" and "those stepping" in, agrees with both, and can be construed with either – an ambiguity that took considerable ingenuity to create' (Graham 2010: 190). Using sibilant sounds, 'alliterations and iterated staccato syllables' Heraclitus evokes the sound of a stream to say, 'stable structures and cognizers coexist with, and are somehow constituted by, changing conditions' (2010: 191):

> There was so much that was real that was not real at all.
> He wanted to feel the same way over and over.
>
> He wanted the river to go on flowing the same way,
> To keep on flowing[.]

> (*SCP*: 425)

Like Yeats in 'Sailing to Byzantium', Stevens imagines a metallic future self, 'released from destruction', 'Breathing his bronzen breath at the azury centre of time'. Both Yeats and Stevens know the impossibility of 'a permanent realization' (*SCP*: 425) in nature as Wordsworth would believe that in his brooding poems 'Abundant recompence' (*LB1*: 206) is to be found for the loss of youth. Such is the later affluence of Yeats and Stevens: they choose 'the universe of the soul of which all art is an embodiment' (Raine 1999: 40). Stevens's work explores the relation between this unspoken site or source of his poems and the poems themselves, caught in the evasions or ironies of earth, body and language, as they provide us with access to truth. The stability of truth is somehow constituted by changing conditions: concealment is an essential constituent of its unconcealment. Stevens's poems brood upon this irony: they foreground the evasiveness of language to explore just how art can be the embodiment of the universe of the soul. His work is concerned with hypostasis, symbolized by a man in a river, both of which change and stay the same in different ways as, say, a man would age if he stayed in that river but the river would look much the same, but the river is constituted a river because its waters continually change around that stationary thing, the man.

The hearsay that transmits Heraclitus to us makes him a lover:

> of all the mighty world
> Of eye and ear, both what they half-create,

> And what perceive; well pleased to recognize
> In nature and the language of the sense,
> The anchor of my purest thoughts, the nurse,
> The guide, the guardian of my heart, and soul
> Of all my moral being.

(LB1: 207–8)

As Cleanthes is reported to have continued his comparison of Zeno and Heraclitus, he makes both sound like Wordsworth in 'Tintern Abbey': 'And souls too are nourished by moist exhalations. Now Zeno like Heraclitus declares the soul to be an exhalation, and he says it is perceptive' because it 'is able to be impressed through sense organs by things that exist and subsist . . . ; for these things are proper to the soul' (Graham 2010: 183). Wordsworth's description of the Wanderer's childhood, and how 'the foundations of his mind were laid' in solitary communion with natural forms, written before Wordsworth embarked on *The Prelude*, but later published in revised form as part of *The Excursion*, proceeds from the same understanding of what is proper to the soul:

> In such communion, not from terror free,
> While yet a child, and long before his time,
> Had he perceived the presence and the power
> Of greatness; and deep feelings had impressed
> So vividly great objects that they lay
> Upon his mind like substances, whose presence
> Perplexed the bodily sense. He had received
> A precious gift; for, as he grew in years,
> With these impressions would he still compare
> All his remembrances, thoughts, shapes, and forms;
> And, being still unsatisfied with aught
> Of dimmer character, he thence attained
> An active power to fasten images
> Upon his brain; and on their pictured lines
> Intensely brooded, even till they acquired
> The liveliness of dreams.

(1849–50: vi. 14–15)

I am not sure that Stevens would have been overly pleased to hear us say that Wordsworth's lines are impressed on his poems in the same manner as 'deep feelings' had 'impressed' 'great objects' or natural forms on the Wanderer's mind. What can we say instead? In 'The Countryman' Swatara is addressed, not as if it is a person wearing a cap and cape, but as a 'black river', moving 'without crystal', unlike the 'fluent mundo' that 'will have stopped revolving except in crystal' when called 'by name', 'Descending, out of the cap of midnight, | Toward the cape at which | You enter the swarthy sea' (*SCP*: 428). Rather than step into the river, a 'countryman' walks beside Swatara:

> He broods of neither cap nor cape,
> But only of your swarthy motion,
> But always of the swarthy water,
> Of which Swatara is the breathing,
> The name.

> (*SCP*: 428–9)

Wordsworth's Wanderer, brooding 'in the after-day | Of boyhood' (1849–50: 15), is an antetype of Stevens's silent countryman who will eventually greet the angel of reality. As in correspondences discerned between the Old and New Testaments, the relation between Stevens's and Wordsworth's figures does not necessarily have anything to do with causality. They are connected by meaning; by their poets' commitment to the 'moving soul', the 'swarthy water' of 'an ebbing and a flowing mind', which they labour to keep within their poems:

> many an hour in caves forlorn,
> And 'mid the hollow depths of naked crags
> He sate, and even in their fixed lineaments,
> Or from the power of a peculiar eye,
> Or by creative feeling overborne,
> Or by predominance of thought oppressed,
> Even in their fixed and steady lineaments
> He traced an ebbing and a flowing mind,
> Expression ever varying!

> (*1849–50*: vi. 15)

Both figures, 'being still unsatisfied with aught | Of dimmer character', trace 'Some lineament or character, || Some affluence, if only half-perceived' (*SCP*: 532–3) in the natural forms upon which they brood: for a countryman, 'Being there is being in a place, | As of a character everywhere' (*SCP*: 429).

In the first part of 'Our Stars Come from Ireland', 'Tom McGreevy, in America, Thinks of Himself as a Boy', it is asked: 'What would the water have been, | Without that that he makes of it?' (*SCP*: 455). We come upon 'him that I loved' stretched over the waves across the Atlantic:

> The stars are washing up from Ireland
> And through and over the puddles of Swatara
> And Schuylkill. The sound of him
> Comes from a great distance and is heard.

> (*SCP*: 455)

Again, 'Deepe calleth unto deepe', gathering poets, 'Brooding sounds of river noises', their Welsh or Pennsylvanian rivers, 'puddles' at 'The sound of him'; 'at the noyse of thy water-spouts'.

The first two poems and the penultimate poem of Stevens's final collection, 'The Rock', first published as part of the *Collected Poems* in 1954, take up the theme. In 'An Old Man Asleep', the 'Bands of black men', from 'The Sick Man', a late poem uncollected at Stevens's death, that 'seem to be drifting in the air, | In the South', are not 'Playing mouth-organs in the night or, now, guitars' (*OP*: 118), but singing 'Ol' man river', as Stevens finds, 'Here in the North', 'The words of winter in which these two will come together' (*OP*: 118). 'The two worlds are asleep, are sleeping, now', as if possessed by a 'dumb sense': 'The self and the earth' – 'The river motion, the drowsy motion of the river R' (*SCP*: 501).

R is for '*Regeneratio*' (Bayley 1912: i. 43): for a Renaissance whose egg will hatch, not burst (see *E&I*: 466–9). What of Heidegger's 'strife' of world and earth? It is reconfigured as a river of earth that rolls back on itself in vision. Oscar Hammerstein II's song includes the Judgement Day and the river Jordan. Stevens's late poems apprehend the Last Judgement that has already occurred and do not long to cross a river that is not Pennsylvanian or in Connecticut. It is certain that that these long rivers will keep forever rolling; 'and again I hear | These waters, rolling from their mountain-springs | With a sweet inland murmur' (*LB1*: 201), affording vision:

> And I have felt
> A presence that disturbs me with the joy
> Of elevated thoughts; a sense sublime
> Of something far more deeply interfused,
> Whose dwelling is the light of setting suns,
> And the round ocean, and the living air,

And the blue sky, and in the mind of man,
A motion and a spirit, that impels
All thinking things, all objects of all thought,
And rolls through all things.

                                        (*LB1*: 207)

R is for rolling: for Wordsworth's 'rolls' in 'Tintern Abbey' that connects 'A presence' with the river Wye, which is not 'undulant', 'not
affected by the tides a few miles above Tintern', as he tells us in his
footnote (*LB1*: 201). Such 'river motion' is and is not 'A motion': 'The
swarthy water | That flows round the earth and through the skies, |
Twisting among the universal spaces, || Is not Swatara. It is being';
'where from secret springs | The source of human thought its tribute
brings | Of waters, – with a sound but half its own' (Shelley 1967, 'Mont
Blanc': 532). Pretending to locate with confidence their evasive subjects,
criticism tends to ignore with deliberation the acausal implications of
Wordsworth's, Shelley's or Stevens's poems. Modern readers talk of a
chain of influence, a concatenation of poets through the generations,
but forget about 'a mighty scheme of truth', and, knowingly or not, they
construct models of influence out of Renaissance practices of imitation
and allusion. Like Freud's theories upon which it is often based, influence criticism is often inhibited by personality, causality and rhetoric.

It is tempting to paint the 'sylvan Wye' with its hermit in the woods
as a bucolic model for the figure and its inner double in the woods by
the river of 'Metaphor as Degeneration'. It seems natural to trace the
flowing of these rivers from one poem to another. But these river poems
carry us in the opposite direction, to the irrational and supernatural,
away from the sea of time and space, or memory and reason. The
second figure in 'Metaphor as Degeneration' is an undisclosed future
reader at the beginning of the unborn kind, a second self of the poet,
not a relic of literature like its marble prototype at the end of the decaying kind: the figures enact a movement from the influence of memory
to inspiration. When the Wye's rolling motion is transfigured by vision
into 'A motion', we apprehend the spirit of Wordsworth, but conjoined
with 'The everlasting universe of things' that 'Flows through the mind',
that 'rolls its rapid waves' upriver inwards, 'Twisting among the universal spaces', and it, not Wordsworth, stirs 'The river motion, the drowsy
motion of the river R'. At the confluence of river 'why?' and river 'are',
we navigate the generic Rio Grande of Being. But on rivers of such
influence, such drifting on a topos, or into an archetype, we experience

synchronicity. Yeats would deliberately climb such streams; Stevens finds, in the evasions of language, the landless, waterless ocean in the sky. As both poets would have understood, if Shelley is recalling Wordsworth it is to reach the acausal realm from which Wordsworth speaks, to escape memory in order to find inspiration. All three make Wordsworth's poems 'the work of Divine Inspiration' (Letter from Crabb Robinson to Dorothy Wordsworth, quoted in Daruwala 1998: 197), when the 'Natural Man' does not rise up to speak so fully of himself.

The second poem of 'The Rock', 'The Irish Cliffs of Moher', is an attempt to awake from the drowsy state of the first. Stevens was inspired to write this poem of the generations and inheritance by a postcard he received of 'the worn cliffs towering up over the Atlantic. It was like a gust of freedom, a return to the spacious, solitary world in which we used to exist' (*SL*: 760–1). Despite its claims, this a poem full of the 'somnambu-lations | Of poetry', including Stevens's own 'Somnambulisma' and 'Our Stars Come from Ireland'. The form of 'The Irish Cliffs' seems a version of 'God Is Good', returning us to the beginning of *Transport to Summer*:

> Who is my father in this world, in this house,
> At the spirit's base?
>
> My father's father, his father's father, his –
> Shadows like winds
>
> Go back to a parent before thought, before speech,
> At the head of the past.

> > > > (*SCP*: 501)

Vaughan's 'Mans fall, and Recovery' is a prototype for these two poems while providing explication of 'The Irish Cliffs'. Vaughan broods upon lines from St Paul: 'As by the offence of one, the fault came on all men to condemnation; So by the Righteousness of one, the benefit abounded towards all men to the Justification of life' (as presented by Vaughan; Romans 5. 19). The poet speaks as Everyman, conjoining these two: 'Farewell you Everlasting hills! I'm Cast | Here under Clouds' (1957: 411), laments that voice, as Adam, at its beginning, but then he spans Old and New Testaments, not just to observe, but to proclaim as, 'God (made man)':

> Yet have I found
> A plenteous way, (thanks to that holy one!)

> To cancell all that e're was writ in stone,
> > His saving wound
> Wept bloud, that broke this Adamant, and gave
> To sinners Confidence, life to the grave;
> > This makes me span
> My fathers journeys, and in one faire step
> O're all their pilgrimage, and labours leap,
> > For God (made man,)
> Reduc'd th'Extent of works of faith; so made
> Of their *Red Sea*, a *Spring*; I wash, they wade.

> > > > (1957: 412)

Both 'The Irish Cliffs' and 'Mans fall, and Recovery' are about cause and effect and that which enters the world of causality to break such a chain; it is appropriate then that they should have a meaningful acausal relationship. Vaughan's 'Everlasting hills' obscured by 'Clouds' match Stevens's 'cliffs of Moher rising out of the mist'. As both poets 'span [their] fathers journeys' they are concerned with first parents, but they also find ways of breaking 'this Adamant', the chain of causality, begun by Adam and of hardest substance, determining the way in which we perceive the world in the west.

At the end of Vaughan's poem we find another source of Stevens's river R beneath 'The redness': 'a *Spring*' that Vaughan made, with 'His saving wound', 'Of their *Red Sea*'. Like Yeats these poets climb the river of life through the generations to make the 'moving soul' of a *Collected Poems*, 'that age-long memoried self', the feeding source to which a life should labour: 'God (made man)'. Such apprehension brings poems together in the 'intensest rendezvous' and we discern 'the miraculous influence' of 'Final Soliloquy of the Interior Paramour':

> Here, now, we forget each other and ourselves.
> We feel the obscurity of an order, a whole,
> A knowledge, that which arranged the rendezvous[,]
>
> Within its vital boundary, in the mind.
> We say God and the imagination are one . . .

> > > > (*SCP*: 524)

As Vaughan admits, 'This makes me span | My fathers journeys'. Such rendezvous between poets leaps over their labours in time, 'For God (made man,) | Reduc'd th'Extent of works of faith'.

The penultimate poem of the *Collected Poems* is of 'a great river this side of Stygia': 'The River of Rivers in Connecticut', not 'the fairest of all rivers' (*1850*, i. 270) but the 'relation of all relations' (Heidegger 1971: 107). The poem's position within the book demonstrates the importance that these river poems of being began to assume for Stevens:

> It is the third commonness with light and air,
> A curriculum, a vigor, a local abstraction . . .
> Call it, once more, a river, an unnamed flowing,
>
> Space-filled, reflecting the seasons, the folk-lore
> Of each of the senses; call it, again and again,
> The river that flows nowhere, like a sea.

> > (*SCP*: 533)

We shall see in Chapter 4 how Stevens transforms 'a sea' into 'A bird's cry' that sounds like a chorister's 'c' preceding 'the choir' in the very last poem of the *Collected Poems*. It is, as in Vaughan, a sea that becomes a source. The poem's title, 'The River of Rivers', announces that we are at once in the realm of fairytale, as in 'Metaphor as Degeneration' with its 'greenest', but we are also 'in Connecticut'. We have moved from Stevens's Pennsylvanian creeks of his childhood to the landscape of his adulthood around Farmington and Haddam; it is also the landscape of Virgil and Dante. Do we find in 'The River of Rivers' the same turning on Satan's tail as in Dante and Yeats? Stevens is writing a poetry of the earth, evasive in its turnings, but in order to come upon the truth.

Among Stevens's late poems that were not included in 'The Rock', 'The Dove in Spring' takes up again the brooding that had been immersed in the waters of Stevens's river poems of being:

> Brooder, brooder, deep beneath its walls –
> A small howling of the dove
> Makes something of the little there,
>
> The little and the dark, and that
> In which it is and that in which
> It is established.

> > (*OP*: 124)

We are back with the dove of the first section of 'Notes', now regenerated after its conjoining with the dove in the belly. The dove becomes another kind of cockerel, its howling awakes us to a different kind of reality:

> There is this bubbling before the sun,
> This howling at one's ear, too far
> For daylight and too near for sleep.

(OP: 125)

This dove is a type of 'the sibyl of the self', her shape:

> Is a blind thing fumbling for its form,
> A form that is lame, a hand, a back,
> A dream too poor, too destitute
> To be remembered, the old shape
> Worn and leaning to nothingness,
> A woman looking down the road,
> A child asleep in its own life.

(OP: 130)

Such is the spiritual affluence of late Stevens. The self needs a sibyl because Stevens's poems wake readers to apprehend 'fearless immortal spirit'. This last section of 'The Sail of Ulysses' provides the title for the last of Stevens's brooding poems, 'A Child Asleep in Its Own Life'. The river has now vanished into 'that single mind', twisting among its universal spaces, so that the scholar-fisherman can grasp the invisible but substantial interiority of a life. Among the familiar old men, it is 'one, unnamed' that 'broods | On all the rest, in heavy thought':

> He regards them
> Outwardly and knows them inwardly,
>
> The sole emperor of what they are,
> Distant, yet close enough to wake
> The chords above your bed to-night.

(OP: 132)

One hears 'disclose', the old word for hatching an egg, behind 'Distant, yet close' in the penultimate line. But the poem broods upon that which will not be disclosed. If it sounds like a riddle, the poem is not

simply a puzzle to be solved. It is about its own restraint and inward-
ness as it complicates Wordsworth's famous maxim that 'The Child is
Father of the Man' (*1815*: i. 3) to disclose darkly the beginning of the
unborn kind.

We can turn again to Vaughan for explication of this poem as it crystallizes Stevens's other brooding poems:

> What sublime truths, and wholesome themes,
> Lodge in thy mystical, deep streams!
> Such as dull man can never finde
> Unless that Spirit lead his minde,
> Which first upon thy face did move,
> And hatch'd all with his quickning love.
>
> (1957: 538)

The 'one, unnamed' is 'A hatching', that which is disclosed when an
everyday self of 'dull man' is lead to, and incubated by, 'that age-long
memoried self' or 'that Spirit' to become a soul. Like Yeats, Stevens
understands that his task as poet is to make his soul, and 'to wake
| The chords' above a sleeping audience, evoking love, which operates
with imagination, and 'proceeds | More from the brooding Soul, and is
divine' (*1805*, xiii. 164–5). In his 'hearing' we hear that which orches-
trates such a project 'Rise liquidly in liquid lingerings, | Like watery
words awash', on a wave of rhythm that flows back into itself, and
'Deepe calleth unto deepe':

> With what deep murmurs through times silent stealth
> Doth thy transparent, cool and watry wealth
>   Here flowing fall,
>   And chide, and call,
> As if his liquid, loose Retinue staid
> Lingring, and were of this steep place afraid,
>   The common pass
>   Where, clear as glass,
>   All must descend
>   Not to an end:
> But quickned by this deep and rocky grave,
> Rise to a longer course more bright and brave.
>
> (Vaughan 1957: 537)

Not for such a fall would Wordsworth 'murmur: other gifts | Have followed, for such loss, I would believe, | Abundant recompence' (*LB1*: 206), and Stevens's later affluence is also such 'watry wealth' risen or 'quickened by this deep and rocky grave'. Vaughan's brooding on the Old and New Testaments provides explication that hatches future poets. The 'deep murmurs' that 'flowing fall, | And chide and call' through Stevens, Yeats, Wordsworth, Milton, Vaughan and others are 'impalpable, incommensurable' (Waley 1934: 170), beyond cause and effect, but they also linger in our liquid words well-disposed, 'Distant, yet close enough to wake | The chords above your bed to-night', disclosing readers who 'from their native selves can send abroad | Like transformations, for themselves create | A like existence, and, whene'er it is | Created for them, catch it by an instinct' (*1805*, xiii. 93–6).

3
'Cuchulain Comforted'

Yeats and Cuchulain

Before 'Cuchulain Comforted', Yeats made five plays and one poem about Cuchulain. Their development and diversity demonstrate the modern poet's 'full-blooded and intensely personal use of myth', and show correspondingly its 'extraordinary imaginative resilience and flexibility' (Kennelly 1994: 162). We see 'a certain arbitrary discretion' at work in the poem as Yeats devises the extraordinary theme of Cuchulain's posthumous existence, just outside of his 'national history or mythology' (Shelley 1967: 204), to give it a Dantean form and setting:

> A man that had six mortal wounds, a man
> Violent and famous, strode among the dead;
> Eyes stared out of the branches and were gone.
>
> Then certain Shrouds that muttered head to head
> Came and were gone. He leant upon a tree
> As though to meditate on wounds and blood.
>
> A Shroud that seemed to have authority
> Among those bird-like things came, and let fall
> A bundle of linen. Shrouds by two and three
>
> Came creeping up because the man was still.
> And thereupon that linen-carrier said:
> 'Your life can grow much sweeter if you will
>
> 'Obey our ancient rule and make a shroud;
> Mainly because of what we only know
> The rattle of those arms makes us afraid.

'We thread the needles' eyes, and all we do
All must together do.' That done, the man
Took up the nearest and began to sew.

'Now must we sing and sing the best we can,
But first you must be told our character:
Convicted cowards all, by kindred slain

'Or driven from home and left to die in fear.'
They sang, but had nor human tunes nor words,
Though all was done in common as before;

They had changed their throats and had the throats of birds.

(*YCP*: 395–6)[1]

During his last days, the poet was sewing for himself a shroud; composing a poem that comes 'by two and three', as if following an old pattern, its metrical and alliterative title of two three syllable words, the first double stitch. The second stitch, like all strong stitches, is epanaleptic: the first two words of the first line are reiterated by its last two; then 'strode' in the second line is pulled through as 'stared' in the third; the three words at the end of that line, 'and were gone', are repeated, after 'head to head', during the first words of the second line of the second stanza, 'Came and were gone'; repetition of the word 'came' continues such fastening. The *terza rima* too comes by two and three as a kind of suture, its three rhymes always stitching two stanzas together, and its associations with the afterlife joining the lips of 'six mortal wounds', which were made by another kind of stitching or stabbing. When in 'Adam's Curse' Yeats defends poetry against 'bankers, schoolmasters, and clergymen', the 'noisy set' who think that poets are idlers, he says, 'A line will take us hours maybe; | Yet if it does not seem a moment's thought, | Our stitching and unstitching has been naught' (*YCP*: 89 and 88). Making poetry is as gruelling as scrubbing floors, breaking stones or sewing, more demanding than the pursuit of any profession, and its needlework should not be on display. But in 'Cuchulain Comforted' we are meant to see the poet's stitching of 'a moment's thought'. A domestic female activity becomes, if not heroic, at least the activity of a hero in the poem. Each of Yeats's poems is stitched, and also a single stitch, joining his *Collected Poems*. The last two poems he composed become the final double stitch. Yeats is fastening off with formal flourish while recalling Dante in different ways: 'qui farem punto, come buon sartore | che com' elli ha del panno fa la gonna' (*Paradiso*, xxxii. 140–1); here we shall make a final stitch like a good tailor who has made of cloth the skirt.[2]

Reading the poem's stitched lines, their repetitions spiral in time, a shape whose 'geometric complexities' are also 'spatial analogues of the temporal paradox of *terza rima* forward motion which recapitulates the beginning in the end' (Freccero 1986: 263). This paradox in the form of the poem uncovers its theme. 'Cuchulain Comforted' looks back to work at the beginning in order to move on at the end. Yeats's first engagements with the Cuchulain myth, in the poem 'Cuchulain's Fight with the Sea' and in the play *On Baile's Strand*, are brought together at the end of his life in his final play *The Death of Cuchulain* and its 'kind of sequel' (*YL*: 922). The very title of Yeats's final play recalls 'The Death of Cuhoollin', the original title of 'Cuchulain's Fight with the Sea', and it brings back a blind man from *On Baile's Strand* to kill off the hero. As the play's coda, 'Cuchulain Comforted' is a recapitulation of the cycle, summing up of Yeats's experience in the death of Cuchulain, but also specifically a return to his very first Cuchulain poem, written before Lady Gregory had published *Cuchulain of Muirthemne*. The poem is the last judgement on a life's work, 'strange too, something new' (*YL*: 922).

The figure of epanalepsis, called 'Eccho sound' or 'the slow return' (Puttenham 2007: 144), in the first line of 'Cuchulain Comforted', catches a figure in 'The Death of Cuhoollin', not Cuchulain or his son, but 'A man' who turns out to be 'Aleel, the swineherd':

> A man came slowly from the setting sun,
> To Emer of Borda, in her clay-piled dun,
> And found her dyeing cloth with subtle care,
> And said, casting aside his draggled hair:
> 'I am Aleel, the swineherd, whom you bid
> 'Go dwell upon the sea cliffs, vapour hid;
> 'But now my years of watching are no more.'

> (*VP*: 105; *1895*: 202)

This third figure, the first figure in the early poem, is like the first rhyme of *terza rima* that prefigures or determines the next two. But he is not to be found in Yeats's written sources (Curtin 1890 and *The Yellow Book of Lecan*). Perhaps Yeats figured him from the swineherd Eumaeus, Odysseus' loyal servant to whom he presents himself, disguised as a withered old man, on his return to Ithaca. Blanchot asks, 'What would happen if Ulysses [that 'decadent Greek ... who should never have figured among the heroes of the *Iliad*'] and Homer, instead of being two distinct characters, shared their roles and became one and the same person?' (Blanchot 1992: 62; 60). Then Homer's *Odyssey* is addressed to Eumaeus by Odysseus disguised as an old man. Blanchot's understanding of narration configures the movement of *terza rima* and the relation of 'Cuchulain Comforted' to 'Cuchulain's Fight'. The swineherd in the action of Yeats's early poem foreshadows Cuchulain's son whom we encounter as we anticipate the older Cuchulain, a figure that must always pre-exist the others. In 'Cuchulain Comforted' Yeats addresses a pre-echo of an earlier self; like Homer he tells a tale for the swineherd.

'Narration ['Le récit'] is not the account of an event but the event itself, its imminence, the site where it will occur – it is a happening about to happen whose magnetic power may enable the narration to happen ['événement encore à venir et par la puissance attirante duquel le récit peut espérer, lui aussi, se réaliser']' (Blanchot 1992: 62; Blanchot 1971: 14). Like the relation of God and the imagination, 'Topologically, the movement between this *récit* and its event is that of a spiral whose spiralling inwards is ceaseless, asymptotic' (Timothy Clark 1992: 86). Yeats's relation to and of Cuchulain is prefigured by Homer's relation to and of Odysseus. In the afterlife of the heroic self, withered old men tell spiralling tales. When Yeats completes his final double stitch with his last poem 'The Black Tower', he eventually becomes the old cook, the 'lying hound', that is, Cuchulain in disguise, familiarly Cuch', a friend one imagines once of the swineherd. Does Yeats thus make Odysseus, Homer and Eumaeus one person in the imagination? 'Cuchulain Comforted' is a tale told of Cuchulain by Yeats for the tower's old cook: three figures in one. The hidden law of all narration, 'sans doute une sorte d'extravagance' (Blanchot 1971: 14), without doubt a sort of wandering out of bounds, conducts itself on Heidegger's wave that 'in its rise causes all the movement of Saying to flow back to its ever more hidden source' (1971: 160):

> Narration is movement towards a point which is not only unknown, ignored and strange but such that it seems to have no prior reality apart from this movement, yet is so compulsive that the narration's appeal depends on it to the extent that it cannot even 'begin' before it has reached it, while it is only the narration and the unpredictable movement of the narration which provide the space where this point becomes real, powerful and appealing. (Blanchot 1992: 62)

Stanzas interlocked by *terza rima* function like the interlocking gyres expounded in *A Vision*.[3] This geometric symbol of the 'double cone or vortex' (*VB*: 70) used by Yeats's 'instructors' to help him understand a man's life and historical epochs also describes the relation between 'Cuchulain Comforted' and 'Cuchulain's Fight'. Each poem moves towards a new and strange point to be found in the other. The later poem recites the earlier one, it summons it to appear for last judgement, so that it may tell over its story of a fight between a father and son, one killing the other and then being killed. But such a story is the poet's own antagonistic development, as in his late poems he 'enumerate[s] old themes' (*YCP*: 391): this relation between an old man and a young man becomes the event that each poem relates of and to a poet young and old. In Yeats's private but perennial philosophy, which is 'there [in *The Death of Cuchulain*] but there must be no sign of it', 'all things are made of the conflict of two states of consciousness, beings or persons which die each other's life, live each other's death. That is true of life and death themselves. Two cones (or whirls), the apex of each in the other's base' (*YL*: 917–18).

As 'Cuchulain Comforted' and 'Cuchulain's Fight' interlock, the events leading to Cuchulain's death interlock with the moments after his death. But this contrary whirling of two spirals as each poem lives the other's death and dies the other's life is but in asymptotic relation itself to Yeats's life as he dies out of the life of his penultimate poem. 'These pairs of opposites whirl in contrary directions, *Will* and *Mask* from right to left, *Creative Mind* and *Body of Fate* like the hands of a clock, from left to right' (*VB*: 74). Yeats lives his alter ego Cuchulain's death as the hero dies the poet's life. One poem summons another to its court of judgement just as orthodox Christianity would have us stand at the end with our life's story, our 'Recorded time' (*F*; *Macbeth*, V. v. 21), or our soul's actions, reported by the recording angel to the Last Judgement 'when time has stopped and all is changed eternally' (Brooke 1990: 204). Does Yeats desire to break 'this Adamant' (Vaughan 1957: 412), our chain of causality linking the generations? Yeats is concerned with what Plotinus also calls the soul in judgement (*VB*: 219; see Plotinus 1992, III. 4. 6: 213), apprehension that the last judgement has already occurred, and he finds that in such a situation his art has 'a certain arbitrary discretion'.

Yeats dictated the prose 'Subject' for 'Cuchulain Comforted' to his wife 'one morning at Ideal Sejour', on or before 10 January 1939:

> A shade recently arrived went through a valley in the Country of the Dead; he had six mortal wounds, but had been a tall, strong, handsome man. Other shades looked at him from among the trees.

Sometimes they went near to him and then went away quickly. At last he sat down, he seemed very tired. Gradually the shades gathered round him, and one of them who seemed to have some authority among the others laid a parcel of linen at his feet. One of the others said 'I am not so afraid of him now that he is sitting still. It was the way his arms rattled.['] Then another shade said: 'you would be much more comfortable if you would make a shroud and wear it instead of the arms. We have brought you some linen. If you make it yourself you will be much happier, but of course we wi[l]l thread the needles. We do everything together, so everyone of us will th[r]ead a needle, so when we have laid them at your feet you will take whichever you like best.['] The man with the six wounds saw that nobody had ever threaded needles so swiftly and so smoothly. He took the threaded needles and began to s[e]w, and one of the shades said: 'we will sing to you while you sew; but you will like to know who we are. We are the people who run away from battles. Some of us have been put to death as cowards, but others have hidden, and some even died without people knowing they were cowards.['] Then they began to sing, and they did not sing like men or women, but like linnets that had been stood on a perch and taught by a good singing master. (Pethica 1997: 467)

The 'Comforted' in the poem's final title recalls Christ's promising of 'the Comforter' (John 15. 26). In the prose draft Cuchulain could be made comfortable simply by changing armour for shroud. Yeats may well have been thinking near his death of 'The Order for the Burial of the Dead' in the Prayer Book proposed in 1928: 'a valley in the Country of the Dead' recalls Psalm 23, to be read '*After they are come into the church*' (BCP 1928: 423): 'Yea, though I walk through the valley of the shadow of death, I will fear no evil: for thou art with me; thy rod and thy staff comfort me' (BCP 1928: 426). Raine wonders what we are to make of this prose draft, this 'amazing phantasmagoria, in which details from Yeats's reading over years . . . are combined in a manner totally different from the way in which a poet working simply from these sources would set about making notes of the elements to be included in his work'. She sees that 'although the dramatic coherence of the theme suggests a dream', it is scarcely possible that a dream could pull together 'so many threads of learning':

I suggest that he here describes a 'path-working' of the kind that as a member of the Magical Order of the Golden Dawn he had learned to perform; an imaginative reverie half-spontaneous and yet at the same time conscious, in which themes will rise from the sleeping mind which is yet to some extent directed by the waking; or perhaps the other way, the sleeping mind tells the story and yet takes the images it requires from the stock of knowledge possessed by the waking consciousness. (1986: 259)

A poem poised on the cusp of two worlds is conceived in a liminal state.

For Vendler, 'The surprising thing about Yeats's prose sketch is how *few* words and phrases it provided for the poem' (2007: 373), but this is because many phrases and words come from 'Cuchulain's Fight'. This earlier poem is a first version that comes towards Yeats, like an attendant herald 'vapour hid', when he turns from the prose sketch to making 'Cuchulain Comforted'; in another kind of 'path-working', the conscious self is joined, in the technical crises of creating the poem out of its theme, with a longer, if not age-long, memoried self. Through the opening of the final version of the much revised earlier poem we discern the misted contours of the later work:

> A man came slowly from the setting sun,
> To Emer, raddling raiment in her dun,
> And said, 'I am that swineherd whom you bid
> Go watch the road between the wood and tide,
> But now I have no need to watch it more.'
>
> Then Emer cast the web upon the floor,
> And raising arms all raddled with the dye,
> Parted her lips with a loud sudden cry.
>
> That swineherd stared upon her face and said,
> 'No man alive, no man among the dead,
> Has won the gold his cars of battle bring.'
>
> (*YCP*: 37–8)

The epanalepsis that makes the first line of 'Cuchulain Comforted' from 'A man' in the first line of 'Cuchulain's Fight' may well have been suggested by repetition in the earlier poem's 'No man alive, no man among the dead'. Just such a line may have been rattling around Yeats's head, assuming in a ghastly manner literal and anagogical senses, as he lay in what would soon become his death-bed in January 1939, and providing also the last three words of line 2 of 'Cuchulain Comforted'.

As the earlier poem proceeds we can detect more and more pre-echoes of the later one:

> 'But if your master comes home triumphing
> Why must you blench and shake from foot to crown?'
>
> Thereon he shook the more and cast him down
> Upon the web-heaped floor, and cried his word:
> 'With him is one sweet-throated like a bird.'
>
> 'You dare me to my face,' and thereupon
> She smote with raddled fist, and where her son
> Herded the cattle came with stumbling feet,
> And cried with angry voice, 'It is not meet
> To idle life away, a common herd.'

(YCP: 38)

Emer is dyeing cloth rather than sewing, but her casting down of the cloth prefigures the authoritative Shroud in 'Cuchulain Comforted' letting fall a bundle of linen at Cuchulain's feet, which he will take up, in contrast to the swineherd's casting of himself down 'Upon the web-heaped floor'. His shaking becomes those arms rattling in the later poem, the word 'rattling' a synaesthetic transmutation of the earlier 'raddling', although we assume that the linen of 'Cuchulain Comforted' is white and not raddled, until we pursue Porphyry's interpretation of sea-purple cloth woven in the cave of the nymphs. Yeats takes up the swineherd's 'With him is one sweet throated like a bird' to make the 'linen-carrier' say, 'Your life can grow much sweeter', and to make the final line, 'They had changed their throats and had the throats of birds.' The word 'thereupon' also appears in both poems. A common herd is an ordinary herdsman but it also suggests the common, cowardly herd of Shrouds that Cuchulain must join in the later poem: both poems evoke the one in many and the many in one. For 'a man to die', like Yeats in the first month of 1939, 'Cuchulain's Fight' must continue to sound ominous:

> 'I have long waited, mother, for that word:
> But wherefore now?'
>   'There is a man to die;
> You have the heaviest arm under the sky.'
>
> 'Whether under its daylight or its stars
> My father stands amid his battle-cars.'

'But you have grown to be the taller man.'

'Yet somewhere under starlight or the sun
My father stands.'
                                    'Aged, worn out with wars
On foot, on horseback or in battle-cars.'

'I only ask what way my journey lies,
For He who made you bitter made you wise.'

                                                        (*YCP*: 38)

Later in the poem, Cuchulain sends someone to inquire the identity
of his son who is camped between the wood and the beach: 'One went
and came', pre-echoing the later poem's terse constructions 'Came and
were gone', 'came and let fall', and 'That done, the man'. Such verbal
correspondences reveal the poems' coming and going to each other,
'the apex of each vortex in the middle of the other's base' (*VB*: 68).
The earlier poem begins to take on eerily personal resonances for the
dying poet in the act of composing what would become his penultimate
poem. Yeats had repeatedly revised 'The Death of Cuhoollin' until it
became 'Cuchulain's Fight' and the spirits who dictated *A Vision* told
Yeats that each part of his retelling of the Cuchulain cycle mirrored his
development. The relation that exists between 'Cuchulain Comforted'
and 'Cuchulain's Fight' draws out of the earlier poem a final and ghastly
sense for Yeats in January 1939. Death approaches the poet as the event
that the poems spiral in their movement of asymptotic detour.
    As each poem interprets the other we discover Yeats's license. We are
permitted to read him at the limits of his own freedom from his earlier
poems, paradoxically chained, but not in 'this Adamant' of causality, to
the 'site of the unspoken statement' (Heidegger 1971: 161) from which
they are released: 'Ever to come, ever past, ever present in a beginning so
sudden that it leaves one breathless, and yet spread out like an eternal
return and rebirth . . . ; such is the event the narration would describe
['tel est l'événement dont le récit est l'approche']' (Blanchot 1992: 65;
Blanchot 1971: 19). When Cuchulain is informed in 'Cuchulain's Fight'
that the stranger camped by the shore only 'gives his name | At the
sword-point, and waits till we have found | Some feasting man that the
same oath has bound', he 'cried, "I am the only man | Of all this host so
bound from childhood on"' (*YCP*: 39). As Wordsworth declares, at the
end of the poem that begins *Poems* (1815), lines also used to preface the
last poem of that first collected edition, 'The Child is Father of the Man;

| And I could wish my days to be | Bound each to each by natural piety' (*1815*: i. 3 and ii. 346). In 'Cuchulain Comforted' its acausal event at once provides and breaks the bond of narration.

In his penultimate poem, Yeats brings himself to judgement before his enduring arbiter, the Cuchulain cycle, and his poem arbitrarily judges Cuchulain in a realm where he is licensed to roam beyond his myth. In turn, a modern audience is judged. Yeats's long and creative relation to Cuchulain prompts an allegorical reading of the poem: it tells the story of the dead poet among his future readers, subject to our 'certain arbitrary discretion': generally, 'convicted cowards all', 'All think what other people think' (*YCP*: 158), unless creatively each learns to 'Scorn the sort now growing up' (*YCP*: 400) and 'Bring the soul of man to God' (*YCP*: 399). Yeats foresees the dark wood of our world, '<When> Imaginative Art & Science & all Intellectual Gifts all the Gifts of the Holy Ghost are [*depisd*] lookd upon as of no use & only Contention remains to Man'; but, as Blake understood, 'then the Last Judgment begins & its Vision is seen by the [*Imaginative Eye*] of Every one according to the situation he holds' (Erdman: 554).

If the gifts of 'the Comforter, which is the holy Ghost' (John 14. 26), 'even the Spirit of trueth' (15. 26), are looked down upon then the Last Judgement has already begun. The beginning of Cuchulain's Purgatory is of his own making, as Blake saw that we make our world, and each sees Yeats's poem according to the situation he holds. The careful disposition of Yeats's poem is that which comforts: his 'prepared position', for later readers, 'one of the greatest consolations of Yeats's *Collected Poems*'. On this occasion, we are meant to see the poem's stitches, beautifully stitched as they are, and Yeats's 'almost military forethought' (Heaney 1984) put on display accesses an irrational mode or supernatural coherence, that which makes us human, since 'we are such stuffe | As dreames are made on' (*F*; *The Tempest*, IV. i. 156–7). The self-destroying labour of technique that Yeats expended in composing his poems means that they are made over to 'age-long memoried self', the greatest help for those that come after, if they will labour to make their souls.

'Now must we sing'

Because we no longer discover the still unpurified dead through our own and others' dreams, and those in freedom through contemplation, religion cannot answer the atheist, and philosophy talks about a first cause or a final purpose, when we would know what we were a little before conception, what we shall be a little after burial. (*VB*: 223)

Yeats divides the period between death and birth 'into states analogous to the six solar months between Aries and Libra' (*VB*: 223). 'Cuchulain Comforted', like the 'shew' that 'imports the Argument of the Play' (*F*; *Hamlet*, iii. ii. 149–50), foreshadows the next steps for Yeats, to be undertaken a couple of weeks after its composition, 'a little after [his] burial'. We see in miniature the posthumous purgation of a Spirit, between lives, which may take centuries. Following the Spirit of Yeats's second self, the poem moves first of all from the first state of *The Vision of the Blood Kindred* and the *Meditation*, after death in Aries, to the second state, which includes the *Return*, the *Dreaming Back*, and the *Phantasmagoria*: 'a man | Violent and famous, strode among the dead' and then 'He leant upon a tree | As though to meditate on wounds and blood', reliving past events of his previous life. When he is invited by the Shrouds, his cowardly opposites, to sit down with them, he enters the third state, the *Shiftings*, and 'his nature is reversed' (*VB*: 231); 'it may renounce the form of a man' (*VB*: 224). During this process, it finds the 'complete equilibrium' (*VB*: 232) of the fourth state, the *Marriage* or the *Beatitude*: 'They sang but had nor human tunes nor words'. Then it can enter the *Purification*: 'All memory has vanished, the *Spirit* no longer knows what its name has been, it is at last free and in relation to *Spirits* free like itself' (*VB*: 233); 'They had changed their throats and had the throats of birds', their song symbolizing the freedom of such Spirits. By the end of the poem, the Spirit is 'now almost united to *Husk* and *Passionate Body*' (*VB*: 234–5), that which it has been sewing among birds who are their own augurs; 'One must suppose such spirits gathered into bands – for as yet they are without individuality' (*VB*: 235): it has been prepared for the final state of *Foreknowledge*. Only 'During its sleep in the womb the *Spirit* accepts its future life, declares it just' (*VB*: 235), and physical birth, after the action of the poem, will be in Libra, according to the purgatorial solar month, not the month of birth in this world.

The opening of Canto II of Dante's *Purgatorio* is also exact about recording the position of the sun between the same signs. The events that Dante relates on the shore of Purgatory presage Yeats's poem in the dark wood as Botticelli's sylvan *Primavera* is related to his marine *Birth of Venus*:

> As more and more toward us came, more bright
> Appear'd the bird of God, nor could the eye
> Endure his splendour near: I mine bent down.
> He drove ashore in a small bark so swift
> And light, that in its course no wave it drank.
> The heavenly steersman at the prow was seen,

Visibly written Blessed in his looks.
Within, a hundred spirits and more there sat.
        'In exitu Israel de Ægypto,'
All with one voice together sang, with what
In the remainder of that hymn is writ.
Then soon as with the sign of holy cross
He bless'd them, they at once leap'd out on land:
He, swiftly as he came, return'd. The crew,
There left, appear'd astounded with the place,
Gazing around, as one who sees new sights.

(Cary: 153)

It seems that during his waking reverie that produced the prose draft and while making the poem, this scene was reorganized as if Yeats was already in the state of the *Dreaming Back*. The heavenly steersman becomes a man whose actions in 'Cuchulain Comforted' resemble those of the many newly deposited on shore in Dante. Their singing 'together' in the boat occurs at the end of Yeats's poem, when the collective zoomorphic transformation of the Shrouds, 'together' sewing and singing, also recalls 'l'uccel divino' (*Purgatorio*, ii. 38), the angelic pilot described as divine bird. One of 'that strange tribe' approaches Dante, prefiguring 'A Shroud that seemed to have authority' in 'Cuchulain Comforted':

Then one I saw darting before the rest
With such fond ardour to embrace me, I
To do the like was moved. O shadows vain!
Except in outward semblance: thrice my hands
I clasp'd behind it, they as oft return'd
Empty into my breast again. Surprise
I need must think was painted in my looks,
For that the shadow smiled and backward drew.
To follow it I hasten'd, but with voice
Of sweetness it enjoin'd me to desist.

(Cary: 154)

The 'voice | Of sweetness' that enjoins is in chiasmal relation to the voice of authority that tempts with the prospect of sweetness, and comes at the end of all these 'other parallels, each slight in itself, but having a cumulative plausibility' (T. S. Eliot, quoted in Ricks 1996: xxviii); except that I do not just argue that Yeats, like Eliot, writes poems 'Formd by the Daughters of Memory', drawing unconsciously or consciously on Dante in writing 'Cuchulain Comforted'. The relation between the two works might be better presented by turning to medieval methods of biblical interpretation.

An explanation of the *Comedy* is explained in the Epistle to Can Grande, by making reference to the same psalm sung by the souls in the boat; the writer considers 'When Israel went out of Egypt, the house of Jacob from a people of strange language' (Psalm 113. 1 [Psalm 114. 1 in KJV]):

> if we consider the letter alone, the thing signified to us is the going out of the children of Israel from Egypt in the time of Moses; if the allegory, our redemption through Christ is signified; if the moral sense, the conversion of the soul from the sorrow and misery of sin to a state of grace is signified; if the anagogical, the passing of the sanctified soul from the bondage of the corruption of this world to the liberty of everlasting glory is signified. (Dante 1920: 199)

Aquinas sees the Bible in a twofold light, making a distinction between its literal sense and its spiritual sense, which 'is based on and presupposes the literal sense'; 'qui super litteralem fundatur et eum supponit' (Aquinas 1964, I. i. 10: i. 38–9).[4] When he divides the spiritual sense into three, he refines his definitions in relation to time: out of its literal meaning in everyday or historical time, the reader of scripture discovers the allegorical or typological sense, which connects the old testament with the new, the moral or tropological sense, which allows us to apply the Bible to our lives today, and the anagogical sense, which is eschatological, that is, to do with eternal things to come. According to this fourfold method of interpretation, by one act of reading we might realize two or four kinds of time, but anagogy does not apprehend us without our first comprehending the text's literal meaning, its historical truth. Aquinas justifies the polysemantic nature of the Bible by drawing attention to its divine authority. In the *Comedy* Dante makes 'the allegory of the poets . . . (a metaphorical narrative sense)' serve 'an allegory of the theologians (a true ultimate literal or historical/theological sense, all metaphors stripped away)'. Poetic fictions that make use of metaphors as well as 'figural allegory, in which the literal sense was historically true' (*Paradiso*: 10) can possess fourfold meaning. 'The pilgrim's journey is . . . a system of metaphors for the process by which a living man, on earth, comes to understand the nature of the cosmos and the state of souls after death' (*Paradiso*: 9–10).

'Cuchulain Comforted' is a polysemantic poem for the modern era, its '*doctrinal content*' (*Paradiso*: 8) put into poetic action but literally true.

Yeats's literal theme is the same as Dante's in the *Comedy*: 'the state of souls after death, pure and simple. For on and about that the argument of the whole work turns'; 'status animarum post mortem simpliciter sumptus. Nam de illo et circa illum totius operis versatur processus' (Dante 1920: 200; 174). Allegorically speaking, there are differences between the poems. Dante explained to Can Grande, 'If, however, the work be regarded from the allegorical point of view, the subject is man according as by his merits or demerits in the exercise of his free will he is deserving of reward or punishment by justice' (Dante 1920: 200). In Yeats's poem the loss of freedom of will is the allegorical theme rather than any gaining or losing of merit through such freedom:

> The dead, as the passionate necessity wears out, come into a measure of freedom and may turn the impulse of events, started while living, in some new direction, but they cannot originate except through the living. Then gradually they perceive, although they are still but living in their memories, harmonies, symbols, and patterns, as though all were being refashioned by an artist[.] (*M*: 355–6)

Blake's argument with Swedenborg was that man is not subject to the justice of being rewarded or punished in terms of the theologians' conceptions of Heaven and Hell. The experience of the dead is also the experience of reading and writing a poem; it is the crisis that joins paradoxically 'our trivial daily mind' to 'age-long memoried self': as we move from the moral sense to an anagogical understanding, we come to see anagogy as transforming, from the beginning as at the end, tropology and typology. Now the literal theme of a poem is the status of the soul after death, then its anagogical sense necessarily comes first:

> Hitherto shade has communicated with shade in moments of common memory that recur like the figures of a dance in terror or in joy, but now they run together like to like, and their covens and fleets have rhythm and pattern. This running together and running of all to a centre, and yet without loss of identity, has been prepared for by their exploration of their moral life, of its beneficiaries and its victims, and even of all its untrodden paths, and all their thoughts have moulded the vehicle and become event and circumstance. (*M*: 356)

In Canto II of the *Purgatorio*, 'The singing of the souls in the angelic boat ... takes place in a literal situation that corresponds to the anagogical sense of the psalm set forth in the Epistle' (*Purgatorio*: 14).

We can read Yeats's poem in the same direction as Dante advises we read the *Comedy* in the *Convivio*: 'In this kind of explication, the literal should always come first, as being the sense in whose meaning the others are enclosed, and without which it would be impossible and illogical to attend to the other senses, and especially the allegorical' (Dante 1990: 41). If we take the literal subject of 'Cuchulain Comforted' to be a fable, then the poem is about Cuchulain's immediate posthumous existence, it is a coda to the early poem and the late play, both called 'The Death of Cuchulain': in a dark wood a fatally wounded man in armour is convinced to sew a new linen costume by a flock of Shrouds with whom he sings at the end. Typologically, as I will argue later, 'Cuchulain Comforted' conjoins the Isis cult and Christ's resurrection in the context of the Ulster cycle of stories. If read for its tropological sense, the poem converts the soul from the struggle and misery of sin or life to the status of communal grace or at least purgation. Its anagogical sense is its unfolding of the Divine Humanity. From the letter, the poem is about a dead hero settling down to work with the flocks of his Purgatory. If read from the spirit, it is about any individual's acceptance today of his communal posthumous opposite, as the artist must come to terms with his audience, conjoining everyday self and 'age-long memoried self', in visionary apprehension of the one-in-many and the many-in-one.

The problem with this movement of interpretation, from literal sense to reach anagogical sense, is that if the fiction of the poem is that it is nonfiction, and its subject is the status of the soul after death, then exposition must be anagogical, that is to say, eschatological, from the beginning. 'Dante clearly understood that the interdependence of the four narratives [in Psalm 113] permitted any one of them to be treated as a literal sense evoking one or more of the others' (*Purgatorio*: 14). This 'structure of mutual implication of his system of belief, as of his poetic text, exists independently of its truth, which is always a matter of faith . . . . Therefore other fictions can be brought into the powerful matrix of these associations' (*Purgatorio*: 15). Transmuting this powerful matrix for his own syncretic purposes, Blake's mode of exposition is in the opposite direction to Dante's official line of explication:

> The Last Judgment is not Fable or Allegory but Vision Fable or ·Allegory are a totally distinct & inferior kind of Poetry. Vision or Imagination is a Representation of what Eternally Exists. Really and Unchangeably. Fable or Allegory is Formd by the Daughters of Memory. Imagination is Surrounded by the daughters of Inspiration who in the aggregate are calld Jerusalem[.] (Erdman: 554)

Blake's poems begin as 'Vision'; as Yeats understood, he 'composed in a state of vision' (*M*: 358). Anagogy, which must remain for Dante his poem's last and obscurest sense, is the impetus for Blake's art: his work delineates fourfold vision that transforms history. Is the same true of Yeats's practice? It would seem that the literal truth of 'Cuchulain Comforted' is a fiction: it features a character from mythology. But this character had long been Yeats's alter ego, and now he has died; Raine believes the prose draft to be an imaginative reverie, and Yeats was to die soon after composing the poem: 'in Yeats, no less than in Dante and in Virgil himself, it is the belief of the poet in the reality of that situation [the discarnate state] as a part of human experience that makes his words, not fanciful but "tongued with fire"' (Raine 1974: 22).

For Blake, anagogy, which reveals the highest sense of the poem, does not occur hereafter as in Dante's scheme. It is not eschatological in any conventional sense and it is therefore more immediate than allegory as Dante and modern theorists understand that term. For Blake, anagogy is an event that unfolds according to what Blanchot identifies as the hidden law of all narration, transforming fable into 'Vision': it is an event to come that has already happened; it is the beginning of the unborn kind of sense, coming after to vivify literal sense at the end of the decaying kind.[5] For Dante, the anagogical sense is found only after the end of time; it is, therefore, allegorical. After Blake, it is ever to come, ever past, ever present in a sudden beginning, 'and yet spread out like an eternal return and rebirth': it is 'Vision', 'Ever expanding in the Bosom of God, the Human Imagination'. For Blake, the Last Judgement is a moment in each day that the industrious find, and that makes anagogy the immanent sense of a work of art. His work thus marks the beginning of the new inner church when the four final things – Death, Judgement, Heaven and Hell – are inside us now. For Plotinus and Blake, 'the judgement resides in the Soul' because 'virtue and vice are not something imported into the Soul – as heat and cold, blackness or whiteness are importations into the body' (Plotinus 1992: 227 and 230).

My question is, would even the ailing, ageing Yeats have concurred with Plotinus that 'For ourselves, it could never be in our system – or in our liking – to bring the Soul down to participation in such modes and modifications as the warmth and cold of material frames' (1992: 227)? 'But Love has pitched his mansion in | The place of excrement' (*YCP*: 295), retorts Crazy Jane to the Bishop who sounds a bit too like Plotinus. Very late Yeats seems to delight in the derision of 'A sort of battered kettle at the heel' (*YCP*: 219); as he knew over ten years before 'Cuchulain Comforted', he will never quite 'bid the Muse go back, | Choose Plato and Plotinus for a friend' (*YCP*: 218). By 'tracing the themes of Yeats's Platonism' in 'Cuchulain Comforted', Raine comes 'full circle to the root of his anti-Platonism; not, I need hardly say, the anti-Platonism of the plain man and the positivist philosopher (they are much the same) . . . . Rather Yeats refused Plato's out and out denial of the value of the lower world and the experience of the soul in its mortal phase' (1986: 284).

Dante also valued 'the lower world' of literary history. The matrix of mutual implication that makes his system of belief allows the *Comedy* to include non-Christian texts:

> The status of pagan myth . . . is of course centrally important for Dante; for him it represented the crystallized wisdom of the ancient world. One of his most original achievements is the way the entire *Aeneid* is drawn into this signifying matrix, as prefiguring, in the history of poetry, the *Comedy* itself. Thus the extraordinary freedom of Dante's poetic imagination and of his manipulation of traditional modes of allegory utterly transcends any rigid formula. (*Purgatorio*: 15)

Martinez and Durling sketch a system of poetic relations that moves along the fourfold method of interpretation, from the literal history of poetry to the anagogical freedom that Dante finds within tradition after he has made Virgil his prototype. If such interpretation moves in the opposite direction, beginning with anagogy, or vision of that which is to come, already expanding within the human imagination, then poets are influenced not by our past but by eternity, which was traditionally of the future; they are not surrounded by the daughters of memory but by the daughters of inspiration:

> Now I a fourfold vision see
> And a fourfold vision is given to me
> Tis fourfold in my supreme delight
> And three fold in soft Beulahs night
> And twofold Always. May God us keep
> From Single vision & Newtons sleep[.]
>
> (Erdman: 722)

Blake understood 'Christianity as a progressive revelation' (Raine 1991: 94) and would have recognized his own and Dante's work as establishing different ages. Blake's 'Last Judgment was not an outer event, in time and in history, but an inner event, which would not dramatically, but gradually, make itself apparent also in the outer world of history. A new church is thus a new consciousness' (Raine 1991: 78–9). This new eschatology changes anagogy irrevocably: the highest form of allegory becomes 'Vision', the beginning of explication, an enfolding of all three spiritual senses, as it transforms gradually, that is, historically, the literal sense of things. For Blake, the role of secular poetry is to wake us up to this state of vision that has already occurred:

> There is a Moment in each Day that Satan cannot find
> Nor can his Watch Fiends find it, but the industrious find
> This Moment & it multiply. & when it once is found
> It renovates every Moment of the Day if rightly placed[.]

> (Blake, *Milton*, plate 35: 283)

In 'Cuchulain Comforted', as in other last poems by both Yeats and Stevens, this moment is rightly placed; it is of the time of Blake's fable-transforming vision, when anagogy renovates tropology and typology in the poet's work, so that he is justified in the high claims that he makes for art, literally. Yeats's poem has the same literal subject as Dante's poem: they are both concerned with last things. But, like Blake, Yeats acknowledges the literal truth of his poem as vision from the beginning; vision that transforms allegory, opening the eschatology of anagogy inwards, so that the Last Judgement is an inner event to come that has already happened. Literally, Yeats sees, at the end of his life, that our time is '<When> Imaginative Art & Science & all Intellectual Gifts all the Gifts of the Holy Ghost are [*despisd*] lookd upon as of no use & only contention remains to Man': 'Where the swan drifts upon a darkening flood' (*YCP*: 276), and we are 'thrown upon this filthy modern tide' (*YCP*: 376). But does that mean 'then the Last Judgment begins & its Vision is seen by the [*Imaginative Eye*] of Every one according to the situation he holds'? 'Cuchulain Comforted' is polysemantic in a regenerative manner. It allows us to discern, judge and be judged, working in the same way as Blake's poems that ring meanings down the fourfold scale of biblical exegesis, to apprehend twofold vision. The poem is about a man's growing awareness of the Divine Humanity within. Already at the end of the decaying kind that precedes the beginning of the unborn kind, Yeats takes as his subject the highest form of allegory, anagogy, as it transforms itself in the human imagination, at once in historical time, and in soft Beulah's light, the time of the threefold spiritual sense of a work, so that all men partake of eschatological vision. Late Stevens undertakes the same project. At the end of his life, conjuring his imaginary second self and aware that 'Man

can embody truth but he cannot know it' (*YL*: 922), Yeats remained true
to his early dogma:

> 'Because those imaginary people are created out of the deepest
> instinct of man, to be his measure and his norm, whatever I can
> imagine those mouths speaking may be the nearest I can go to truth'.
> When I listened they seemed always to speak of one thing only: they,
> their loves, every incident of their lives, were steeped in the super-
> natural. (*Au*: 116)

Unfolded linen

When he printed another copy of *The Marriage of Heaven and Hell* in
1794, Blake was careful to insert, above the text of plate 3, the original
date of composition, 1790. Underneath he proclaims:

> As a new heaven is begun, and it is now thirty-three years since its
> advent: the Eternal Hell revives. And lo! Swedenborg is the Angel sitting
> at the tomb: his writings are the linen clothes folded up. (Blake: 109)

Blake was born 28 November 1757; Swedenborg understood the beginning of the new church to be that year. A relation is established between
Christ and Blake, which we come to consider in terms of Yeats and
Cuchulain. By drawing attention to the date of his poem, Blake makes
himself, cryptically, emblem for all creative artists, for all of us after
the death of Christ as 'fellow-heirs with Christ'; Blake's birth, like every
birth, marks 'a continuance of the Incarnation' (Raine 1991: 92). Blake
is saying, damningly, that Christ has fled, has already arisen, from
Swedenborg's work. His writings have no divine soul: it is not good to
be an Angel in *The Marriage of Heaven and Hell* since, on plate 21,

> I have always found that Angels have the vanity to speak of them-
> selves as the only wise; this they do with a confident insolence
> sprouting from systematic reasoning; Thus Swedenborg boasts that
> what he writes is new; tho' it is only the Contents or Index of already
> publish'd books[.] (Blake: 127)

The Angel sitting in Christ's empty sepulchre, whose 'countenance
was like lightning, and his raiment white as snowe' (Matthew 28. 3), as if
made out of Christ's discarded linen winding-sheet, heralds resurrected

Christ and foreshadows the linen-carrier in 'Cuchulain Comforted'. That Shroud is made out of a shroud but has a different function to the angel, inviting a hero who is becoming unwittingly Christ-like ('leant upon a tree | As though to meditate on wounds and blood') to do what the Spirit of Christ might. After the Crucifixion, from an unorthodox perspective, the Resurrection but prefigures His reincarnation in everyone: Yeats's poem makes us think of Christ sitting down, like Cuchulain with his communal opposite, to sew a shroud, emblem of each human life after Christ, if we understand a shroud also as a body, a mortal thing to clothe 'fearless immortal Spirit'. Thus engaged the Shrouds, the one-in-many and the many-in-one, 'sing and sing the best we can', like the souls in the boat steered by the bright angel to Purgatory:

> 'In exitu Isräel de Aegypto'
> cantavan tutti insieme ad una voce
> con quanto di quel salmo è poscia scripto.
>
> (*Purgatorio*, ii. 46–8)

We discern a typological relation between Psalm 113 and accounts of the Resurrection, especially since all of that psalm 'was traditionally sung in the vesper service on Sundays; according to the opening [of Canto II of the *Purgatorio*], the time in Jerusalem is that of vespers. Presumably the souls are singing the more elaborate psalmody customary on Easter Sunday' (*Purgatorio*: 44). The casting down of linen to be sewn while singing likewise places 'Cuchulain Comforted' in relation to Easter Sunday: a day out of time. My interpretation begins to sound like early Christian and medieval biblical exegesis, but I believe that Yeats intended that we so read his poem.

The spiritual capability of 'Cuchulain Comforted' relies on its technical achievement. As a critic well trained in the Aristotelian vein of interpretation I can identify and comment on the form of the poem. Later I discuss the significance of *terza rima* and we can continue to notice other stitches on show since 'Cuchulain Comforted' employs many schemes: epanalepsis in the first line, intermittent alliteration ('character | Convicted cowards'), significant enjambment ('let fall | A bundle'), parallelism throughout, parenthesis in the second line of the seventh stanza, sibilance in the last line of the sixth stanza and the first line of the seventh, and so on. We can classify the poem as an elegy or 'self-elegy', modifying the prose draft's 'palpable aura of dilatory Irish folk-tale, so clearly present in its homely specification . . . its colloquial hyperbole ... its frequent repetitions, and its social prescriptions' (Vendler 2007: 375 and 374); and all the while we are 'adapting conceptual tools' developed for the study of 'persuasive prose', which it is clear that Yeats employs. Vendler's analysis of the poem is a textbook example of Aristotelian criticism at work; an approach based on the noticing of 'schemes of tropes, levels of style, figures of speech and thought, criteria of genre, methods of moving the emotions of an audience' (Struck 2004: 2). Adopting the mask of another kind of interpreter, to extract some of the poem's hidden wisdom, I say that these stitches are one means of ensuring that the poem becomes the human divine. Our mode of persuasion that faces the world is made by the poem into lines that face eternity. The hypostatic union of the poem's well-stitched form and content makes it emblematic of Christ's continuous incarnation in us all, not Resurrection, after His Crucifixion. As Blake understood, the new church manifests itself in such interpretation of tradition within poems as each reader makes her soul.

Of all the gospels, John makes the most of Christ's linen shroud. Joseph and Nicodemus took

> the body of Jesus, & wound it in linnen clothes, with the spices, as the maner of the Jewes is to burie: Now in the place where he was crucified, there was a garden, and in the garden a new Sepulchre, wherein was never man yet layd. There laid they Jesus therefore, because of the Jewes preparation day, for the Sepulchre was nigh at hand. (John 19. 40–2)

Time passes before the new chapter begins:

> The first day of the weeke, commeth Mary Magdalene earely when it was yet darke, unto the Sepulchre, and seeth the stone taken away from the Sepulchre. Then she runneth, and commeth to Simon Peter, and to the other disciple, whom Jesus loved[.] (John 20. 1–2)

They run together to the sepulchre, the other disciple arriving first:

> And he stouping downe and looking in, saw the linnen clothes lying, yet went he not in. Then commeth Simon Peter following him, and went into the Sepulchre, and seeth the linen clothes lie, And the napkin that was about his head, not lying with the linnen clothes, but wrapped together in a place by it selfe. Then went in also that other disciple which came first to the Sepulchre, and he saw, and beleeved.

For as yet they knew not the Scripture, that hee must rise againe from the dead. Then the disciples went away againe unto their owne home. (John 20. 5–10)

Strangely like the two disciples, Augustine is in too much of a hurry to bother to interpret the linen clothes[6] that they witness: 'Think we these things are without significance? Let me not be supposed to think so. But we are hastening on to other matters' (Augustine 1848–9: ii. 1050). In his exegesis of John, Aquinas does not see the meaning of the linen clothes as self-manifest (Augustine 1848–9: ii. 1050), and he is captivated by various details, lingering exegetically, like Mary Magdalene by the sepulchre. He begins by interpreting the linen clothes lying in the tomb as 'the figures or foreshadowings of all the mysteries' (Aquinas 2010, 2480: iii. 255), coming before Blake in making a connection between linen clothes and writings. Peter, representing the Gentiles, sees the linen clothes of the Old Testament as well as the napkin of the New '*not lying with the linen cloths, and rolled up, having a place by itself*, because the divinity of Christ is covered over, and it is apart from every creature because of its excellence' (Aquinas 2010, 2483: iii. 256). Blake, who believed in 'Christ, the human imagination' (*Ex*: 44), would have begun to diverge from Aquinas on these points. Peter 'saw the napkin *rolled up*, to form a circle. And when linen is rolled this way one can not see its beginning or end, for the eminence of the divinity neither begins nor ends' (Aquinas 2010, 2483: iii. 256). Not rolled up, but folded up linen, Swedenborg's project, in Blake's eyes, makes creases so that the material can be stored away neatly. Allegorically speaking, to fold is to create illusory division, as between good and evil; to partition what is eternal 'with a confident insolence sprouting from systematic reasoning'; to formulate merely 'the Contents or Index of already publish'd books', including the Bible.

Yeats rehearsed Blake's verdict of Swedenborg as 'but "the linen clothes folded up" or the angel sitting by the tomb, after Christ, the human imagination, had arisen. . . . We come [to the peaceful Swedenborgian Heaven] . . . by no obedience but by the energy that "is eternal delight"' (*Ex*: 44). If 'We say God and the imagination are one', then the old moral distinctions must be re-examined: Blake 'would have us talk no more "of the good man and the bad," but only of "the wise man and the foolish," and he cries, "Go put off holiness and put on intellect"' (*Ex*: 44). Blake's writings do not abide the orthodoxy of Aquinas or even Swedenborg; in Blake's eyes, Aquinas' explications of the Bible would begin to appear anti-explications: it is as if Aquinas writes to fold the

Bible up rather than unfold it out because he denies the comfort of the continuous incarnation of Christ, apprehension of which, visionary art labours to awaken in its readers: 'Higher than all souls that seem to theology to have found a final state, above good and evil, neither accused, nor yet accusing, live those who have come to freedom, their senses sharpened by eternity, piping or dancing or "like the gay fishes on the wave when the moon sucks up the dew"' (*Ex*: 44).

Finally, in John, it is Mary who sees beyond the linen clothes and the napkin left behind and who is vouchsafed a vision of their transmutation into two angels. She then sees and hears Christ Himself:

> But Mary stood without at the sepulchre, weeping: & as shee wept, she stouped downe, and looked into the Sepulchre, And seeth two Angels in white, sitting, the one at the head, and the other at the feete, where the body of Jesus had layen: And they say unto her, Woman, why weepest thou? Shee saith unto them, Because they have taken away my Lord, and I know not where they have laied him. And when she had thus said, she turned herselfe backe, and saw Jesus standing, and knew not that it was Jesus. Jesus saith unto her, Woman, why weepest thou? whom seekest thou? She supposing him to be the gardiner, saith unto him, Sir, if thou have borne him hence, tell me where thou hast laied him, and I will take him away. Jesus saith unto her, Mary. She turned herselfe, and saith unto him, Rabboni, which is to say, Master. (John 20. 11–16)

Reading Swedenborg's writings, Blake finds himself in the position of Peter and the other disciple, perplexed, seeing nothing but linen clothes, even if he and we 'believed, with a true faith'. Blake's writings are designed to be read as vision, the kind of vision afforded to Mary of two angels in white sitting inside the sepulchre, before Christ who stands in the light without, as long as we too wait at the opening. Remaining on this threshold we see how Plato's parable of the cave could be transformed in Mary's vision, turning from the dark to the garden, and it takes Mary's patience to make Blake's syncretic, visionary texts, which appear heretical to orthodoxy. Raine says:

> In some respects Swedenborg's Christianity lies within the mainstream of orthodoxy. Blake indeed reproached Swedenborg because he had not in fact taught anything new. . . . What Blake chiefly held against Swedenborg was that he lays excessive stress on moral virtue, placing the virtuous in the heavens and evil-doers in the hells. Blake

himself saw . . . Divine Humanity as embracing the wholeness of life, both heaven and hell, reason and energy, the darkness and the light in a holiness and a wholeness beyond what humankind calls good and evil in terms of the moral laws of this world. (Raine 1991: 94)

Whereas Aquinas presents, in his allegorical interpretation of the linen in John, an essentially tranquil God and a Redeemer whose sufferings are separate from our sufferings, Blake is close to Jung's anagogical reading of the Bible in *Answer to Job*, both seeing 'Christian Revelation as incomplete': 'God, in the shape of the Holy Ghost, puts up his tent in man, for he is obviously minded to realize himself continually not only in Adam's descendants, but in an indefinitely large number of believers, and possibly mankind as a whole' (Jung 2002: 64). Orthodox Christian doctrine since Aquinas practises and encourages the worship of the Son at the expense of the presence of the Holy Spirit within the soul: 'The action of the Paraclete, metaphysically so important, is wholly undesirable for the good organisation of a Church, for it eludes all control' (Henry Corbin, quoted in Raine 1991: 93). In a vivifying way Christian revelation is still incomplete. Blake saw that Christ is not merely an historical figure, nor a kind of classical demigod to be worshipped, but an emblem of 'the Divine Human, [that] is born, lives and dies in every life' (Raine 1991: 94–5), and art has a role to awaken man in this state already regained.

In the Vulgata, 'linnen clothes lying' is 'posita linteamina' (John 20. 5). The ninth meaning of *pono* in *L&S* is '*To lay aside, take off, put down, lay down*, etc.', near to Yeats's 'let fall' in 'Cuchulain Comforted'. It can also mean to lay out for the grave. That Swedenborg's writings should be the linen clothes folded up is a double damnation: not only has Christ left Swedenborg's works but he has folded up that which can only remind us of His material absence. Rather than vouchsafing to us a vision of linen clothes transmuted into being, Swedenborg merely folds up what is literally there, thus limiting what future readers can apprehend of vision. Swedenborg is a partial witness because he has come away from the sepulchre too soon like Peter and John, believing but perplexed; Blake waits like Mary, weeping behind, and sees the linen clothes transformed into visionary figures, turning finally to discover a gardener who is Christ: his work apprehends Jesus the Imagination in everyone. A book is always in danger of being just a book, something to close and to put back; to fold up in orthodox interpretations that do not thus truly explicate. Blake demands that we learn to read his work as a human form divine, as something that is born, lives and dies in every life, and is incomplete without a reader. I make this digression into Blake's judgement of Swedenborg, in relation to Aquinas's exegesis of John, because I ask, what would Blake have made of Yeats's penultimate poem? 'Cuchulain Comforted' takes up and unfolds the linen left in the sepulchre. Its hero begins to sew as Yeats finds at the very end of his life what 'higher Argument | Remaines' (*PL*, ix. 42–3). Would Blake have apprehended Yeats's poems as he does 'particles' of light in a letter to Butts, 'Astonishd Amazd | For each was a Man | Human formd', or the light glancing off the waves, 'Heavenly Men beaming bright' that 'Appeard as One Man' (Erdman 712–13)? In this divine man or human divine all lives are contained. How is Cuchulain comforted? Does Yeats apprehend Christ's words of comfort in the fourth gospel? Does the poem apprehend the indwelling holy ghost?

My explication of 'Cuchulain Comforted' moves between the literal, analytical or Aristotelian stage of interpretation and the anagogical, interpretive or Porphyrian mode: fourfold medieval Biblical exegesis makes use of both kinds of reading. Yeats's craft, the technique identified by our Aristotelian training, ensures that the more than human it that speaks whenever man speaks, speaks through his poems so that we discern tradition, or ancient wisdom from the future. 'Yeats was a highly sophisticated, highly conscious symbolist' who 'would not deviate from his "traditional" meanings' (Wilson 1960: 15 and 14) in his poems and in his interpretations of the works of others, including especially Shelley and Botticelli. As the poet asserted in his 1898 essay, 'Symbolism in Painting':

> All art that is not mere story-telling, or mere portraiture, is symbolic, and has the purpose of those symbolic talismans which mediaeval magicians made with complex colours and forms, and bade their patients ponder over daily, and guard with holy secrecy; for it entangles, in complex colours and forms, a part of the Divine Essence. (*E&I*: 148)

Yeats remained a symbolist after the symbolist movement because his early and late master was Blake, not French. Brown talks of Yeats, after the early years of the twentieth century, discovering 'the limitations of symbolism' (1999: 80). I would argue that Yeats discovers rather the limitations of his own early use of symbolism, because of his deepening understanding of symbolism in terms of fourfold vision that foregrounds anagogy, in an immediate eschatology, to transform a poem's moral meaning, its fable, and literal history: 'The abstract joy, | The half-read wisdom of daemonic images, | Suffice the ageing man as once the growing boy' (*YCP*: 232). Yeats is better at disguising symbols in later poems that are in fact organized from the beginning to make mounting use of their profound power. I use the fourfold method of interpretation, as it is regenerated or reversed by Blake, to explicate Yeats because he has taken up the end of his master's 'golden string' (Blake, *Jerusalem*, plate 77: 374).

Yeats's penultimate poem is full of the end of John, from the 'Comforted' of the title to the linen shroud that is taken up. John is an important gospel for interpreting Blake and Yeats because the comfort that it teaches, 'the spirit of trueth' (16. 13), the Holy Ghost that Jesus sends his disciples, 'envisages a continuing realization of God in his children, which amounts to a continuance of the Incarnation' (Raine 1991: 92). Jesus said to his disciples towards the end of that gospel: 'it is expedient for you that I goe away: for if I goe not away, the Comforter will not come unto you: but if I depart, I will send him unto you' (John 16. 7). The mundane sequel to 'Cuchulain Comforted', 'The Black Tower', like *Macbeth*, marks our time when Christ has gone but the Comforter has not yet come unto us. I read Yeats in relation to the tradition, including Swedenborg, Blake and Jung, that apprehends the 'progressive indwelling' (Corbin quoted in Raine 1991: 93) of the holy spirit in man. Christ says soon after he talks of the Comforter, 'I have yet many things to say unto you, but ye cannot beare them now' (John 16. 12). To read Blake is to learn to bear such things. Blake is a radical Christian and his prophecies are essentially 'of good cheare' since he knows that Christ has 'overcome the world' (16. 33). With Yeats we seem to be in the hinterland of vision. His poems can register the confusion of the modern world, echoing the disciples: 'Then saide some of his disciples among themselves, What is this that he saith unto us, A little while, and ye shal not see me: and againe, a litle while, and ye shall see me: and, because I goe to the Father?' (16. 17).

In 'Cuchulain Comforted' the hero gives himself over to the communal work of others and the poet leaves a final draft of his poem to his literary executors for us all to read. Since 'the vision hasteneth to an end', St Bernard says to Dante:

> 'Here we break off, as the good workman doth,
> That shapes the cloak according to the cloth;
> And to the Primal Love our ken shall rise;
> That thou mayst penetrate the brightness, far
> As sight can bear thee.'

> (Cary: 438)

Yeats's late poems are in travail and have sorrow (John 16. 21); they also teach us to 'Beare free and patient thoughts' (*F*; *King Lear*, IV. vi. 79). The travail of 'Cuchulain Comforted' brings forth its comfort. There are no gods or goddesses in the poem because 'There is one, unnamed, that broods | On all the rest, in heavy thought' (*OP*: 132). The hero is sewing his next body with Shrouds in a wood, if viewed from the cave of generation. There is no relief but delivery. Yeats had already discerned the hinterland of vision, the wood of 'Cuchulain Comforted', through the Neoplatonic cave that is disguised as a stable in Botticelli's *Mystic Nativity*, which he would have scrutinized in the National Gallery, London: 'Certainly the glimpse of forest trees, dim in the evening night, through the far entrance, and the deliberate strangeness everywhere, gives one an emotion of mystery which is new to painting' (*VA*: 203).[7] Yeats looks closer:

> There is a Greek inscription at the top of the picture which says that Botticelli's world is in the 'second woe' of the Apocalypse, and that after certain other Apocalyptic events the Christ of the picture will appear. He had found, maybe in some utterance of Savonarola's, a promise of an ultimate Marriage of Heaven and Earth, of sacred and profane, and pictures it by the Angels and shepherds embracing, and as I suggest by Cave and Manger. (*VA*: 202–3)

'Cuchulain Comforted' allows a figure passage from our world to tread the path of the immortals, as it sews story or history and symbol, literal and anagogic senses, together. It is also as if the poet has passed through the picture plane to view the middle ground of Botticelli's painting from its obscure background. But within a dark wood we are likely to forget that Christ's sepulchre in the middle ground is also the stable that is His birthplace. Like the Shrouds in his poem, Yeats stares out, at once hiding from and ready to occupy interpretation. Each reader must make the journey around a point, from sepulchre through wood to manger, for herself.

Linen taken up

When Yeats wonders whether some 'Florentine Platonist' had read Porphyry's *On the Cave of the Nymphs* to Botticelli, before he painted his *Mystic Nativity*, because 'I seem to recognise it in that curious cave, with a thatched roof over the nearer entrance to make it resemble the conventional manger' (*VA*: 202), he is also wondering about the poet's making use of such disguises. The cave of the nymphs is made to resemble conventional images in various poems. From the viewpoint of Yeats's tower, for example, it is downstream, 'Under my window-ledge' (*YCP*: 275). I would now attempt a Porphyrian explication of 'Cuchulain Comforted'. If a soul's passage through the six stages between death and birth is but an extension, or dark doubling, of its tripartite spiritual pilgrimage on this earth then my interpretation already comes close to that of a 'Florentine Platonist'.[8] Such an approach might be questioned by some of Yeats's critics today, but it is the poet's preferred way of understanding and making works of art and literature. Yeats does not quite 'resuscitate and preserve the pagan form in all its seemingly un-Christian splendour, while reading into it a secret meaning consistent with Christian theology', as the 'humanist artists of Italy' (Wind 1958: 49) strove to do, because his work does not pretend orthodoxy. But such a syncretic technique informs his poems that find correspondences between diverse traditions in order to read into them secret meanings.

Yeats's late poems come after 'certain other Apocalyptic events', from Dante to Blake, to conjoin 'Heaven and Earth', like Botticelli's angels embracing the shepherds at the mystic second nativity. The linen in 'Cuchulain Comforted' is stitched at once into a winding-sheet and swaddling linen; it evokes the Neoplatonic cave by making readers think initially of Christ's sepulchre, the stone rolled away in this poem for us to discern Botticelli's wood, to be found at the back of the *Mystic Nativity*, as well as in his *Primavera*, a reproduction of which Yeats had on his wall at Riversdale (see Wellesley 1964: 100): 'Eyes stared out of the branches and were gone'. As we discern a relation between Cuchulain and Christ, 'Cuchulain Comforted' makes John available for a Neoplatonic reading. My interpretation asks with Yeats, 'How can the arts overcome the slow dying of men's hearts that we call the progress of the world, and lay their hands upon men's heart-strings again, without becoming the garment of religion as in old times?' (*E&I*: 162–3). It would be a mistake to think this a question that could have been asked only in the late 1890s; it is a question posed by Botticelli when he used the medieval template of the Baptism of Christ for his *Birth of Venus*; and it is a question that Yeats pondered still, near his death, as he composed 'Cuchulain Comforted', a poem full of a homely and religious material: its bird-like things sew linen, which, although the garment of religion, becomes, if rightly seen, even etymologically, the lines and lineaments of another kind of art altogether.

A shroud is the soul's vestment; from a Neoplatonic perspective Cuchulain would be sewing his next body in the poem since he is still caught in metempsychosis. If Christ's incarnation is continuous in us all after His death, how does that change a pagan understanding of reincarnation? Blake would answer, the linen clothes in John are to be taken up creatively by everyone after Christ so that God as 'Jesus, the Imagination' 'is born in every birth, not in one only' (Raine 1991: 94–5), and during the course of all of our reincarnations. Christ's sepulchre becomes a birthplace as in *Mystic Nativity*. Raine sees that the Shrouds in 'Cuchulain Comforted'

> partake in that Platonic ambiguity of those who 'in the words of Heraclitus "live each other's death, die each other's life".' The first, most striking meaning, which has given these beings that awe-inspiring numinosity indicated by the capital letter, must be the poet's premonition of his own approaching death. It is 'Our graves that shroud us from the searching sun'; but conversely the body is the shroud of the soul in generation. (Raine 1986: 267)

The Shrouds in 'Cuchulain Comforted' are ambiguous. But 'Christianity, in its popular forms at all events, has never sufficiently understood what Jung has called the ambivalence of the archetypes. No psychic energy, or mood of the soul, is merely good or merely evil; the face turned depends upon circumstances' (Raine 1970: 56). Such insight is part of Blake's judgement of Swedenborg: that he folds up the linen clothes, limiting Christ's teaching by laying excessive stress on moral virtue, rather than engaging in true explication that allows for ambivalence; such insight also changes our apprehension of the Last Judgement. For Paul, in his second epistle to the Corinthians, clothing does, however, seem to have a vital ambivalence like the Shrouds in Yeats's poem: we groan 'to be clothed upon' with raiment of Heaven, but we also groan because we are clothed with mortality (see 2 Corinthians 5. 1–4).

A Neoplatonist Christian would argue that metempsychosis is but one aspect of the continuous incarnation of Christ in us all. The hypostasis of Christ, apprehended as emblem for the lives of all afterwards, since 'We say God and the imagination are one', can be included in Plotinus' description of Soul:

> 'Formed from the undivided essence and the essence divided among bodies': this description of Soul must therefore mean that it has phases above and below, that it is attached to the Supreme and yet reaches down to this sphere, like a radius from a centre. (Plotinus, IV. i. i: 292)

Yeats's geometric model for this movement, divinely dictated to him, conjoins circular or spherical eternity with linear or sequential time, to make the two interlocking gyres; the movement of each gyre conjoins time and eternity and their spiralling of different phases of the soul is played out in the *terza rima* of 'Cuchulain Comforted':

> Thus it is that, entering this realm, [Soul] possesses still the vision inherent to that superior phase in virtue of which it unchangingly maintains its integral nature. Even here it is not exclusively the part-ible soul: it is still the impartible as well: what in it knows partition is parted without partibility; undivided as giving itself to the entire body, a whole to a whole, it is divided as being effective in every part. (Plotinus, IV. i. i: 292)

As Mircea Eliade says, 'the "intervention of God in history", that is, the divine revelation vouchsafed *in Time*, renews and confirms a "non-temporal situation"' (1991: 168). My explication builds on Eliade's argument that 'history does not radically modify the structure of an "immanent" symbolism. History continually adds new meanings to it, but these do not destroy the structure of the symbol.' The sacred history of Christianity, 'although in the eyes of an alien observer it looks like a local history, is also an exemplary history, because it takes up and perfects . . . trans-temporal Images' (1991: 161 and 168–9). Continuous incarnation of Christ confirms metempsychosis. We find ourselves again in a realm of acausality.

The linen-carriers in 'Cuchulain Comforted' have a meaningful but not necessarily causal relation to the linen-wearing initiates of the Isis cult as described in Apuleius' *Metamorphoses*. If we compare Apuleius and John then we find the vivifying ambivalence of linen in Yeats's poem. Botticelli provides a precedent for such typology in art. The ass's vision of Isis, the night before the transformative procession, was one of the models for his Neoplatonic painting, *The Birth of Venus*, which compositionally is a covert Baptism;[9] and so the ass, type of the uniniti-ated younger Botticelli who painted *The Birth of Venus* and *La Primavera*, is of central importance in the apocalyptic but syncretic *Mystic Nativity*, making the new Christ and Mary exist simultaneously as Lucius, type of the radiant initiate, and Isis, type of the white goddess. If one conjoins *The Birth of Venus* and *La Primavera* then the twelve figures represent the triple rhythm of the life cycle of a soul or initiation (see Wind 1958: 44). I would argue that *Mystic Nativity* is a complex apocalyptic and Christian sequel to these pagan paintings, using Apuleius among other sources. Yeats conjured themes for his own poems in the same manner that Ficino may have devised complex allegorical subjects for Botticelli to paint. For example, the figure of Mercury in *La Primavera*, dispersing mist in the tree tops with his caduceus, assumes a pose that suggests, and especially in a postcard reproduction, Cuchulain who leant upon a tree because 'The *Spirit* is still unsatisfied, until after the third state, which corresponds to Gemini, called the *Shiftings*, where the *Spirit* is purified of good and evil' (*VB*: 231); according to Ficino the constellation Gemini is ruled by the sign Mercury: like *La Primavera*, 'Cuchulain Comforted' tells of the period between death and birth in a wood. We shall see that Yeats's next and final poem, 'The Black Tower', returns to the first part of the soul's life cycle when '*winds come up from the shore*' as in *The Birth of Venus*.

In chiasmal relation to Mary Magdalene's encounter with the resurrected Christ (preceded by the vision of the angels wearing white who are spiritual embodiments of Christ's cast-off linen clothes), Isis appears above the moonlit sea in answer to asinine Lucius' plea, made on the shore and 'from the depth of misery and spiritual degradation' (Graves 1999: 65). 'Her vestiment was of fine silke yeelding divers colours' (Apuleius 1922: 219) or 'Her robe, woven of sheer linen, was of many colours, here shining with white brilliance'; 'Tunica multicolor, bysso tenui pertexta, nunc albo candore lucida' (Apuleius 1989: ii. 296–7); according to *L&S*, *byssus* is 'the linen made from' 'a fine kind of flax': 'sometime yellow, sometime rosie, sometime flamy, and sometime (which troubled my spirit sore) darke and obscure' (Apuleius 1922: 219). Before 'a flippant communication under the moon' (*SCP*: 418), turning from the sky above the beach, 'With its frigid brilliances, its blue-red sweeps | And gusts of great enkindlings, its polar green, | The color of ice and fire and solitude' (SCP: 413), Stevens's 'scholar of one candle sees | An Arctic effulgence flaring on the frame | Of everything he is. And he feels afraid' (*SCP*: 417); 'The Polar Dragon slept': 'Great Powers of falling wave and wind and windy fire, | With your harmonious choir | Encircle her I love and sing her into peace, | That my old care may cease' (*YCP*: 80). Near death Yeats heeds St Bernard in the penultimate canto of Dante's *Paradiso*: 'Cuchulain Comforted' is the poet stopping, like a good tailor who makes a final stitch, before the divine effulgence of the visionary rose of constellated saints, and accepting the hinterland of Purgatory, which is immediately to come.

Lucius as ass sees Isis as 'one person manifests the aspect of all gods and goddesses'; 'deorum dearumque facies uniformis' (Apuleius 1989: ii. 298–9): the one-in-many and the many-in-one, which expresses the synchronism (not synchronicity) of 'Cuchulain Comforted'; its symbolic apprehension of different traditions within its action of letting linen fall and taking it up to sew. As we turn from John to Apuleius, I am interested, tropologically, in the way a reader's mind is engaged by what Yeats calls a 'new science' – in fact, as he well knew, a very old one – as it is awakened by a poem that conjoins the natural and the supernatural, while sewing together, in a typological manner, stories from different traditions, but only in order to apprehend, anagogically, 'Christ . . . flowing, concrete, phenomenal' (*E&I*: 518). Likewise the linen winding-clothes of John become linen swaddling-clothes in Botticelli's *Mystic Nativity*. Each stares at that which is already born within when the elevated and centrally placed ass and the baby, from distinct traditions, gaze at each other in Botticelli's painting. Our material-ist, atheist, patched culture stares back at *Mystic Nativity* unable to explicate its hidden syncretism, at the asinine end of the decaying kind, before the beginning of the unborn kind. Then again, 'Man is but an Asse, if he goe about to expound this dreame' (*F*; *A Midsummer-Night's Dream*, IV. i. 211).

The attendants of Isis, in the procession the day after the ass's vision, like the angels in the sepulchre, are types of the linen-carriers in Yeats's poem, wearing rather than sewing *linteae vestis*:

> Then came the great company of men and women, which had taken divine orders, whose garments glistered all the streets over ['linteae vestis candore puro luminosi']. The women had their haire annointed and their heads covered with linnen: but the men had their crowns shaven, which were the terrene stars of the goddesse, holding in their hands instruments of brasse, silver and gold, which rendered a pleas-ant sound. The principall Priests which were apparelled with white surplesses hanging downe to the ground, bare the relikes of the puis-sant goddesse. (Apuleius 1922: 222–3; Apuleius 1989: 310)

Yeats long associated the Gospels with Apuleius' story:

> Because the Rose, the flower sacred to the Virgin Mary, and the flower that Apuleius' adventurer ate, when he was changed out of the ass's shape and received into the fellowship of Isis, is the western Flower of Life, I have imagined it growing upon the Tree of Life. I once stood beside a man in Ireland when he saw it growing there in a vision, that seemed to have rapt him out of his body. (*VP*: 811)

Raine says, 'Yeats did not exclude Christianity, if understood against a background not of history but of a mystical understanding such as the Celtic church inherited from the Druids' (Raine 1999: 33). Introducing his poems in 1937, Yeats carefully explained:

> Behind all Irish history hangs a great tapestry, even Christianity had to accept it and be itself pictured there. Nobody looking at its dim

folds can say where Christianity begins and Druidism ends . . . . Into
this tradition, oral and written, went in later years fragments of Neo-
Platonism, cabbalistic words . . . . That tapestry filled the scene at the
birth of modern Irish literature . . . it is there . . . in all but my later
poetry. (*E&I*: 513–14)

If this tapestry does not fill the scene of 'Cuchulain Comforted',
is it that the Shrouds sewing of shrouds changes such a back-drop?
In Yeats's poem a dead hero is invited to sew a winding-cloth into
swaddling-clothes, during the process of his soul's purgation of its last
life, in preparation for the next. The sepulchre is also the cave of generation in Botticelli's *Mystic Nativity*, through which we discern the setting
of 'Cuchulain Comforted', its figures emerging from and transforming
the flat composition of the tapestry-like wood in the *Primavera*. Out of
Christian and pagan symbols, Yeats makes a poem of the continuous
incarnation of Christ and metempsychosis; such mystical understanding in the poem takes 'Druidism' that is 'shut off in dead history' to
apprehend a Christ that is Blake's 'Human Imagination':

I am convinced that in two or three generations it will become
generally known that the mechanical theory has no reality, that
the natural and supernatural are knit together, that to escape
a dangerous fanaticism we must study a new science; at that moment
Europeans may find something attractive in a Christ posed against
a background not of Judaism but of Druidism, not shut off in dead
history, but flowing, concrete, phenomenal.
    I was born into this faith, have lived in it, and shall die in it; my
Christ, a legitimate deduction from the Creed of St. Patrick as I think,
is that Unity of Being Dante compared to a perfectly proportioned
human body, Blake's 'Imagination,' what the Upanishads have
named 'Self': nor is this unity distant and therefore intellectually
understandable, but imminent, differing from man to man and age
to age, taking upon itself pain and ugliness, 'eye of newt, and toe of
frog.' (*E&I*: 518)

It may be that this imminence accounts for the absence of Christ or
Isis from 'Cuchulain Comforted': we are to feel the cold but real comfort
of the paraclete within; that Jesus the Imagination takes on mortal pain.
Yeats is making symbolic poetry that can withstand, and sustain us as
we are 'thrown upon[,] this filthy modern tide' (*YCP*: 376), at the end of
the decaying kind. 'Cuchulain Comforted' and 'The Black Tower' are the

culmination of Yeats's late project to make his soul by writing poems that embody truth in its pain and ugliness as he sought to embody truth at the completion of his life (*YL*: 922). The mockery of poems from *The Tower* onwards makes 'Unity of Being', ironically, imminent, by dispensing with the intellectually understandable. In one of Aquinas' interpretations of John, 'the napkin' discarded in the sepulchre, 'which workers use to wipe the sweat off their faces can be understood to indicate the labour of God. For while God always remains tranquil, he presents himself as labouring and burdened when he endures the stubborn depravity of mankind' (Aquinas 2010, 2484: iii. 256). Yeats does not comprehend Aquinas' tranquil God who is 'all transcendence' (*YCP*: 533), but he would understand God 'labouring and burdened'; like Jung, Yeats apprehends Christ within men, 'flowing, concrete, phenomenal': the taking up of linen to sew in 'Cuchulain Comforted' is a deliberate act of explication and making, an unfolding of what is folded up by Aquinas' or Swedenborg's latent orthodoxy, and a creative emblem of Christ's continuous incarnation in the context of a pagan understanding of the purging of a soul between lives.

In Apuleius, after the Ass has eaten of the roses, the newly transformed, nakedly human, Lucius is given an initiate's linen dress, by order of the priest from the astonished procession. In John the linen discarded by the resurrected Christ becomes the white garments of attendant angels. In 'Cuchulain Comforted' the just dead hero takes up linen let fallen by initiate-like Shrouds, that is, bird-like things made out of linen, who are afraid of the rattle of his armour. As the hero sews his new clothing, he is zoomorphized into a bird. Yeats's poem stitches together the linen from divergent traditions; the typology that it thus establishes should have a tropological effect in its anagogical setting: the wood of last things, beyond the sepulchre, but before the cave of generation, which, as Botticelli's painting establishes, is one and the same place. We can apply Yeats's understanding of Blake in relation to Swedenborg: 'His own memory being full of images from painting and from poetry, he discovered more profound "correspondences"' (*Ex*: 44), which draw us out of the past into the realm of vision. Within 'Cuchulain Comforted' exist manifold stories, each deepening the others, and making the symbol of linen properly ambivalent as in Paul: linen is at once the discarded form of one kind of history and the vestment of spiritual life; 'For, we that are in this tabernacle, doe grone, being burdened, not for that wee would bee unclothed, but clothed upon, that mortalitie might bee swallowed up of life' (2 Corinthians 5. 4).

Fittingly, at the end of his life Yeats turns from the symbol of the rose to the symbol of linen cloth just as the ass eats roses and the then transformed Lucius, his name suggesting that his countenance is like lightening, is given linen. Yeats thus characteristically conflates the cult of Isis with the Resurrection of Christ: his poem enacts a symbolic marriage, bright bride and spouse both clothed in transfigured linen. Yeats was alive to Blake's distinction between allegory and symbol, quoting Blake's 'A Vision of The Last Judgment' at the beginning of his essay, 'Symbolism in Painting', and his interpreters should be careful not to make his poems 'the playthings of the allegorist or the pedant, and soon pass away' (*E&I*: 161). As critic and poet he was careful to know the process of his apprehension of 'Vision or Imagination', 'Surrounded by the daughters of Inspiration': 'innumerable meanings . . . alike in the emotions and the intellect, move visibly through my mind, and move invisibly beyond the threshold of sleep, casting lights and shadows of an indefinable wisdom on what had seemed before, it may be, but sterility and noisy violence' (*E&I*: 161). As Wilson puts it, Yeats 'thought that any symbol which at some time or other in the world's history had been part of religion would retain forever, through Anima Mundi, a peculiar depth and power of communication' (1960: 13).

I am not maintaining that these are the only two or three sources for the linen in 'Cuchulain Comforted'. But I am interested in their correspondence; in the way that the stories of Christ's Resurrection and casting down of linen, and Apuleius' vision of Isis, his transformation and taking up of linen, now live together in the poem.[10] Their correspondence points the way to a properly anagogical reading of the poem, transforming its tropological value, its typology and literal history. What moves visibly and invisibly through our minds as the symbolic potential of the poem reveals itself to us? Our interpretation of the poem would do well to concentrate on the associations of the poem itself, believing that they express something specific from 'age-long memoried self'. A poem is like a dream to an extent; Yeats exploited a magical state of half-reverie, or 'path-working', to make his prose draft of 'Cuchulain Comforted'. Sometimes it helps us to think of a poem as an object. Sometimes it does not. A poem can grow in the ear, like Rilke's tall tree (see 2006: 16–17), from our conscious and reasonable comprehension of it, until we apprehend the paradox that it commands, from the beginning, the celestial realms of anagogy. Attention to detail admits us to see, if but darkly, secret things. Such interpretation allows a poem in turn to interpret us. Chasing sources is one step on this path of explication. The next is to notice how correspondences between different systems of thought act on our minds and join our everyday way of thinking to 'age-long memoried self'. Poems like dreams have different senses. We are well trained by Aristotle to notice formal qualities; we are well schooled to discuss a poem's conscious structure. But we must not forget that the deliberately old-fashioned forms of Yeats's poems, all of which are written to 'the dance music of the ages' (Wellesley 1964: 114), knit the natural and the supernatural together, and his themes are conscious attempts to plumb what we now call the unconscious, but Blake called, Jesus the Imagination, or the Divine Humanity.

Yeats's explicators do well to learn from magic, a private but perennial practice that transforms rhetoric, our everyday mode of public discourse. We must use as guides such modes of explication as Porphyry's allegorical reading of Homer, in order to move between a literal sense of a work and the realm of anagogy: as long as anagogy is not to come as medieval interpreters of the Bible believed, but is, as Blake believed, already on hand. Jung's collective unconsciousness, what Yeats calls 'age-long memoried self', is but the same well from which Porphyry drew meaning to find anagogical sense in Homer. Modern criticism is, generally speaking, still Aristotelian: we 'generate an approach to poetry and a method for studying it by adapting conceptual tools first developed for the study of the public delivery of persuasive prose' (Struck 2004: 2). Yeats understood, 'We make out of the quarrel with others, rhetoric, but of the quarrel with ourselves, poetry' (*M*: 331). A second kind of criticism, now and then, 'shares conceptual tools with other well-attested fields of interpretive inquiry in the ancient world, including divination, magic, religious rite, and certain traditions of esoteric philosophy' (Struck 2004: 4). Allegory (or the threefold spiritual sense of a work, or magic, or divination, call it what you will) transforms oratory. Yeats makes interpretation move between these two realms of explication.

Homer's cave on the shore of Ithaca that so enthralled Porphyry, in which the returning Odysseus leaves his treasure, before meeting the swineherd Eumaeus, 'has two mouths. The one that looks north is the way down for men. The other, facing south, is for the gods; and as immortals come in by this way men do not trespass there' (*Odyssey*: 171–2). As such a cave 'Cuchulain Comforted' looks out into the wood at the back of Botticelli's *Mystic Nativity*. Before Botticelli's picture we are at the other entrance for mortals, like the new Christ. Yeats's penultimate poem too provides access for gods and men; it is the time and place when and where they are knit together. As we read the poem, we find passage between the mundane and the dark wood of the afterlife, from one plane to another, we also move between the poem's deployment of allegory and rhetoric, the one transforming the other.

In 'Cuchulain Comforted' Christ and Isis are absent but the presence of linen deepens its typological sense, calling into play the two traditions. If we compare Yeats's prose draft with the poem, we see the poet making more apparent the allusions to John as he makes the poem. The tree and the wounds and blood evoke Christ's Passion on the cross; the linen is strangely emphasized and shade is changed to Shroud, as if these ghosts are already the shrouds that they sew out of linen: they recall the white angels in John, made out of Christ's linen winding sheet. Likewise the finished poem brings the reader closer to Apuleius. In the prose version 'A man' is 'A shade' at the beginning: in the poem he undergoes possibly three transformations from man to Shroud to bird. The zoomorphic transformation is emphasized in the poem (in the prose draft the shades merely sing like linnets, in the poem they had changed their throats); the transfiguration from man to Shroud to bird reverses the ass transformed back to Lucius who in turn becomes linen-wearing initiate of the Isis cult. That we are afforded no vision of Isis or Christ in Yeats's poem is significant in itself: we are in a posthumous hinterland of vision; the poem's theme is but one episode of 'the Theme': the story of 'the God of the Waxing Year' and his rival, 'the God of the Waning Year', in relation to the 'all-powerful Threefold Goddess' (Graves 1999: 20).

In John, Joseph takes down Jesus' body from the cross and wraps it in linen for burial. The linen is then put off in the Resurrection, the cloth discarded and the napkin rolled. These items of linen become, in my interpretation, angels. In Apuleius, we see visionary linen first, in the ass's vision of Isis. The next day in the procession both priests and initiates wear linen like their goddess. Once the ass is transformed back to Lucius after eating the roses, the naked man, born again is given linen to hide his nakedness. 'Cuchulain Comforted' holds these two episodes from the ends of stories about death and re-birth in perpetual chiasmal relationship: in the poem linen is put down and taken up as one man interacts with the many. There is a danger that using the linen to bring in Apuleius and John to play, we remain in the realm of fable. Allegorically speaking, we are doing no more than establishing a typological relation between two traditions within the text. But linen is a material of last and first things: death and birth; 'Thy swathing linnen, and thy winding sheet' (Lovelace 1930: 29). Linen must be put off before Judgement, Heaven and Hell, and then once that is all over, put on again in a kind of re-birth. Cloth of linen is a twofold symbol. Clothing can traditionally symbolize the body in which the soul is closed. In John it stands for the missing body of Jesus. But vision sees the discarded shroud as a supernatural being, or the divine human, 'that mortalitie might bee swallowed up of life' (2 Corinthians 5. 4).

The twofoldness of linen, as symbol of two kinds of bodies, makes it essential to a soul's progress through the six states between death and life. In the *Meditation* of the first state, 'the *Spirit* and *Celestial Body* appear': 'If the *Passionate Body* does not *disappear*, the *Spirit* finds the *Celestial Body*, only after long and perhaps painful dreams of the past, and it is because of such dreams that the second state is sometimes called the *Dreaming Back*.' In 'Cuchulain Comforted' we first encounter Cuchulain as he enters this state of *Dreaming Back*, leaning against a tree, meditating on wounds and blood. He represents literally and mystically a passionate body; as Cuchulain dreams over his past, he resembles the last stage of Christ's Passion: 'a tree' symbolizing the cross. Yeats notes that 'The more complete the *Dreaming Back* the more complete the *Return* and the more happy or fortunate the next incarnation' (*VB*: 223, 224–5 and 227). In a footnote to this sentence he provides a key to the symbol of linen in 'Cuchulain Comforted', corresponding with Blake's verdict that Swedenborg's writings are the linen clothes folded up:

> Compare the account of the *Dreaming Back* in Swedenborg's *Heaven and Hell*. My account differs from his mainly because he denied or ignored rebirth. Somebody has suggested that he kept silent deliberately, that it was amongst those subjects that he thought forbidden. It is more likely that his instructors were silent. They spoke to the Christian Churches, explaining the 'linen clothes folded up', and even what they said or sought to say was half-transformed into an opium dream by the faith of those Churches in the literal inspiration of the Bible. (*VB*: 227–8)

During the *Shiftings*, the third state of the soul after death, 'the *Spirit* is purified of good and evil. In so far as the man did good without knowing evil, or evil without knowing good, his nature is reversed until that knowledge is obtained'; like Blake, this state transmutes Swedenborg's too orthodox views of good and evil, it is an unfolding of the linen clothes. The following state, the *Marriage* or the *Beatitude*, 'is said to pass in unconsciousness, or in a moment of consciousness': '"The *Celestial Body* is the Divine Cloak lent to all, it falls away at the consummation and Christ is revealed", words which seem to echo Bardesan's "Hymn of the Soul", where a King's son asleep in Egypt (physical life) is sent a cloak which is also an image of his body. He sets out to his father's kingdom wrapped in the cloak' (*VB*: 231 and 232–3). The casting down of linen before the hero marks the appearance of the Celestial Body in the poem, and out of it Cuchulain sews such a cloak, with the other Shrouds, in preparation for his purification and foreknowledge, which comes as augury, the hero transformed into bird. Such a cloak is also an image of the soul's new body, prefiguring its rebirth that Yeats thought Swedenborg denied.

When Yeats was editing Blake with Edwin J. Ellis in the 1890s he was also engaging at one remove with Swedenborg's work; with Ellis he was running to discover Swedenborg's linen clothes as Simon Peter and the other disciple, whom Jesus loved, ran both together to the sepulchre after Mary Magdalene's news in John. The patient poet eventually becomes Mary Magdalene; he is afforded a vision of the Divine Human. Where Swedenborg saw strict division, folding up the linen clothes, Blake would marry Heaven and Hell, transfiguring his master's teachings into a new garment. Yeats writes out of the tradition that Blake thus establishes. Yeats acknowledges the literal truth of his poem as vision from the beginning; vision that transforms allegory, opening the eschatology of anagogy inwards, so that the Last Judgement is an inner event to come that has already happened. The literal sense of 'Cuchulain Comforted' was revealed to the poet in an anagogical manner by his instructors from the other world. Yeats was well versed in eschatology, the science of last things. But 'He that commeth after me, was before me because he was yer then I' (Tyndale 2008: sig. cxix^v): the event to come that has already happened is an expanding of God in the human imagination, the crisis that joins 'trivial daily mind' and 'buried self' in the creative act today.

Blake's 'golden string' that we wind into a ball as we backtrack our way out of the labyrinth is used by the Shrouds in 'Cuchulain Comforted' to thread the needles' eyes. If we so thread it, the needle's eye is another way out of the labyrinth. Raine elaborates the symbol as I would meditate upon linen in the poem:

> In the Gospel it is through the needle's eye that a man enters the Kingdom of Heaven. The image suggests also the narrow entrance of womb and passage-grave, the dimensionless *punctum* through which life comes and goes. Above all, the needle's eye is apt to receive the thread of destiny spun by the Fates that runs on 'Plato's spindle' from birth to death, and, in the 'dreaming back', when 'time is unwound' from death to birth. (Raine 1986: 276)

My explication sees 'Cuchulain Comforted' as an attempt to find the kingdom of God through a needle's eye; readers discover 'The everlasting universe of things' (Shelley 1967: 532) in its details because the poem possesses 'the perfections that escape analysis, the subtleties that have a new meaning every day' (*E&I*: 164). In the cave of generation there is spinning and sewing: 'The goddesses of fate spin the thread of human life' (Eliade 1991: 114). Alcinous proposes to the 'Captains and Counsellors of the Phaeacians' that they will safeguard Odysseus home on the final stretch to Ithaca, but 'After which he must suffer whatever Destiny and the relentless Fate spun for him with the first thread of life when he came from his mother's womb' (*Odyssey*: 89–90). Sure enough, after he is landed on his island, Odysseus finds the cave that so enthralled Porphyry with its 'great looms of stone where the Nymphs [whom we call Naiads] weave marvellous fabrics of sea-purple' (*Odyssey*: 171). As Porphyry explains,

> the purple garments plainly appear to be the flesh with which we are invested; and which is woven as it were and grows by the connecting and vivifying power of the blood, diffused through every part. . . . Add too that the body is a garment with which the soul is invested; a circumstance indeed wonderful to the sight, whether we regard its composition, or consider the connecting band by which it is knit to the soul. (Taylor 1969: 305)

Thread is a twofold symbol. As in Paul we groan for the stitching of two kinds of garments. In the end the strongest line is the one established by Shakespeare: 'Nor shall death brag thou wandr'st in his shade, | When in eternall lines to time thou grow'st' (Q 1609). The lineaments of sonnet 18 are covered by the linen of 'Cuchulain Comforted', another poem that makes death die for us. Like Dante and Blake, Yeats's penultimate poem brings other fictions into its 'powerful matrix' of 'mutual implication'.

'Behold a wonder worthy of the rhyme'

Yeats's use of Dante's 'rhyme' also recalls Shelley's last poem, 'The Triumph of Life', where 'The grove ‖ Grew dense with shadows to its inmost covers' (Shelley 1967: 518–19). Both Shelley and Yeats people the dark wood of Canto I of the *Inferno* with the spirits encountered before Acheron in Canto III, among whom Dante recognizes 'the shade of him, who to base fear | Yielding, abjured his high estate' (Cary: 11). 'Each at [Charon's] beck, as falcon at his call', the shades descend to the shore, 'As fall off the light autumnal leaves, | One still another following, till the bough | Strews all its honours on the earth beneath' (Cary: 12); in 'Cuchulain Comforted' 'bird-like things' emerge from branches, come creeping up to a man, one letting fall a bundle of linen beneath the tree against which he leans.

Where do we find sewing in Dante? There is the image of an ageing tailor peering at his needle, before Dante's recognition of Brunetto Latini, in *Inferno*, xv. 20–1 (see Albright 1994: 818). When Virgil and Dante meet Statius in Canto XXI of *Purgatorio* they talk of poetic influence and the spinning of the fates, and Virgil's questioning 'threaded the needle of my desire'; 'per la cruna | del mio disio' (*Purgatorio*, xxi. 37–8). It is fitting that Yeats's penultimate poem should also correspond with the penultimate canto of the *Paradiso*, when St Bernard halts his description of the saints in the Rose:

> Ma perché 'l tempo fugge che t'assonna
> qui farem punto, come buon sartore
> che com' elli ha del panno fa la gonna,
>
> e drizzeremo li occhi al primo amore,
> si che guardando verso lui penètri
> quant' è possibil per lo suo fulgore.
>
> (*Paradiso*, xxxii. 139–44)

In his introduction to a translation that Yeats read, John William Mackail comments:

> it has been found remarkable – it has even been thought a curious defect of judgement or of taste – that at the very consummation of the Beatific Vision the one image used by St. Bernard is almost prosaic in its bald simplicity:
>
>   . . .
>
> > 'Good tailors we, an end must make,
> > And so, to fit the gown,
> > Use but the cloth we own.'

. . . But the touch here is probably a calculated one. It is a specific instance of what becomes more and more the burden of the whole poem as it approaches its conclusion, *All' alta fantasia qui mancò possa*, 'Here failed the vision.' In the last resort he becomes careless of any verbal or rhetorical artifices. The simplest language comes nearest to expressing what is beyond expression. (1915: xxix–xxx)

Near death Yeats also valued 'bald simplicity' with a calculated touch and the translation's half-rhyme of gown and own sounds Yeatsian. As we have seen, in 'Adam's Curse', Yeats thought of a poet as a good tailor, or at least seamstress, and here in Dante such a tailor can help repair Adam's curse. In 'Cuchulain Comforted', the poet will make a stitch (stitch a final stitch) like a good tailor that has, from the cloth, made the skirt. Cuchulain is given his bundle of linen and as he begins to sew, St Bernard stops stitching, so to speak, in order to direct his and Dante's eyes 'to the Primal Love, so that, looking towards Him, thou mayst penetrate, as far as that can be, into His effulgence' (Sinclair 1961: iii. 469–71). To bring this climactic moment of the *Comedy* into play is to provide a counterpoint that sounds in a poignant manner. Yeats confessed that he was no Dante scholar, but 'Cuchulain Comforted' conjoins the beginning of the *Inferno* with the end of the *Paradiso* in the same manner as it gathers, at the end of Yeats's life, his very first poem about Cuchulain, making his hero pass through specific stages of the afterlife. As we witness again Yeats's stitching, the pattern of the poem becomes even more complex. Yeats's poem connects the climax of the *Comedy* with the climax of Apuleius' *Metamorphoses*:

> the great Priest which bare the restoration of my human shape, by the commandment of the goddes, approached . . . bearing . . . a garland of Roses to give me, to the end I might be delivered from cruel fortune . . . . Then I not returning hastilie . . . but going softly through the prease of the people, which gave me place on every side, went after the Priest. The priest being admonished the night before, as I might well perceive ['At sacerdos, ut reapse cognoscere potui, nocturni commonefactus oraculi miratusque congruentiam mandati muneris'] . . . thrust out the garland of roses into my mouth, I (trembling) devoured with a great affection . . . my deforme and Assie face abated[.] (Apuleius 1922: 223–4; Apuleius 1989: 314–16)

St Bernard, the angels in John, and 'A Shroud that seemed to have authority' perform the same function as the priest. In late Yeats his once beloved symbol of the rose is not abandoned but deferred. Out of Dante's artisanal figure of speech used to cut short a description of the visionary Rose and out of the costume of Apuleius' initiates of Isis and her priest who bears a garland of roses, a zoomorphic poem is made that prepares, not for the Resurrection, but transformation through deliverance of the Divine Human. Reading Yeats's poem we behold coincidence of vision. Lucius' description of 'the priest, who, as I could tell from the facts, remembering the oracle he had received in his dream and marvelling at the coincidence with the instructions he had received, stopped at once and spontaneously stretched out his hand and held the wreath of roses right in front of my face' (Apuleius 1989: 315–17), fits both Yeats and his readers in relation to the poem that takes on transformations of its own. Yeats has not deliberately conjoined two traditions by writing under the direction of the daughters of memory, rather his poem circles a syncretic and acausal realm, guided by the daughters of inspiration. Joining his everyday self to that age-long memoried self, Yeats has made something, with a 'moving soul' of its own, with which we should learn to speak.

The real sewing in the *Comedy* is its rhyme: 'the apparent coherence of Dante's belief is at least in part a projection of the coherence of his poem' (Freccero 1986: 260). As early as Chaucer's 'A Complaint to his Lady', its third part 'yknit' in *terza rima* (Chaucer 1987: 642), and Wyatt's 'My mothers maydes when they did sowe and spynne' (Wyatt 1969: 91), the chain rhyme of the form is associated, at least unconsciously by poets, with sewing. If Yeats's faith has a geometrical form it is the interlocking gyres, spiralling with the apocalyptic asymptotic movement, which Blanchot also identifies in narrative, towards an ending that cannot have begun before one has reached it. It is fitting then that he should turn to *terza rima* at the very end, a rhyme scheme that is always 'At the earliest ending' (*SCP*: 534). Its forward motion, which is at the same time recapitulatory, 'can also serve as the spatial representation of narrative logic, particularly autobiography' (Freccero 1986: 263), a movement that we have already traced in Blanchot's reading of Homer's relation to and of Odysseus. 'The narrative structure we have been describing, like the verse pattern, privileges the ending, the moment of closure and makes it coincide with the beginning. This logical reversal is theologically the movement of conversion, of death and resurrection' (Freccero 1986: 264).

When Yeats returns to the Cuchulain myth at the very end of his life, his 'trivial daily mind' and 'buried self' join at the crisis of death. The theme of his penultimate poem turns out to be the continuity and discontinuity of the autobiographical form:

> Like the process of autobiography, conversion begins with two subjects: the sinner who is and the saint who will be, like the pilgrim who is and the author who will be. . . . Logically, the movement is twofold, chronologically it is one, for the first step toward salvation is the first away from sin. (Freccero 1986: 266)

Such movement is at the end of the decaying kind as it precedes the beginning of the unborn kind. '*Conversion* is the technical term of the theologians to describe the way the Old Testament was transformed in the light of the New' (Freccero 1986: 266), as Blake transforms Swedenborg's writings. Ireneaus saw Christian history as recapitulation: 'It means not just flowing backward to the beginning, but movement forward in time as the integration of the beginning in the end, and this is the significance of the movement itself, insofar as it is at once in time and above time' (von Balthasar 1968: 116): 'This theory of history is the foundation of biblical allegory, God's way of writing narrative, with things rather than signs' (Freccero 1986: 267). The origin of the Greek word for history as recapitulation is a rhetorical term found in Aristotle. When Yeats transmutes rhetoric in 'Cuchulain Comforted' we register the difference between 'A man' and 'a man', 'till one greater Man | Restore us' (*PL*, i. 4–5):

What if Christ and Oedipus . . . are the two scales of a balance, the two butt-ends of a seesaw? What if every two thousand and odd years something happens in the world to make one sacred, the other secular . . .? What if there is an arithmetic or geometry that can exactly measure the slope of a balance, the dip of a scale, and so date the coming of that something? (*VB*: 28–9)

When Dante moved from Latin to the vernacular, he also applied sacred rules of interpretation to secular poetry. The *terza rima* that he devised in the process possesses a geometry that can just as well balance Christ and Oedipus, or Cuchulain and Isis. What is true of a man's life is true of an age, and of ages changing into ages.

4

'Not Ideas about the Thing but the Thing Itself'

The end of the decaying kind

'Not Ideas' unfolds in and out of everyday conceptions of time. According to normal methods of measuring time, the poem marks the time of the approach of morn, specifically the March morning of the vernal equinox that heralds the first season of the year; since it is the period around sunrise, as an almanac would tell us, the clock has just turned, or is just about to turn, six. Stevens's poem is as exact as Dante's 'elaborately astronomical' beginning to Canto II of *Purgatorio*, his 'first representation of the redeemed life' (Sinclair 1961: ii. 41): the speaker wakes to the zodiacal constellation of Aries; to the time of the first house, which is also the first stage of the period between death and birth (see *VB*: 223). 'Not Ideas' tells of a time that precedes its telling while occurring hereafter, changing the very language that makes it known:

> At the earliest ending of winter,
> In March, a scrawny cry from outside
> Seemed like a sound in his mind.
>
> He knew that he heard it,
> A bird's cry, at daylight or before,
> In the early March wind.
>
> The sun was rising at six,
> No longer a battered panache above snow . . .
> It would have been outside.
>
> It was not from the vast ventriloquism
> Of sleep's faded papier-mâché . . .
> The sun was coming from outside.

That scrawny cry – it was
A chorister whose c preceded the choir.
It was part of the colossal sun,

Surrounded by its choral rings,
Still far away. It was like
A new knowledge of reality.

(*SCP*: 534)

Holly Stevens tells us that the poem was written especially for an issue of *Trinity Review*, published in May 1954, 'like a very rich chocolate cake' (*SL*: 835), celebrating Stevens's forthcoming seventy-fifth birthday. In preparing his *Collected Poems*, to be published on that birthday in October, Stevens may have been tempted to regard the book half-light-heartedly as 'a missal for brooding sight': 'I play. But this is what I think', he confesses of 'The Man with the Blue Guitar' in 1937 (*SCP*: 178). Chosen by the poet to close that book, 'Not Ideas' can be read at once as part of the canonical hours, and at the end of all divine offices, in praise of the 'scrawny cry' of a new born epistemology. The poem contains hymns to be sung at Lauds as recommended by the Roman Breviary: when the reader is invited to play 'That scholar hungriest for that book, | ... | Or, at the least, ... | ... that latined phrase' (*SCP*: 178). It also echoes our very last response in Thomas Cranmer's 1549 rendering of 'The Order for the Burial of the Dead' in The Book of Common Prayer: '*Prieste*. O lorde, graciously heare my prayer. | *Aunswere*. And let my crye come unto thee' (BCP 1549: sig. cxlix[v]). Reluctantly consenting in April 1954 to the publication of what he envisaged by May as *The Whole of Harmonium*, Stevens ends the book with a grave allusion, playfully to 'face the fact' (*SL*: 829): a *Collected Poems* is one way of laying a septuagenarian poet to rest; 'He knew that he heard it', the hollow echo or harsh allusion, 'That scrawny cry – it was' – 'And let my crye come unto thee.' Stevens was to die at the end of the summer the following year. The correspondences that I explore next comprehend this other kind of cry.

At the end of a poet's life, 'Not Ideas' is also of the beginning. Heidegger's 1953 explication of another poet's lines can be appropriated:

The end is here not the sequel and the dying away of the beginning. The end precedes, namely as the end of the decaying kind, the beginning of the unborn kind. Yet the beginning has already overtaken the end as the earlier earliness. [Das Ende ist hier nicht die Folge und das Verklingen des Anbeginns. Das Ende geht, nämlich als das Ende des verwesenden Geschlechtes, dem Anbeginn des ungeborenen Geschlechtes vorauf. Der Anbeginn hat jedoch als die frühere Frühe das Ende schon überholt.] (Adapted from 1971: 176; 2007: 57)[1]

For Stevens, in the spring and early summer of 1954, Heidegger's books remained unobtainable and the man himself was presumed Swiss (lecturing, the poet mistakenly believed, in Fribourg not Freiberg), an explicator of Hölderlin who was also 'a myth, like so many things in philosophy' (*SL*: 839). To adapt the words of this philosopher whom Stevens did not read, the poem begins at the end yet overtaken by the beginning it precedes, the earlier earliness already at the ending: 'At the earliest ending', when 'was' becomes, as 'it was', repeated, heralds 'A new knowledge of reality'. The end of one kind of time and the beginning of another are conjoined by the different kinds of relations 'Not Ideas' creates with other poems and hymns. Let us begin with the end of the decaying kind and its attendant allusions, a choir full of poems that gathers to respond, 'And let my crye come unto thee', to be distinguished from the influence of hymns that are distilled in the poem.

'*A Cry within of Women.*' 'What is that noyse?' asks Macbeth (proleptically, the line before the stage direction in *The First Folio*). 'It is the cry of women, my good lord', assures Seyton, exiting to investigate. 'The time ha's beene, my sences would have cool'd | To heare a Night-shrieke' but now Macbeth is so sated with horrors that he does not start at such a sound. 'Wherefore was that cry?' he asks upon Seyton's return. 'The Queene (my lord) is dead' (*F*; *Macbeth*, V. v. 7–16). Macbeth's lament is at the tired and despairing end of the decaying kind with which this chapter begins; it comprehends the kind of poem 'Not Ideas' might have become, without its apprehension of the beginning of the unborn kind, as exemplified by the much earlier 'Depression before Spring' when 'The cock crows | But no queen rises' (*SCP*: 63). After seventy-five years of mornings it is significant by the end of the poem that 'It was not from the vast ventriloquism | Of sleep's faded papier-mâché . . . ', that 'a sound' was not 'a Night-shrieke', although to begin with the cry appears to come from *Macbeth*:

> She should have dy'de heereafter;
> There would have beene a time for such a word:
> To morrow, and to morrow, and to morrow,
> Creepes in this petty pace from day to day,

To the last Syllable of Recorded time:
And all our yesterdayes, have lighted Fooles
The way to dusty death.

(V. v. 17–23)

In a play of cries, and unborn metaphorical babies, this cry is a hollow reminder of that noise at an odd hour that Macbeth will never hear, it is a sound marking a double death since his wife dies issueless. On waking to yet another tomorrow, which has become today, in order to join all our yesterdays, 'He knew that he heard it' in 'Not Ideas', that is, a cry from outside that seemed like a sound in his mind, like the ambiguous stage direction, '*A Cry within of Women*', that precedes Macbeth's appalling heap of days. Although in Stevens's poem that scrawny cry is also a child's cry, until it is identified as a bird's cry in line 5, the reader must first hear the poem's very real lamentation in order to understand the 'fructifying virtue' of the sound, its twofold significance, as it brings itself to the 'heereafter' when 'There would have beene a time for such a word'. As the beginning of 'The Man on the Dump' proves, Macbeth's hopeless catalogue of tomorrows was a commonplace for Stevens of dusty belatedness, of despairing of saying anything fresh because 'The freshness of night has been fresh a long time' (*SCP*: 202): 'Day creeps down. The moon is creeping up' (*SCP*: 201). To risk doubling what is already in two, there are two twilights in 'Not Ideas'. At the opposite end of the diurnal time of the poem, that is, its spring dawn setting, which makes the poem an alembic containing old hymns that flow in and well up, which I will explore later as the beginning of the unborn kind, is the terrible twilight of evening in autumn, which stands for a man's life. This second twilight is evoked in Stevens's poem as it calls to three crepuscular and autumnal poems, Whitman's 'Bardic Symbols', Keats's 'To Autumn' and Shakespeare's 'Sonnet 73', and to the apocalyptic 'Alphonso of Castile' by Emerson, poems that Stevens returned to again and again and so 'bloom' (Keats 1820, 'To Autumn': 138) the *Collected Poems* in the form of 'pure explication de texte' his 'principal form of piety' (*SL*: 793).

The reader of 'Not Ideas' must hear 'The cry that contains its converse in itself' in Canto VIII of 'An Ordinary Evening in New Haven', that which Bloom discerns as the 'prevalent and central' cry in Stevens:

Our breath is like a desperate element
That we must calm, the origin of a mother tongue

> With which to speak to her, the capable
> In the midst of foreignness, the syllable
> Of recognition, avowal, impassioned cry,
>
> The cry that contains its converse in itself,
> In which looks and feelings mingle and are part
> As a quick answer modifies a question,
>
> Not wholly spoken in a conversation between
> Two bodies disembodied in their talk,
> Too fragile, too immediate for any speech.

> (*SCP*: 470–1)

For Bloom the cry takes Stevens 'back to Whitman's fierce old mother, the sea, crying out in the night for her sons, the poets, who have been cast away from her, who have fallen down into the occasions that are the cries of their poems' (1977: 316). The critic falls down into the etymology of 'occasion' while drawing our attention to the opening of Canto XII of 'An Ordinary Evening': 'The poem is the cry of its occasion, | Part of the res itself and not about it' (*SCP*: 473), the origin of 'Not Ideas' in Stevens's own work, making clear that the poem's cry is part of its title. The origin of all that is good in Stevens for Bloom is Whitman: 'hostile to all suggestions that he owed anything to his reading of precursor poets, [he] would have left us nothing of value but for Walt Whitman' (1997: xxiii); and here specifically 'Bardic Symbols', later collected as the second poem of 'Sea-drift' in the 'Death-bed Edition' of *Leaves of Grass*. As Bloom rightly emphasizes, the cry in Stevens is 'the syllable | Of recognition, avowal' (*SCP*: 471). A cry repeated in such a sibilant poem as 'Not Ideas', like the cry of Canto VIII of 'An Ordinary Evening', should be recognized at first, but only at first, as a calling upon Whitman, as precedent and solace:

> As I ebbed with an ebb of the ocean of life,
> As I wended the shores I know,
> As I walked where the sea-ripples wash you, Paumanok
> Where they rustle up, hoarse and sibilant,
> Where the fierce old mother endlessly cries for her castaways[.]

> (Whitman 1860, ii. 1–5: 445)

We should reread the rest of Whitman's poem, 'musing late in the autumn day', and measure it against 'Not Ideas' as both poets measure preceding poems. The endless crying of the 'hoarse and sibilant', 'fierce old mother' sea, whose sound 'preceded' the letter c as the comedian, both in *Harmonium* and in 'Not Ideas', is not as deathly sterile as the crying in *Macbeth*, giving birth as it does to such a jocund pun between poems. But the sibilant calling to Whitman at once masks and unveils a doubt that can only be spoken of thus in Stevens's poem about the collected poems that precede it, 'here preceding what follows':

> Oh, baffled, lost,
> Bent to the very earth, here preceding what follows,
> Terrified with myself that I have dared to open my mouth,
> Aware now, that amid all the blab whose echoes recoil upon me,
>   I have not once had the least idea who or what I am,
> But that before all my insolent poems the real me still stands
>   untouched, untold, altogether unreached[.]
>
> (Whitman 1860, vi. 1–5: 445–6)

The hoarse undercurrent of Whitman's poem in 'Not Ideas', as it half-recognizes that it is 'Terrified with myself', is accompanied by a terrible silence, in another poem, by a calling to the absence of choirs that cannot call back, to choristers who no longer sing in the bare ruined choirs of trees or derelict abbeys, in 'Sonnet 73'. The very absence of song in Shakespeare's poem joins Whitman's croaking as a poignant counter-point to the colossal choral rings at dawn in spring of Stevens's poem:

> That time of yeeare thou maist in me behold,
> When yellow leaves, or none, or few, doe hange
> Upon those boughes which shake against the could,
> Bare rn'wd quiers, where late the sweet birds sang.
> In me thou seest the twi-light of such day,
> As after Sun-set fadeth in the West,
> Which by and by blacke night doth take away,
> Deaths second selfe that seals up all in rest.
>
> (Q 1609)

As he confesses in 'Michael', Wordsworth writes 'For the delight of a few natural hearts', Milton's 'fit audience . . . though few', 'And with yet fonder feeling, for the sake | Of youthful Poets, who among these Hills | Will be my second self when I am gone', the two or three allusions making sure that he is not only of the 'happy few' who read Milton and Shakespeare continuously and deeply, but that he is the 'second self' of the two poets, as unborn youthful poets will, in turn, become after his death his second self, a 'band of brothers' (*F*; *Henry V*, IV. iii. 60) who seem to speak with one voice. 'Not Ideas' partakes of Wordsworth's 'vivifying Virtue' at his death as it also explicates 'Sonnet 73', transforming the mere arrest in love of its speaker's decay; it is of those youthful poets, 'Among the second selves' (*OP*: 119), of the unborn kind already to be found at the end of the decaying kind. It speaks of the Romantic that sees through Shakespeare and Milton as in a renovating of the canon; it 'seest' the twilight of Shakespeare's sibilant octet along with an ebb of Whitman's sea at evening, but as one become again an abecedarian; it is a final poem that finds it is already at the beginning; when such day in me thou *ceased*, 'And still more' (Keats 1820, 'To Autumn': 137), when Stevens's c preceded, by making new, Shakespeare's vandalized church and vanished Catholic choir: it is where, late, the sweet birds can sing, 'will never cease' (Keats, 'To Autumn': 137). That this cry before and after two or three kinds of choirs is 'scrawny' and not 'sweet' heralds the crisis that joins late and early, 'At the earliest ending', at the crack of dawn, the word piping us down a telling path of poems.

On the numerologically significant twenty fourth day of creation, Adam, like the protagonist of 'Not Ideas', is awoken at six, 'that sweet hour of Prime', not by a bird that precedes, but by the 'shrill Matin Song' itself, 'Of Birds on every bough' (*PL*, v. 170, 7, and 8). Milton is restoring the shaking boughs of Shakespeare's bare ruined choirs and with the strange word 'Matin', allowing a connection between the dawn chorus and hymns sung in church at Matins. As in 'L'Allegro' and its shrill cock this shrillness is Georgic, Milton translating Virgil's *arguta*. In the first book of the *Georgics*, 'arguta lacus circumvolitavit hirundo' (Virgil, *Georgics*, i. 377: i. 124). There is a transmutation and proliferation of Virgil's 'twittering swallow [that] flits round the pools' (Virgil: i. 125) in the last stanza of Keats's 'To Autumn' with its 'wailful choir' of 'small gnats' 'Among the river sallows', and 'gathering swallows' that 'twitter in the skies', preceded by 'The red-breast' that 'whistles from a garden-croft' (Keats 1820: 139); choristers who are also crepuscular precursors of the aubade to come in 'Not Ideas', 'as Stevens draws the ode forward from its sunset into a new sunrise' (Vendler 1980: 193).

Stevens's translation of *arguta* is 'scrawny', an American pronunciation of an English dialect word, *scranny*, meaning thin or scraggy, and, like Milton's 'scrannel' in 'Lycidas', derived from the Norwegian word for lean or shrivelled, *skran*:

> And when they list, their lean and flashy songs
> Grate on their scrannel Pipes of wretched straw,

> The hungry Sheep look up, and are not fed,
> But swoln with wind, and the rank mist they draw,
> Rot inwardly, and foul contagion spread[.]
>
> (*1645*: i. 62)[2]

The word that we are tracing is infectious like an outbreak of murrain in sheep. We might say that Stevens catches the disease from his proximity to Emerson who picked up 'scrawny', as a mutant strain of 'scrannel', in 'Alphonso of Castile'. The stern foremost-looking speaker of this poem lives and learns, 'Seeing nature go astern. | Things deteriorate in kind'; the world, apocalyptically, is coming down with something, 'Imps, at high Midsummer, blot | Half the sun's disk with a spot':

> Roses bleach, the goats are dry,
> Lisbon quakes, the people cry.
> Yon pale, scrawny fisher fools,
> Gaunt as bitterns in the pools,
> Are no brothers of my blood; –
> They discredit Adamhood.
>
> (1883–4: ix. 25–6)

Emerson's conjuring of 'Imps, at high Midsummer' is an allusion that announces his poem as an imitation of the first fairy scene in Shakespeare's *A Midsummer-Night's Dream*. The rhyming tetrameter couplets are derived from Puck's manner of speaking but the theme is Titania's complaint about Oberon's disruption of the dancing of 'our ringlets to the whistling Winde', 'in the beached margent of the sea' (*F*; *A Midsummer-Night's Dream*, II. i. 86 and 85), the cause of the recent flooding, diseases and disturbance of the seasons. Infected by Milton's 'scrannel', Emerson also notices that which infected 'Lycidas'. Milton remembers Titania's argument: 'Therefore the Windes, piping to us in vain, | As in revenge, have suck'd up from the sea | Contagious fog-ges'; their rain causing the rivers to flood so that 'the greene Corne | Hath rotted, ere his youth attain'd a beard: | The fold stands empty in the drowned field, | And Crowes are fatted with the murrion flocke' (*F*; *A Midsummer-Night's Dream*, II. i. 88–90, and 94–7).

If belated poets 'Grate on their scrannel Pipes of wretched straw', 'They discredit Adamhood', 'rising at six'. But Milton's allusion to Shakespeare is salutary; it counteracts another kind of deleterious influence, and Stevens appropriates the turn in Emerson from 'cry' to

'Yon pale scrawny' as we might take a vaccine; the words scrawny and cry act as a preparation of the causative organism or substance of a disease that we are treated with, in order to prevent the rot: 'That scrawny cry' was and was not from that 'vast ventriloquism', sucked up or spoken from that bloated, hollow belly. Stevens, like Milton, uses a word that means thin or meagre with the sense harsh or unmelodious although he suppresses the 'scrannel' that became poetic after Milton. The scrawniness is a kind of hollow allusion. The poems alluded to by the word scrawny are like the play of thoughts as we wake; as the Latin etymon of allusion suggests, they dally with us as they rush, flash and touch lightly upon their subject, flowing in from various sources as a profusion converging on and literally filling up the hollow word 'scrawny'. We must allow their shrill song in order to discern at the end the thing itself, 'That scrawny cry' inside but so commingled with the cries that make 'one mutuall cry' from outside (F; *A Midsummer-Night's Dream*, IV. i. 121).

   To a seventy-five year old poet his *Collected Poems* might appear in one light like a vast ventriloquism of sleep's faded papier-mâché. Mouth closed, one can make a papier-mâché puppet appear to speak, and a book made out of printed paper also has a poet's voice, or is it that Stevens fears, in this last poem of the book, that he speaks, only as a dummy can, with the voices of others? We shall see at the end how this solipsistic fear is unfounded. 'Not Ideas' can be read as an allegory of the relation between allusion and influence, and the distinguishing of one's own voice, that 'sound in his mind', from the cries that become one cry, of other poets outside. 'He knew that he heard it', but if readers can identify elements from other sources in the poem, it is impossible to say how deliberate is the incorporation, unlike the allusions made by Emerson that announce 'Alphonso of Castile' as an imitation of Shakespeare. Like the difference between mechanical and chemical digestion, which typifies the different degrees of assimilation in English of the foreign words -*mâché* and *ventri-*,[3] some of the poems and hymns in 'Not Ideas' are more fully digested than others. As a *scrawny* cry the cry in 'Not Ideas' calls to a musical discord in a chasm across the generations, a hollow in which we hear echoes of many voices making one mutual cry in the cavern of the ear, and in this hollow the waking poet wonders about the possibility of making anything out of nothing itself.

The beginning of the unborn kind

The step before normal time to true time in 'Not Ideas' is a movement in the poem after the everyday, at the ill end of the decaying kind that is overtaken by the beginning of the unborn kind. Let us defer again to Heidegger in determining the poem's displacement of reason, played out as its figure is apprehended between waking and sleeping: 'True time . . . is the arrival of that which has been. This is not what is past, but rather the gathering of essential being, which precedes all arrival in gathering itself into the shelter of what it was earlier, before the given moment'; 'die wahre Zeit ist Ankunft des Gewesenen. Dieses ist nicht das Vergangene, sondern die Versammlung des Wesenden, die aller Ankunft voraufgeht, indem sie als solche Versammlung sich in ihr je Früheres zurückbirgt' (1971: 176–7; 2007: 57): -*er* is literally 'At the earliest ending' of the poem, as the ending of the earliest line's ending, 'of winter', which 'seemed like a sound' earlier in the line, in 'earliest', derived from *ere*. In his 1526 edition of The New Testament, Tyndale has John the Baptist proclaim at the beginning of John, 'He that commeth after me, was before me because he was yer then I'. Like John in Tyndale, Stevens's poem steps back to that 'before' which 'commeth after', as 'yer' or ere, at the end of winter, happened upon in the changing form of the language that takes the step from the time of everyday representation: to *er*, not to *time*, not to *me*, not to the last, but literally speaking to the first syllable in reverse, of 'Recorded time' and 'recognition'. We find ourselves as we read in a realm described by Stevens in 'Long and Sluggish Lines', a poem of the month before 'Not Ideas': 'The life of the poem in the mind has not yet begun. || You were not born yet when the trees were crystal | Nor are you now, in this wakefulness inside a sleep' (*SCP*: 522).

By the fifth line of the poem we learn that 'a scrawny cry from outside' in line 2 is 'A bird's cry'. Between these two occasions of 'cry' we have 'a sound', a word that should be sounded. Auspiciously or inauspiciously a scrawny cry, not song but call, sounds a mind using old and new methods. The cry is a sound that sinks straight in the ocean of the mind like the lead and line but it resounds as a sounding that echoes from the sea-bottom, and 'Deepe calleth unto deepe' (Psalm 42. 7). Dark and auricular deeps precede the visible surface of things but in a poem whose play of light and sound ends in their pre-existent, synaesthetic and oracular union.[4] The poem is about our more than auricular relationship with oracular tidings. Although we learn of the seasonal before the diurnal at the opening, this reversal is unexpected only in retrospect: the speaker is stirred after a night's sleep as if he is the year waking from winter, and a day that is a year can also stand for a man's life. Seasonal change is related to the diurnal round as sound is to light. Ceaselessly occurring at the earliest ending of winter and of sleep, this poem unfolds a vast story in a small manner, of what is scrawny heralding the colossal from outside but 'like | A new knowledge of reality' inside. It is unexpected only in retrospect because the poem plays backwards the time of prolepsis; not like reason 'looking before and after' (Q 1604; *Hamlet*, IV. iv. 37) but looking after something heard 'at daylight, or before'.

As we have seen, the delay in identification of the cry until the fifth line means that other cries have time to intrude: beyond the cry so 'prevalent and central' in Stevens that comes from Whitman, we hear cries from a cry of 'encircling hounds', the crying of the infant Christ,[5] auricularly, or even, etymologically, a kind of Roman supplication, imploring the aid of the clamorous Quirites. During the penultimate stage of the 'pre-history' (*SCP*: 522) of 'That scrawny cry', in which each identification precedes the preceding one, we are told that it was 'A chorister whose c preceded the choir'. Since 'Not Ideas' is set in March and at daylight or before, it follows that, without being a hymn, it comprehends the traditional morning hymn to be sung at Lauds on Tuesdays, Mars's day: 'Ales diei nuntius', which is part of Prudentius' longer 'Hymnus ad galli cantum'. It turns out that 'that scrawny cry' is cock-crow;[6] '*Hark, hark, I heare, the straine of strutting Chanticlere | cry cockadidle-dowe*', as Ariel sings, like Stevens, hearing the cock cry, not crow; the 'Burthen' that sounds 'dispersedly' (*F*; *The Tempest*, I. ii. 384–6 and 382) in the poem is a scrawny chicken's ki-ki-ri-ki:

> Ales diei nuntius
> lucem propinquam praecinit;
> nos excitator mentium
> iam Christus ad vitam vocat.

The bird that heralds day forewarns that dawn is at hand; now Christ, the awakener of our souls, calls us to life. (Prudentius 1949–53: i. 6–7)

In the synaesthetic dawn of Canto VII of 'An Ordinary Evening in New Haven' there is a compounding of 'the imagination's Latin with | The lingua franca et jocundissima' (*SCP*: 397) and 'lucem propinquam *praecinit*' 'becomes, | In misted contours' (*SCP*: 470), 'that latined phrase', 'cock-c*ry pinked* out *pastily*' (*SCP*: 470) as Stevens names the bird that Prudentius does not until verse x of his hymn. 'Not Ideas' is in this kind of propinquity. We hear 'praecinit', as a word that *sings before*, but also along with, Stevens's chorister, and that *predicts* the sound of the c that 'preceded' the choir, the euphonic soft c that we say, preceding, but not precluding, the cacophonic hard c of ki-ki-ri-ki that the cock sings, crows or cries, presumably finding the key or ki of C.[7] The first four lines of Prudentius' hymn provide at once the argument and a sound 'in, on or about the words' (*SL*: 352) for the poem as a whole; except it is not Christus but His distilled absence caught in assonance and sibilants, as the sound of c becomes the comedian, including 'all related or derivative sounds' (*SL*: 351), in 'a scrawny cry from outside', 'chorister', 'its choral', that excites our souls and calls us to life.

The influence of hymns is at first aural and only then doctrinal, as Augustine admits, when he remembers the choirs in Milan: 'Those voices flowed into mine ears, and thy truth pleasingly distilled into my heart, which caused the affections of my devotion to overflow, and my tears to run over, and happy did I find myself therein'; 'voces illae influebant auribus meis, et eliquabatur veritas in cor meum, et exaestuabat inde affectus pietatis, et currebant lacrimae, et bene mihi erat cum eis' (1912, IX. vi: ii. 28–9). Augustine's description of the voices that flow in and boil up to steam inside, running down from the listener's eyes in tears as they cool outside, allows a relation between auricular influence and ocular mist that corresponds at once to the synaesthesia and to the influence of early hymns in Stevens's late poem. The listener's heart and mind become an alembic, distilling the influence of voices into tears or, 'in misted contours', vision, 'et bene mihi erat cum eis'. As the sun rises, 'Not Ideas', a still of influence, transmutes that which is auricular, a scrawny cry and the voices of others, into that which is oracular or a new knowledge of reality, another kind of vision. Such inner distillation of hymns counteracts the inward rot caused by lean and flashy songs that Milton speaks of, and fills up the absence of song in 'Sonnet 73'.

As the cock is not named so Christ remains absent. Who is the protagonist of Stevens's poem? The answer comes from a line in 'The Sail of Ulysses', which turns into the title of another late poem or prophecy, 'A Child Asleep in Its Own Life' (*OP*: 132). He is the doubter who comes to understand that 'God and the imagination are one'. At first deluded by a sleepy imagination, so that fantastically 'a scrawny cry from outside | Seemed like a sound in his mind', we can think of his awakening within the poem in relation to the conversion of the sceptical Horatio at the beginning of *Hamlet* who 'saies, 'tis but our Fantasie, | And will not let beleefe take hold of him | Touching this dreaded sight, twice seen of us'. Once Horatio has 'the sensible and true avouch | Of mine owne eyes' he can believe in the 'present Object' of the ghost: something supernatural has been presented to his senses (*F*; *Hamlet*, I. i. 23–5, 57–8 and 156). By the end of 'Not Ideas' a sound that was perceived to be a product of the subjective mind is acknowledged as an objective cry, 'outside' as it is stressed at the end of three lines, and so the he of the poem, as he awakes, believes again in the natural world. But this cry from outside heralds 'something far more deeply interfused' (*LB1*, 'Tintern Abbey': 207), 'like | A new knowledge of reality'. Like reality that contains a new knowledge, it augurs the supernatural and gives us back the world of objects within a sudden magnification that collapses subjectivity: as part of what is 'Still far away' and coming 'from outside' it nonetheless heralds a 'new knowledge' inside, a colossal distension of 'his mind', as it joins with that which decides.

The early part of Stevens's poem, however, occupies the realm of hearsay, to which even Horatio, Marcellus and Barnardo return after the ghost has vanished. 'It was about to speake, when the Cocke crew' (*F*; *Hamlet*, I. i. 147), observes Barnardo, using the formula of 'It was' that is repeated with variations seven times in 'Not Ideas', becoming fixed and involved with '*Anaphora*, or the Figure of Report' (Puttenham 2007: 142) in the last two stanzas. As Horatio and then Marcellus try to make sense of what they have seen, each moves from a firsthand account to explanations gleaned from oral tidings; tradition, rumour and common talk of cock-crow that warns wandering demons and heralds our Saviour's birth: 'HOR. And then it started . . . I have heard . . . MAR. It faded on the crowing of the Cocke . . . Some sayes . . . (they say) . . . HOR. So have I heard, and do in part beleeve it' (*F*; *Hamlet*, I. i. 148–65). As it is said in Stevens's poem, 'He knew that he heard it', that is, in verse x of Prudentius' 'Hymnus ad galli cantum':

> ferunt vagantes daemonas
> laetos tenebris noctium,
> gallo canente exterritos
> sparsim timere et cedere.

They say that evil spirits which roam happily in the darkness of night are terrified when the cock crows, and scatter and flee in fear. (Prudentius 1949–53: i. 8–9)

Shakespeare magnifies Prudentius' little disclaimer 'ferunt' (some say), which removes absolute say-so by reminding us that we are singing hearsay. The Christian Horatio may recall the hymn, as well as the cock in Ambrose's 'Aeterne rerum conditor', the other important early Christian hymn contained in Stevens's poem; although when the choir sings 'hoc omnis errorum chorus | vias nocendi deserit' (Ambrose 1992: 149), 'Through him the entire choir of wanderers | Abandon the ways of wickedness', we think less of wandering demons than that we are chorusing our own allegorical wanderings in sinful error. Certainly as a scholar Horatio draws his 'extravagant and erring spirit' etymologically from both hymns, from 'vagantes daemonas' and from 'erronum chorus', but he is still safe only to say,

> I have heard,
> The Cocke, that is the Trumpet to the day,
> Doth with his lofty and shrill-sounding Throate
> Awake the God of Day: and at his warning,
> Whether in Sea, or Fire, in Earth, or Ayre,
> Th'extravagant, and erring Spirit, hyes
> To his Confine. And of the truth heerein,
> This present Object made probation.

(F; Hamlet, I. i. 149–56)

It is as if Horatio is also saying, I have heard the cock, that is, I have heard only hearsay: since the root of *gallus* (cock) is the same as for *garrio* (to speak, chatter [like chittering birds] or prate [like domestic poultry]), the potentially oracular ghost has been silenced by the cock, that is by merely auricular traditions. But it is hearsay that reminds us how the cock's cry can function as inarticulate but oracular warning: some say, cock-crow scatters the hosts of darkness and thus symbolically it heralds the coming of Christ. Stevens's poem also occurs on this auricular and oracular cusp. As it steps back to an oracular knowledge it discovers a time that does not precede this movement but occurs through an auricular change in the very language that makes that step: a post-articulate crying from within the auricular deeps of the poem precedes our knowledge of a pre-articulate but oracular cry.

'A scrawny cry' is a thin or shrill sound made in a metonymic manner from 'his lofty [upstretched, sky-directed, sky-full or scrawny] and shrill-sounding [scrannel or scrawny] Throate'. But if we hear an allusion to *Hamlet* in the poem, it is contained appropriately enough in 'He knew that he heard it'. If Stevens alludes to Shakespeare and Prudentius, like them, he is also alluding disconcertingly to hearsay, to the 'I have heard . . . some sayes', to 'ferunt', to something by definition without a source; his poem plays with the distinction between allusion and topos, and this playfulness defies category in a sphere of ambiguity that does not provide answers as to whether the poet is making voluntary allusions or not. Tracking allusions, tracing influence, or discussing topoi, we are in the realm of hearsay. We may argue that 'it was' is also part of this allusion deliberately made to encourage conjecture. But then three times by an elegant anaphora is this phrase, 'it was', used in the final two stanzas of Stevens's poem; and thus this figure of auricular report, becomes the auricular 'Figure of Report', turning its hearsay, which we used to call auricular, into an oracular ending. Yet again if we hear an allusion in the poem it turns out to be to, and thus to be, hearsay; anaphora, in its repetitions of 'it was' that move after, bears us back to report that thus becomes increasingly undependable or untraceable but also prophetic. What can we say? We hear in Stevens's poem, language caught in the strange relation between hearsay and prophecy, one always about to overtake the other, in a handing down that also ascends; 'it was as though I came . . . to the roots of the Trees of Knowledge and of Life' (*M*: 138) and 'It was like | A new knowledge of reality.' In the same manner, in Prudentius' hymn, oracular knowledge is not precluded but preceded by auricular report, which comes at the end. 'Not Ideas' concerns itself with the evasions of language in relation to being, which is like knowing the reality that truth loves to conceal itself.

After the three verses of hearsay about the hosts of darkness fleeing at cock-crow, verse xiii of 'Hymnus ad galli cantum' retells the passage in Matthew that gives unifying force to the hymn as a whole, Christ's prediction that Peter will deny knowledge of Him three times before cock-crow:

> quae vis sit huius alitis,
> Salvator ostendit Petro,
> ter antequam gallus canat
> sese negandum praedicans.

What this bird signifies the Saviour showed to Peter, when He declared that ere the cock crew He should be thrice denied. (Prudentius 1949–53: 8–9)[8]

In Stevens's early 'Hymn from a Watermelon Pavilion', which also seems to collate and rewrite different Lauds hymns, including 'Aeterne rerum conditor' and 'Hymnus ad galli cantum', with its 'best cock of red feather | That crew before the clocks', the three denials are transformed into three cries of welcome and resurrection: 'You dweller in the dark cabin, | Rise, since rising will not waken, | And hail, cry hail, cry hail', in response to the 'hail' that either the blackbird or the cock 'creaks' (*SCP*: 89). Prudentius' hymn sustains the metaphor of cock-crow on a basis of prophecy-fulfilment and typology. The three hails of 'Hymn from a Watermelon Pavilion' are, in turn, transformed into the three instances of the word 'cry' in 'Not Ideas', heralding at last, in an auricular but pointedly not an oracular manner, Christus. The sound of His name underscores 'That scrawny cry – it was | A chorister' so stressing His absence, and making Christ into the spectre of a small 'chorister' whose c is a small c as it is correctly denoted in the poem. To adapt the first lines of 'Depression before Spring', another poem that prefigures or typifies 'Not Ideas', by conflating a dawn from during, with a dawn from after, the Passion, the cock crows, but no Christ rises (see *SCP*: 63): 'It was like | A new knowledge of reality'. Now 'That scrawny cry' captures the sound of Christus from old hymns to be sung at dawn, so we discover a chorister singing new words of comfort. Then 'We say God and the Imagination are one . . . ' and changes are wrought in the language of the poem, as it makes the step back to true time, 'To open the Eternal Worlds, to open the immortal Eyes | Of Man inwards into the Worlds of Thought: into Eternity | Ever expanding in the Bosom of God, the Human Imagination' (Blake, *Jerusalem*, plate 5: 302) that is, 'Christ, the human imagination' (*Ex*: 44).

A new knowledge as a last judgement

In 'On the Morning of Christ's Nativity' Milton repeats, in the first verse of 'The Hymn' in his poem, Barnardo's 'It was' formula that precedes hearsay, heralding, by looking before, the 'true time' of the great master's birth (the 'He that commeth after', but was before 'because he was yer then I'). The end precedes, namely as the end of the decaying kind or 'Nature', the beginning of the unborn kind, 'the Heav'n-born-childe':

> It was the Winter wilde,
> While the Heav'n-born-childe,
>   All meanly wrapt in the rude manger lies;
> Nature in aw to him
> Had doff't her gawdy trim
>   With her great Master so to sympathize:
> It was no season then for her
> To wanton with the Sun her lusty Paramour.

(1645: i. 2–3)[9]

'It was the Winter wilde' not 'At the earliest ending of winter', and the scene-setting 'It was' in Milton identifies what 'a scrawny cry' was not or was in Stevens. 'It' in Milton's 'It was' is the time of year, in Stevens's poem it is 'a scrawny cry' that heralds a new knowledge of time. The time of the great master's birth, both in and out of time, corresponds to the 'true time' of Stevens's allusions and self-allusions in 'Not Ideas': that is, the gathering of earlier poems already at the end of the decaying kind (the poet's seventy-fifth birthday and our poetic tradition), in order to witness the birth of the unborn kind: not the publication, but the origination 'of the unspoken statement', 'des ungesprochenen Gedichtes', (Heidegger 1971: 161; Heidegger 2007: 39), of his *Collected Poems* and of our poetic tradition, 'too immediate for any speech'.[10] Like Milton's hymn, 'Not Ideas' 'wears a deliberately commonplace costume, and yet seems . . . to contain something of the essential gaudiness of poetry' (*SL*: 263). Both poems, rather gaudily, are making a show of doffing gaudiness:[11] we have seen how the cry in 'Not Ideas', like the cry in *Macbeth*, is cut in a commonplace fashion from The Book of Common Prayer while the poem digests or distils secretly hymns from the Roman Breviary; even in the seventeenth century, the word doff was 'a literary word with an archaic flavour' (*OED*). When Stevens disclaims but retains his two or three gaudy lines ('No longer a battered panache above snow . . . ' and 'It was not from the vast ventriloquism | Of sleep's faded papier-mâché . . . '), the ellipses at the end of each luxurious show balance extravagance against censoriousness, allowing us to pause and gaze at what is so brilliantly fine but perhaps pointing to excesses already excised, lines or stanzas the poet has struck through before publication.

The ellipses call to and dismiss earlier Stevens poems, in a mode of self-allusion that balances indulgence against expurgation. Beyond 'Hymn from a Watermelon Pavilion' and its somnolent spouse, 'Depression before Spring',[12] there are other gaudy antetypes of the cock and its scrawny cry in 'Not Ideas'. But all of these shadows in Stevens's *Collected Poems* must have 'doff't' their 'gawdy trim' to the late poem in the same manner that Milton has Nature 'With her great Master so to sympathize'. Heidegger says, in the same essay with which the discussion in this chapter began, 'Since the poet's sole statement always remains in the realm of the unspoken, we can discuss its site only by trying to point to it by means of what the individual poems speak'; 'Weil das einzige Gedicht im Ungesprochenen verbleibt, können wir seinen Ort nur auf die Weise erörtern, daß wir versuchen, vom Gesprochenen einzelner Dichtungen her in den Ort zu weisen' (1971: 160; 2007: 38). Like other late poems, including 'The Planet on the Table' and 'As You Leave the Room', 'Not Ideas' reveals Stevens measuring his achievement by wondering about his commitment to the singleness of his unspoken poetic statement. As he gathers earlier poems for publication, the poem that becomes the last poem of his *Collected Poems* also gathers its foreshadowings because 'the discussion of the poetic statement must first pass through the precursory clarification of individual poems' (Heidegger 1971: 160). In Stevens's words, 'We move between these points: | From that ever-early candour to its late plural' (*SCP*: 382), the excitation in the moment of transition 'At the earliest ending'. In 'Not Ideas' we witness poems gathered at the end of the decaying kind precede the unspoken statement before them at the beginning of the unborn kind.

Most readers will think of 'The Snow Man' at the first of the ellipses in 'Not Ideas' but Stevens sounds other poems too. A scrawny cry from outside seemed like a sound in his mind or in his soon to be published *Collected Poems*: 'He knew that he heard it', where was it? Let us open the book and play the game of association. As we have already heard, in 'Depression before Spring', 'The cock crows | But no queen rises'. Although prophetic cock-crow fails to bring poetic brooding in this poem – 'But ki-ki-ri-ki | Brings no rou-cou, | No rou-cou-cou' (*SCP*: 63) – as we have seen in Chapter 2, there is much roucoulement or brooding 'Over his own sweet voice' (*1807*: i. 88) in later Stevens until, in 'The Dove in Spring', 'A small howling of the dove | Makes something of the little there' and 'There is this bubbling before the sun, | This howling at one's ear, too far | For daylight and too near for sleep' (*OP*: 124–5). A cry is a Latinate call to a Middle English howl of Germanic or more accurately echoic origin. But the gaudiest type that prefigures 'Not Ideas' is in 'Bantams in Pine-Woods': the cock 'Chieftain Iffucan of Azcan in caftan | Of tan with henna hackles' (*SCP*: 75) ('No longer a battered panache above snow . . . ') who 'hoos' like the wood-dove that 'used to chant his hoobla-hoo' while, synaesthetically, a version of Whitman's 'fierce old mother', 'the grossest iridescence of ocean | Howls hoo and rises and howls hoo and falls. | Life's nonsense pierces us with strange relation' (*SCP*: 383). Four cantos later in 'Notes toward a Supreme Fiction' 'the cock crows on the left and all | Is well', heralding an early but not quite sufficient climax in the poem:

> Perhaps there are moments of awakening,
> Extreme, fortuitous, personal, in which
>
> We more than awaken, sit on the edge of sleep,
> As on an elevation, and behold
> The academies like structures in a mist.

> (*SCP*: 386)

This movement within Canto VII of 'Notes' is reflected by the movement from Canto VII to canto VIII in 'An Ordinary Evening in New Haven'. 'As that which was incredible becomes, | In misted contours, credible day again' at 'cock-cry', in the next lines, in the next canto, 'We fling ourselves, constantly longing, on this form. | We descend to the street and inhale a health of air | To our sepulchral hollows' (*SCP*: 470). Since 'The tips of cock-cry', as we have seen, are 'pinked out pastily' from Prudentius' Latin, one 'origin' of our 'mother tongue', punningly, is 'In the midst of foreignness', like Whitman's ocean, but 'To our sepulchral hollows', the cry is 'a scrawny cry' and a mist is our breath:

> Our breath is like a desperate element
> That we must calm, the origin of a mother tongue
>
> With which to speak to her, the capable
> In the midst of foreignness, the syllable
> Of recognition, avowal, impassioned cry,
>
> The cry that contains its converse in itself,
> In which looks and feelings mingle and are part
> As a quick answer modifies a question,
>
> Not wholly spoken in a conversation between
> Two bodies disembodied in their talk,
> Too fragile, too immediate for any speech.

As 'Not Ideas' explicates its cry the poet listens for the single statement that speaks through all of his poems but must remain unspoken. We can think of the poems within this last poem of the *Collected Poems* in terms of 'The cry that contains its converse in itself': the poems are in converse contained by its cry, a conversation or communion that is also the converse or opposite of that cry. Stevens says in the lines that come immediately after the above, at the beginning of Canto IX of 'An Ordinary Evening', 'We keep coming back and coming back | To the real: to the hotel instead of the hymns | That fall upon it out of the wind' (*SCP*: 471).

As 'the grossest iridescence of ocean | Howls hoo' in 'Notes'[13] so the 'mimic motion' of water[14] in 'The Idea of Order at Key West' 'Made constant cry, caused constantly a cry, | That was not ours although we understood, | Inhuman, of the veritable ocean' (*SCP*: 128): the inhuman 'Has carried far into his heart' (*LB2*: ii. 15) its voice. It may be that the cry in 'No Possum, No Sop, No Taters' is a crow's cry:

> It is in this solitude, a syllable,
> Out of these gawky flitterings,

Intones its single emptiness,
The savagest hollow of winter-sound.

(*SCP*: 294)

But the leanness and raggedness of 'scrawny', the 'hollow of winter sound'
is also in the 'broken stalks' (broken to make 'scrannel pipes'), from the
standpoint of 'Not Ideas', leafless, having doffed their gaudy trim:

They have heads in which a captive cry

Is merely the moving of a tongue.
Snow sparkles like eyesight falling to earth,
Like seeing fallen brightly away.

(*SCP*: 294)

In 'The Course of a Particular', a late poem mistakenly left out of the
Collected Poems, 'The leaves cry . . . One holds off and merely hears the
cry' (*OP*: 123): the speaker holds off and 'Nature in aw to him | Had
doff't her gawdy trim'. As Stevens explicates again in this poem 'Sonnet
73', the 'late plural' of poems, of leaves of his *Collected Poems*, 'hanging
on branches swept by the wind', returns us to 'that ever-early candor'
(*SCP*: 382): the end of the decaying kind that is overtaken by the beginning of the unborn kind, 'At the earliest ending', the site of Stevens's
unspoken poetic statement. A syllable that intones its single emptiness,
the desperate cry or night-shriek that Stevens finds in Macbeth's last
syllable of recorded time, becomes the syllable of recognition, avowal
of a beginning of the unborn kind. Such a transition has little do with
Bloom's causal concept of Stevens's Freudian, American and quasi-filial
relation with Whitman. That impassioned cry at the end of the *Collected
Poems*, it was the cry that contains its converse in itself; the it of 'it was'
is the inhuman syllable that speaks whenever man speaks of that time
in which a poem attends in order to converse. We keep coming back to
the real and the hymns keep falling upon the hotel out of the wind.

The two ellipses in 'Not Ideas' have a double function, as a poem, unlike
a god, is at once 'superficially explicative' and 'full of the secret of things'
(*OP*: 261); the two instances of three periods are marks of punctuation,
and they serve as a guide to reading the poem as a whole. They indicate
omissions and wrong turnings into gorgeousness half-taken by the poem
itself, while recalling and dismissing the shadows of earlier gorgeous
poems. As aposiopesis, they are also, paradoxically, soundings in the sense

that the poem is a sounding of 'sound', allowing the word to resound in a literal manner. 'Not Ideas' is elliptical, literally and anagogically speaking. Its submerged allusions to Shakespeare, Whitman et al. mean that it lacks words, which must be supplied to complete the sense. Elliptically, in an anagogical sense, the poem (if not Stevens himself) hides at the other equinox (of its ellipse) Christian hymns that at once allow and disallow the colossal or soul-raising, if unexpected and pagan, connotations of 'colossal' in the penultimate stanza. The poem becomes 'a little colossal' (*OP*: 261), to use a late oxymoronic expression of the poet, as it measures individual poems against that which must remain unspoken.

What colossus bestrides the last page of Stevens's *Collected Poems*? John Lemprière's *Bibliotheca classica* points to the bronze statue of Apollo that once stood over Rhodes harbour. It is tempting to say that the choir in 'Not Ideas' will be hymning the god of truth, light and the sun, of prophecy, poetry and music; celebrating at the end a developed daylight version of the more nocturnal god 'of the silver bow' whose rage is identified by Calchas' second sight – itself a gift he owed to Apollo – at the beginning of *The Iliad* (see *Iliad*, i. 36–101: 5–6). As Stevens said, 'The great and true priest of Apollo was he that composed the most moving of Apollo's hymns' (*OP*: 261). But his poem has more to do with the breaking up of this brazen work: '*Apollo* from his shrine | Can no more divine, | With hollow shreik the steep of *Delphos* leaving' (*1645*: i. 9), as Milton proclaims in his hymn. Then again, the cry in Stevens's poem is not the cry of the new born Christ or at the end on the cross as in Mark 15. 37. At the advent of a new knowledge of reality, I contend that the choristers' text in Stevens's poem will be taken, not from the Homeric Hymns, not from Prudentius or Ambrose, but from the end of Blake's 'A Vision of The Last Judgment',[15] something on Steven's mind as early as the 'Extraordinarily brilliant day' of 4 April 1904 when, apocalyptically, half-playfully, 'No doubt, if it had been a bit nearer sunset, the particular hills I gazed at so long would have been very much like the steps to the Throne. And Blake's angels would have been there with their "Holy, Holy, Holy"' (*SL*: 71):

> What it will be Questiond When the Sun rises do you not see a round Disk of fire somewhat like a Guinea O no no I see an Innumerable company of the Heavenly host crying Holy Holy Holy is the Lord God Almighty I question not my Corporeal or Vegetative Eye any more than I would Question a Window concerning a Sight I look thro it & not with it. (Erdman: 565–6)

At the cry that marks the hypostasis of Christ, we hear hymning angels, and the pagan gods flee while the oracles cease, as in many Christian nativity poems and hymns before Milton. But in Stevens as in Blake the 'new knowledge' is that 'God and the imagination are one . . . '. The new knowledge is of a second coming, apocalyptically 'still far away', 'yet close enough to wake | The chords above your bed to-night' (*OP*: 132): as Blake says at the beginning of 'A Vision of The Last Judgment', 'whenever any Individual Rejects Error & Embraces Truth a Last Judgment passes upon that Individual', '& its Vision is seen by the [*Imaginative Eye*] of Every one according to the situation he holds' (Erdman: 562 and 554). We find affluence in a Song of Sixpence as something that once looked 'like a Guinea' becomes 'an Innumerable company', a choir. Stevens's poem 'contains its converse in itself'; it is at the end of the poet's life, gathering his own work and the suitably autumnal poems of others, but it is also inspired like Christian Latin hymns, Milton's 'On the Morning of Christ's Nativity' and his own 'Hymn from a Watermelon Pavilion', in order to apprehend this event about to come that has already happened, and, in an age of disbelief, 'It comes to this that we use the same faculties when we write poetry that we use when we create gods or when we fix the bearing of men in reality' (*OP*: 266).

To 'fix the bearing of men in reality' for Stevens is to believe, as Blake did, that 'The Last Judgment is not Fable or Allegory but Vision':

> Vision or Imagination is a Representation of what Eternally Exists. Really & Unchangeably. Fable or Allegory is Formd by the Daughters of Memory. Imagination is Surrounded by the daughters of Inspiration who in the aggregate are calld Jerusalem. (Erdman: 554)

We must read Stevens's poem not just literally, typologically, and tropologically, but at the highest level of interpretation, anagogically, and we take our cue from the poem itself, since it operates as vision, transforming fable or allegory and a too customary, natural and historical understanding of reality. As the poem sublimates other poems and hymns we see and hear Stevens's 'principal form of piety', his pure 'explication de texte', at work, transforming commonplaces from two interrelated traditions, as the poem is inspired. 'Not Ideas' is not formed by the Daughters of Memory, it is not only made out of certain other poems by the poet making allusions to them, and it is greater even than a distillation of hymns that flow in as influence. It is a poem surrounded by the Daughters of Inspiration at the beginning of the unborn kind in a conversation 'too immediate for any speech' with the Daughters of Memory at the end of the decaying kind. As a discovery of itself in the realm of earlier poems and hymns, it apprehends the unlocalizable cry of a poet's unspoken single statement, his relation to tradition that looks after, changing his second self or future readers hereafter, and as it apprehends the arrival of true time, it passes its last judgement.

'A new church is . . . a new consciousness', explains Raine. The beginning of the unborn kind is 'an epiphany of the Divine Humanity in His full glory in the inner worlds or "heavens". . . . This Last Judgement was not an outer event, in time and in history, but an inner event, which would, not dramatically, but gradually, make itself apparent also in the outer world of history' (Raine 1991: 78–9): it is already at the end of the decaying kind. 'Not Ideas' is on the cusp of these inner and outer times and 'At the earliest ending', 'It was like | A new knowledge of reality'. 'What is under consideration is an event whose nature is rather a subtle change of awareness than a temporal fact' (Raine 1991: 79): 'the gathering of essential being'. The sound of 'That scrawny cry – it was | A chorister whose c preceded the choir' sublimates the name Christus: He is thus interiorized, in every sense of the word, literally, within the poem, and, anagogically, 'We say God and the imagination are one'. I would argue that it is impossible to explicate late Stevens without due consideration of this apprehension.

The time of 'Not Ideas' is the time of equinox, the paradisal time of the year, and as we have seen, although the poem is set at the vernal point it also contains allusively the sun's crossing of the equator in autumn. An equinox is an equal halving of daylight and night-time but also a double thing itself, and in 'Not Ideas' Stevens is perfecting a vernal and transcendental counterpart to Keats's 'To Autumn' (composed between 19 and 21 September). For Stevens an epiphany of the Divine Humanity does not mean that we leave the end of the decaying kind behind, the two kinds of time are inextricably linked, as day depends on night, spring on autumn, one transforming our apprehension of the other. The event of 'Not Ideas' 'leads humankind back to the Paradisal state from which we have fallen' (Raine 1991: 79) but that state is within us, 'in earth' (Matthew 6. 10), and it is occurring now. I end my explication by returning to the 'sweet hour of prime' in Book V of *Paradise Lost*, the hour of sunrise in Stevens's poem, confirming again that it is set in the propinquity of Paradise where the sun always rises at six since day and night are equal; characters in both poems are waking to a time that balances the seasonal disruption in 'Alphonso of Castile' and *A Midsummer-Night's Dream*. After Adam has cheered Eve who is disturbed by proleptic dreams induced by Satan, they sing spontaneously a morning hymn in which we find Blake's Sun or 'Innumerable company of the Heavenly host crying Holy Holy Holy':

> Speak yee who best can tell, ye Sons of light,
> Angels, for yee behold him, and with songs

> And choral symphonies, Day without Night,
> Circle his Throne rejoycing, yee in Heav'n,
> On Earth joyn all ye Creatures to extoll
> Him first, him last, him midst, and without end[.]

> (*PL*, v. 160–5)

We have seen how 'Not Ideas' distils the hymn for Lauds on Tuesdays in the Roman Breviary. The morning hymn in *Paradise Lost* imitates Psalm 148, 'used in Christian worship as the Canticle *Benedicite, omnia opera*, set for Matins as an alternative to the *Te Deum* in The Book of Common Prayer' (Fowler 1998: 290). The unaccompanied setting sun in 'Sonnet 73' is reunited with song as it rises in Milton, Blake and Stevens, and synaesthetically we hear and see 'sound' in the space between the final two stanzas, between 'sun, || Surrounded'. At the earliest ending of 'To morrow, and to morrow, and to morrow' 'Not Ideas' acknowledges within 'Him first, him last, him midst' in order to converse with 'her, the capable'. Stevens finds the converse contained in the cry that Macbeth hears of 'dusty death', the sound of its opposite and the late conversation or communion with that which is unborn, 'without end'.

Socrates' dying words as recorded in the *Phaedo* were 'Crito, we owe a cock to Asclepius; make this offering to him and do not forget' (Plato 1997: 100). Asclepius, the god of healing was Apollo's son and 'this betrays the role attributed to the cock of psychopomp, acting as herald and guiding the dead person's soul to the Otherworld, where it would awaken to a fresh day, the equivalent of rebirth' (Chevalier and Gheerbrant 1982: 209–10). The god of healing like Christ can bring the dead to life and this prefigures our rebirth in heaven. Although 'Not Ideas' is a healing of the sickness variously diagnosed by Whitman, Emerson, Keats, Milton and Shakespeare, it is not about Apollo, Asclepius or Christus. It is a poem that acts as psychopomp for Stevens as 'We keep coming back and coming back | To the real'. Its cry is the last syllable of recorded time but also the syllable of recognition, avowal of the hereafter, really and unchangeably, today.

5
The Very Last Poems

'The Black Tower'

In the final line of Canto VII of the *Inferno*, winding about an arc of the swampy river Styx, 'to a tower's low base [al piè d'una torre] we came' (Cary: 30; *Inferno*, vii. 130). Dante begins Canto VIII by returning 'to a narrative moment logically earlier than the end of the previous canto' (*Inferno*: 134):

My theme pursuing, I relate ['Io dico, seguitando'], that ere
We reach'd the lofty turret's base ['al piè de l'alta torre'], our eyes
Its height ascended, where we mark'd uphung
Two cressets ['due fiammette'], and another saw from far
Return the signal, so remote, that scarce
The eye could catch its beam. I, turning round
To the deep source of knowledge ['al mar di tutto 'l senno'], thus
    inquired:
'Say what this means ["Questo che dice?"]; and what, that other light
In answer set: what agency doth this?'
      'There on the filthy waters ["le sucide onde"],' he replied,
'E'en now what next awaits us thou mayst see,
If the marsh-gender'd fog conceal it not.'
      Never was arrow from the cord dismiss'd,
That ran its way so nimbly through the air,
As a small bark, that through the waves I spied
Toward us coming, under the sole sway
Of one that ferried it, who cried aloud:
'Art thou arrived, fell spirit?'

(Cary: 30–1; *Inferno*, viii. 1–18)

178

The dying Yeats, self-fashioned as 'that wild old wicked man' (*YCP*: 356), would lie down 'where all the ladders start, | In the foul rag-and-bone shop of the heart' (*YCP*: 392): 'What matter if the ditches are impure?' (*YCP*: 266). Had he recalled then Dante's lines, which foreshadow the second canto of the *Purgatorio*, the oarsman's greeting, 'Now you are caught, wicked soul', 'Or se' giunta, anima fella' (*Inferno*, viii. 18: 126–7), shouted as he swiftly propels himself to the tower, they would have taken on a grotesque, almost comical, but undeniably eerie significance. Like Blake, Yeats would have comforted himself in the knowledge that the soul cannot be defiled by the sluttish heart. In any case Phlegyas is mistaken, believing the pilgrim to be a soul condemned to the Styx.

Dante's interlinking of Cantos VII and VIII of the *Inferno* mirrors the chained relationship of 'Cuchulain Comforted' and 'The Black Tower'. Discrepancy about the ordering of Yeats's last poems, leading to the reversal of these two in different editions, compounds their concatenation. Yeats's final two poems are discrete works but they can also form a diptych in the same manner that Botticelli's *The Birth of Venus* and *La Primavera* can be read either separately or continuously with twelve figures. As with much in Botticelli and the wind that blows from the shore through 'The Black Tower', Yeats's tower is an intricate emblem. Generally speaking, the poem's

> symbolism is mixed; much that is Platonic rubs shoulders with much that is not. Where this happens in Yeats, the poem is usually one of a series, and the earlier poems on the theme present the symbolism in more orthodox, 'purer' terms. This is certainly the case with 'The Black Tower', which can only be considered as a unit in a larger pattern. (Wilson 1958: 223)

'The Black Tower' could be the sequel or the prequel to 'Cuchulain Comforted', which is a kind of coda that returns us to the beginning of Yeats's Cuchulain plays and poems. Certainly 'The Black Tower' is the last of his tower poems. Perhaps Yeats understood this poem to be his last. But if it also comes very deliberately at what he perceived as the end of the larger pattern of western literature, does that end precede the beginning of the unborn kind in the poem? 'Questo che dice?'

Two stanzas before the end of Canto VII of the *Inferno*, in the fifth circle of Hell, the angry and sullen gurgle from black slime their hymn or 'dolorous strain . . . in their throats, | But word distinct can utter none'; 'Quest' inno si gorgoglian ne la strozza, | ché dir nol posson con parola integra' (Cary: 30; *Inferno*, vii. 125–6): they are a hellish underwater

version of the bird-like choir in 'Cuchulain Comforted'. Yeats's gro-
tesquely zoomorphic singers, lapsing out of language, would make
fantastic Gothic or Romanesque gargoyles, positioned at the top of the
tower to spout rain above Dante's gargling souls, perpetually drowning
in the filthy waters below, blending their 'murmurs' (*1805*, i. 273). On
the other hand, 'those bird-like things' in 'Cuchulain Comforted' are
transmuted into 'small birds' of the air to be caught by the old cook in
'The Black Tower'.

By comparing 'Cuchulain Comforted' and 'The Black Tower' with
the end of Canto VII and the beginning of Canto VIII in the *Inferno* we
find ourselves between different versions of the two mouths of the cave
of generation that Porphyry identifies in Homer: appropriately water
gurgles through the caverns of afterlife as the pilgrim finds passage
from earth to Heaven. In 'The Black Tower' we enter a related symbol
from which to view the filthy modern tide: Yeats's tower connects
water or earth and sky. Darkly, Dante's outpost tower before Styx and
the gates of Dis, behind which the devils are driven as citizens at war
with another city-state, constitute an infernal and genuinely gothic
landscape that foreshadows the setting of Yeats's often underrated final
poem. We come to what looks like one of the dark towers at the end of
the decaying kind in Hell but then we find ourselves at the beginning
of the unborn kind because a tower is a mixed symbol: cryptically, it is
also a spiritual inversion of the cave of generation; our apprehension
of the cave changes, making it a tower, as we are moved upside down
from one mouth to the other. Yeats's tower is not just one tower from
Dante but encompasses the whole of Dante's symbolic landscape from
Inferno to *Purgatorio*.

When Blake illustrated Dante, he would have interpreted the different
circles of Hell as our world; 'under every *Good* is a hell. i.e. hell is the
outward or external of heaven. & is of the body of the lord. for nothing
is destroyd' (Erdman: 602).[1] As the King observes, Macbeth's 'Castle',
another foreshadowing of Yeats's tower, 'hath a pleasant seat' (*F*; *Macbeth*,
I. vi. 1) and we have witnessed, in Chapter 4, Stevens pass out of this
hellish edifice to hear the beginning of the unborn kind in the cries of
bewailing women inside:

> Dante's hells are the states of souls under the tyranny of the unforgiv-
> ing 'God of the World', 'The Accuser': 'these States Exist now. Man
> Passes on, but States remain for Ever; he passes thro' them like a travel-
> ler who may as well suppose that the places he has passed thro' exist
> no more, as a Man may suppose that the states he has pass'd thro'

Exist no more.' In this, though in no other sense, Hell is eternal. (Raine 1970: 200; Erdman: 556)

With Blake in mind, I come to Yeats's last poem as Dante moves from the fifth to the sixth circles of Hell, calling upon Virgil, 'al mar di tutto 'l senno', to the sea of all wisdom, who answers questions about agency by pointing forward. The symbol of the tower with a light shining is reclaimed by Yeats in earlier poems, drawing on Milton in 'Il Penseroso' among other sources. By 'The Black Tower', 'le sucide onde', the slimy waves, 'this filthy modern tide' (*YCP*: 376), is lapping dangerously close to the sea of knowledge inside the tower that represents from one perspective 'a bulwark against ignorance in the pursuit of wisdom' (Moore 1954: 439). If Yeats is not quite the sea of all wisdom, he is a gate-keeper, proffering the end of a golden string: the pilgrim and Virgil are at first denied entry to Dis, but Yeats writes poems that allow us to find a way out of the labyrinth of our limited metaphysics. We come in this chapter to the foot of a tower at the end.

In the 1950 *Collected Poems*, 'The Black Tower' comes immediately after 'Cuchulain Comforted'; in the 1939 Cuala Press edition of *Last Poems and Two Plays*, it comes immediately before.[2] In both editions it is dated '*January* 21, 1939', although there is no evidence that Yeats would have wished a date appended to the poem in print:

> Say that the men of the old black tower,
> Though they but feed as the goatherd feeds,
> Their money spent, their wine gone sour,
> Lack nothing that a soldier needs,
> That all are oath-bound men:
> Those banners come not in.
>
> *There in the tomb stand the dead upright,*
> *But winds come up from the shore:*
> *They shake when the winds roar,*
> *Old bones upon the mountain shake.*
>
> Those banners come to bribe or threaten,
> Or whisper that a man's a fool
> Who, when his own right king's forgotten,
> Cares what king sets up his rule.
> If he died long ago
> Why do you dread us so?

There in the tomb drops the faint moonlight,
But wind comes up from the shore:
They shake when the winds roar,
Old bones upon the mountain shake.

The tower's old cook that must climb and clamber
Catching small birds in the dew of the morn
When we hale men lie stretched in slumber
Swears that he hears the king's great horn.
But he's a lying hound:
Stand we on guard oath-bound!

There in the tomb the dark grows blacker,
But wind comes up from the shore:
They shake when the winds roar,
Old bones upon the mountain shake.

(*YCP*: 396–7)[3]

The spiral shapes that we traced in Chapter 3 now form a winding stair: a symbol within the symbol of the tower for its old cook to 'climb and clamber'. In 'Cuchulain Comforted' there were trees, in contrast, this poem is set in what man himself builds; 'the tree of life gives place to the edifice of wisdom, whose "winding ancient stair" becomes the "steep ascent" of gnosis as the Biblical Garden of Eden gives place to the terminal image of the City "coming down from heaven", man's completed work' (Raine 1986: 243). We shall see how Stevens's very last poem that contains a palm is not 'Of that Forbidden Tree' because his poem has a 'fructifying virtue' to awaken 'one greater Man' within us to 'regain the blissful Seat' (*PL*, i. 2, 4 and 5); Stevens's organic symbol helps us to apprehend 'a new heaven, and a new earth: for the first heaven, and the first earth were passed away, and there was no more sea' (Revelation 21. 1). Yeats's poem set on the sea is at once of Macbeth's 'Castle' that merely 'hath a pleasant seat' (situation or climate) and like Eden contains 'Death', and of 'the secret top' (*PL*, i. 3 and 6). But in such a dark time as ours, or such a dark poem as 'The Black Tower', even the adept on the stair of gnosis can seem merely antic, senile or outright untrustworthy, a mere servant to those who are caught in death-like sleep.

Eliade understood that 'When the pilgrim climbs' the temple or ziggurat, 'he is coming close to the centre of the world, and on its highest terrace he breaks through into another sphere, transcending profane, heterogeneous space, and entering a "pure earth"' (1958: 376). We have seen Yeats pacing the ruined top of such a tower in Chapter 1. In Dante's *Inferno* such a pilgrimage is inverted, the ever decreasing circles of Hell are a giant ziggurat that reaches to the literal centre of the earth, through which the pilgrim and his guide journey. At the centre this symbolic geography is upturned, the symbol changes; at the 'top' of the inverted tower the pilgrim finds that he is at the bottom: a cave appears with water welling within it. These two symbols interconnect like the interlocking gyres of *A Vision*, the top of one is at the base of the other. Reading Yeats's 'The Black Tower' we are winding through one symbol to find its opposite regenerative aspect; at the end of a man-made form, dead at the top, we discover natural forms restored by the waters of the beginning of the unborn kind: 'small birds in the dew of the morn' or water that seems to descend from Heaven when we wake. The tower's old cook is also ambivalent, he may appear to be an absolute ironist or mocker, but there is a glimpse of transformation as Hell is inverted to discover Purgatory, our materialist descent preceding the ascent of gnosis: 'that other war, where opposites die each other's life, and live each other's death, is a slow-moving thing' (*Ex*: 417).

'The Black Tower' is 'cryptic' (Moore 1954: 438): it is enigmatic, con-cealing perhaps occult wisdom; it employs an occult method of com-municating secret knowledge for a 'fit audience . . . though few' (*PL*, vii. 31). It is also quite literally of the crypt: '*There in the tomb stand the dead stand upright*'; the tomb may be under the black tower, although '*Old bones upon the mountain shake*', as if the crypt is a bare ruin (is the tower on a mountain above the sea?); cryptically, the poet is saying that I have here put that which is usually hidden 'on show' (*YCP*: 391). A cryptic method is foregrounded, cryptically to reveal the occult. That which is underground in Dante, the circles of Hell continuing down to form a massive inverted ziggurat tower, projects above ground in Yeats's last poem as the black tower, an ancient symbol offered in its darker aspect, is shown 'In strong and black relief' (Shelley 1967, 'Julian and Maddalo': 192).[4] Finally, the poem is cryptic because Yeats writes almost from beyond the grave, it is a poem that is drafted and revised on or near his death-bed, threshold of the crypt. It is his final 'remarkable engagement with his impending death his [last] wish to achieve an accomplished closure of his poetic canon' (Pethica 1997: xxiii).

Both 'Cuchulain Comforted' and 'The Black Tower' allow a plurality of voices, the one becomes many in the former so that the many speak as one in the latter. Their message, perhaps communicated to an enemy envoy, in the first and second stanzas at least of 'The Black Tower', is defiant: in brief, we will not surrender (see Vendler 2007: 143). In the third stanza, the tower's old cook is introduced; he is a reincarnation of Cuchulain, his profession sounding literally like a shortened version of the hero's name, although, if 'cook' was a name, then Cuchulain sounds like its diminutive: a relationship between the two is established that mirrors the poet Yeats's relationship to his chosen mask, the hero Cuchulain. The poet engaged in the sedentary drudgery of writing verse (as described in 'Adam's Curse') corresponds in a cryptic way with his active but mythical second self, the ancient Irish hero. By the end of the third stanza the soldiers discredit the cook: 'But he's a lying hound'.

The poem's chorus, repeated three times, twists the linear narrative of its balladical stanzas around a circle of return, making a spiral out of a story that usually has a beginning and an end. I find the first line, varying from chorus to chorus, difficult to scan. Has Yeats created an eerie counterpoint so that two or more rhythms play together at once? Some critics dismiss the poem as unfinished and therefore unmetrical. But the rhythms are strong and of Yeats's late recalcitrant style. Yeats writes as he should read the first line of *Paradise Lost*: he crosses his lines 'with another emphasis, that of passionate prose . . . ; the folk song is still there, but a ghostly voice, an unvariable possibility, an unconscious norm. What moves me and my hearer is a vivid speech that has no laws except that it must not exorcise the ghostly voice' (*E&I*: 524). The colloquial cadence of the individual ego is crossed with the metre of the archetypal unconscious.[5] As the shepherd says of the goatherd (who must feed as the men of the old black tower feed) in 'Shepherd and Goatherd', Yeats has 'measured out the road that the soul treads | When it has vanished from our natural eyes'; and in that manner, the poet has 'talked with apparitions' (*YCP*: 162). The counterpoint of rhythms in the chorus of 'The Black Tower' makes sure that 'The supernatural' stays 'present, cold winds blow across our hands, upon our faces, the thermometer falls': 'the rhythm is old and familiar, imagination must dance, must be carried beyond feeling into the aboriginal ice. Is ice the correct word?' (*E&I*: 523). Like Jonah, a type of Christ, 'I have been cast up out of the whale's belly though I still remember the sound and sway that came from beyond its ribs, and, like the Queen in Paul Fort's ballad, I smell of the fish and the sea' (*E&I*: 524): '"You smell of the sepulchre." "A whale devoured me. Sailor, 'tis not of the sepulchre I smell, but of the sea"' (Fort 1921, 'A Queen in the Sea': 6).

Critics have made numerous conjectures about the literal sense or senses of 'The Black Tower' and its conscious and unconscious influences.[6] Mrs Yeats told A. Norman Jeffares that it 'was on the subject of political propaganda' (Jeffares 1996a: 337, n. 4) and Vendler sums up this mode of interpretation: 'If we ask whether, in life, Yeats had known of an oath-bound remnant of soldiers defending, in defeat, a last outpost under siege, we think immediately of the Easter Rising and the General Post Office in Dublin where its soldiers made a last stand' (2007: 142). Certainly Yeats's positioning of the poem (according to which it is printed in the Cuala Press *Last Poems*), immediately after 'Three Songs to the One Burden' that praises 'Nineteen Sixteen, | Those . . . | . . . | That fought in the Post Office' (Yeats 1939: 7), seems to prepare for an historical reading. James Pethica questions the unqualified heroic status usually assigned to the 'loyal warriors', arguing that 'the poem seems carefully balanced between admiration and criticism of them'. He contends that 'Yeats had thoughts of the rearguard action of his own class in mind, since in early versions the warriors' last battle is strategically sited by "the black pigs dike," a historical dividing line between Protestant Ulster and Southern Ireland' (1997: xxxiv). Others have equated the banners with the flags of a contemporary Nuremberg Rally.

But 'The Black tower' is not just so crudely allegorical: it has another kind of relation to history. Vendler approaches an anagogical interpretation when she posits that the poem is a special kind of ballad; 'a single freeze-frame, immortalizing one moment out of a much longer implied epic tale' (2007: 143). The epic tale would have involved a battle and a retreat: Yeats's soldiers are like Dante's devils who 'consider themselves still in a state of war, driven back into their city walls, with outposts [like the tower in *Inferno*, viii] in the surrounding countryside' (*Inferno*: 134). 'Yeats wrests the innate narrativity of the ballad as far as it can go in the direction of instantaneity' (Vendler 2007: 144). The time of the literal story is sublimated in a moment at the end. The significant 'freeze-frame' that Yeats focuses on is the point that allows the narration to happen (see Blanchot 1992: 62); the beginning of that story is outside of Yeats's poem, but by focusing on the point to which it moves, the poet finds the anagogical beginning, transforming unpredictably the literal sense of his poem.

The poem begins with a command: 'Say'. Vendler has posited the literal sense of the poem as the soldiers' collective and defiant reply to an enemy envoy. But a reader could also ask, is it we who are to say, or is the poet taking dictation? It may be that whoever reads the poem is to take the soldiers' message to the enemy envoy, or, conversely, it may be that each reader is the enemy envoy, confronted with the poet's rendition of the soldiers' message. Beyond this tropological function the word 'Say' makes typological sense. Since the poem revolves around a defining moment from an epic, a moment to which all epics move and without which they cannot even begin, 'Say' is a deliberate invocation of invocations in earlier significant epics. Milton employs the same strategy, using the same word, at the beginning of the 'initium' of *Paradise Lost*, 'introducing the action and giving its cause' (Fowler 1998: 60):

> Say first, for Heav'n hides nothing from thy view
> Nor the deep Tract of Hell, say first what cause
> Mov'd our Grand Parents in that happy State,
> Favour'd of Heav'n so highly, to fall off
> From thir Creator, and transgress his Will
> For one restraint, Lords of the World besides?
> Who first seduc'd them to that foul revolt?
>
> (*PL*, i. 27–33)

The anaphoric repetition of 'say first' builds up the allusion to Virgil as Milton asks his 'Heav'nly Muse' to 'say first what cause': 'Musa, mihi causas memora'; 'Tell me, O Muse, the cause' (Virgil, *Aeneid*, i. 8: i. 262–3). In his very last poem, Yeats is thinking about causes, if but allusively. His reference to Milton and Virgil may be unintentional and, therefore, it says all the more pointedly that the histories within all epic poems, which we think of as causal, are dictated by the Muse who is independent of cause and effect.

Milton's question, 'Who first seduced them to that foul revolt?', comes thirty three lines into *Paradise Lost*, so that it calls to mind, cryptically, Christ's death on the cross and Resurrection, countering the actions of the answer: 'Th' infernal Serpent' (*PL*, i. 34). 'The Black Tower' is also about the seduction of political propaganda and asks one question about the supposedly dead king in the second stanza: 'If he died long ago | Why do you dread us so?' Allegiance to the king who, like Christ, is and is not dead, counters the enemy's satanic overtures. Virginia Moore explains:

> in esoteric literature . . . the deepest principle in man, call it self, ego, or pure spirit, is often . . . designated 'king.' To be oath-bound to a king, therefore, means, among other things, oath-bound to spirit; with the forbidden banners doubtless those of materialism. The king's coming is delayed; that is all. Things must get worse before they can get better. So much for the general meaning. (1954: 439)

According to Blake, Satan is the state into which we are all born, and which we can each escape by rejecting selfish selfhood. 'The Black Tower' is about our time, after Christ has gone away but before we have recognized the arrival of the Comforter within (see John 16. 7), when we seek merely to preserve our everyday selves, and we are susceptible to the propaganda that subjectivity is an ideological project, propaganda so subtle it works by foregrounding propaganda. Moving from *Paradise Lost* to 'The Black Tower', we also move from Genesis to a period prophesied at the end of the Bible. Such a period is our time because it occurs in each of our lives: 'the salvation of the world consists in the salvation of the individual soul' (Jung 2010: 32). Satan's seduction of Adam caused us all to live in our world, no longer ours to exploit when we acknowledge the finitude of causality, a story dictated all along by that immortal self within each of us, call it Muse or king, if each could but listen.

By asking questions in the *initium*, after he has called upon the 'Heav'nly Muse' to 'Sing' (*PL*, i. 6), Milton is drawing into his poem the very beginning of the first western epic right up to Homer's question about the cause of Achilles' anger:

> *Anger – sing, goddess, the anger of Achilles son of Peleus, that accursed anger, which brought the Greeks endless sufferings and sent the mighty souls of many warriors to Hades, leaving their bodies as carrion for the dogs and a feast for the birds; and Zeus' purpose was fulfilled. It all began when Agamemnon lord of men and godlike Achilles quarrelled and parted.*

Which of the gods was it that made them quarrel? (*Iliad*: 4)

Traditionally dogs and birds are psychopomps, as well as scavengers of carrion, and Yeats has both beasts preside over his two death-bed poems. After 'Cuchulain Comforted', which contains bird-like things and is about a mighty warrior in Hades, Yeats writes a poem with a cook described as 'a lying hound': a poem that asks, not which of the gods caused all of this trouble, but where is that god or king, and why are you so frightened of us if he is dead? It has been remarked of the *initium* in *Paradise Lost* that Milton's 'formulaic method involves "a whole segment of western culture", counterpointing Adam's deeds with those of classical heroes. . . . But counterpoint here approaches contrast: in pagan epic it is the gods' anger that needs explanation' (Fowler 1998: 60). In his final lyric poem that uses the ballad form but with a chorus, thus creating that spiralling kind of poem, a lyrical ballad, Yeats has lyric include epic (sometimes it is epic that is praised 'for containing all genres' [Fowler 1998: 467]). Yeats's final poem is of the moment to which the story returns, and without which it cannot begin, to be found within us and our day. The opening 'Say', as economically as Milton's *initium*, swallows a whole segment of western culture and us with it, but in order for us to be reborn and to find 'the blissful Seat' within. Significantly the first word is not 'Sing', although in the Cuala Press edition of *Last Poems*, 'The Black Tower' and 'Cuchulain Comforted' are framed by two sets of three songs with political and spiritual themes. Finding a moment at the end, Yeats makes a road map for the soul. We need no longer ask questions about the gods without. The poem would move us out of the realm of causality to find the human divine within.

Vendler's account of the poem, as a collective reply to an envoy, is right, but she makes the story too distant, too quaint, too Pre-Raphaelite, because she does not include its future readers in the story. Yeats's use of the ballad form implies a narrative, which the poem itself denies us. Instead we are referred to the beginning of that story, at the commencement of the first western epic, by Yeats's opening 'Say'. But that word is also placed to wake us up to our continuing role within that narrative, and its continuing role within us. Homer tells a story and other stories have followed. As we continue to tell these stories, we change history. Our response to the poem is part of that story. We must learn to 'Say' too, as soldiers might awake from their slumber. If the soldiers are 'oath-bound to spirit' but asleep, symbolically speaking, their allegiance is obscured by their ego-hoods. Like the tower they inhabit, they are a mixed symbol.

Since we are mostly asleep ourselves, there is every chance we just recite the poem; like Augustine remembering a psalm at the end of his *Confessions*, the experience of reading the poem should give us a deeper sense of our involvement in time. Yeats is saying, in his last poem, it is up to you how you read my work; my future readers will be among the enemy and among the oath-bound few,[7] and our time is so dark that even my potentially 'fit audience' is asleep in selfhood. A reader makes a decision of allegiance in the manner that she reads 'The Black Tower', and if she sides with Yeats, she might wake up to her life's inner substance out of a shattered ego. When such readers of 'The Black Tower' find the beginning of its story in the inception of western literature, that story finds its denouement within us today. Like Augustine's reconstitution of time as present-past, present-present, and present-future, which I explore in the epilogue, my tropological reading vivifies the other two spiritual senses of 'The Black Tower'. At the end of one kind of story told by others, we find that it begins within each of us today. Can such a spiralling explication of the poem only climb and clamber after its old cook up and down the spiral stair? Yeats's poem is made out of the difference between fiction and history: it is vivified by tensions between its spiritual and literal senses. At the end of a body of work it is a poem that would like to wake its readers to change history, although it is not sure if many are ready. Each reader must figure the poem out for herself. By presenting our situation cryptically, 'The Black Tower' guides to the work that each must undertake alone. It is not meant to console by allowing us satisfying explications: at the end, we must turn from the poem to understand ourselves.

Other dark towers

Poems of the mid nineteenth century can resurface in poems of the mid twentieth century, to voice unconscious doubts about poetic enterprise. Stevens's 'Not Ideas' seems to make Whitman in 'Bardic Symbols' cry out Stevens's qualms about his *Collected Poems*. Yeats's last poem makes Browning, who was for Yeats the equivalent of Whitman for Stevens, exclaim his hopes and fears about a life's work. In each case the later poem makes the earlier poet speak with altered voice.[8] Turning to Browning's 'Childe Roland to the Dark Tower Came' after reading 'The Black Tower', we find a drama that attains almost to dark comedy; we guess 'what skull-like laugh | Would break, what crutch 'gin write my epitaph | For pastime in the dusty thoroughfare' (Browning 1940: 359), for Yeats had recently written his own epitaph on such a dusty thoroughfare between poems, in the poem that should begin *Last Poems*: '*Cast a cold eye | On life, on death. | Horseman, pass by!*' (*YCP*: 401). The cripple at the very beginning of 'Childe Roland', like the swineherd in 'Cuchulain's Fight', is forebear of the cook in 'The Black Tower', a male counterpart of Crazy Jane. In early drafts of 'The Black Tower' there is a figure called 'Old Tom', who eventually merges with the cook (see Pethica 1997: 104–5), underscoring the connection with Browning's poem that bids its readers '*See Edgar's song in* "LEAR"'. We also read Yeats's *Collected Poems* 'acquiescingly' (Browning 1940: 359) to the end; Bloom, a critic obsessed with allegory and memory, would say that Yeats's anxiety is that of influence and Childe Roland is a figure fabled for each poet questing inevitably to his source in Shakespeare. Yeats is drawn fatally back into Browning's allegorical story to find a terrible literal truth in the fable: 'As when a sick man very near to death | Seems dead indeed, and feels begin and end | The tears and takes the farewell of each friend', listening to some outside the sickroom discuss when a day 'Suits best for carrying the corpse away, | With care about the banners, scarves and staves' (Browning 1940: 359).

Besieged in his castle with the aptly named servant Seyton, Macbeth says defiantly:

> Hang out our Banners on the outward walls,
> The Cry is still, they come: our Castles strength
> Will laugh a Siedge to scorne: Heere let them lye,
> Till Famine and the Ague eate them up:
> Were they not forc'd with those that should be ours,
> We might have met them darefull, beard to beard,
> And beate them backward home. What is that noyse?
>   *A Cry within of Women.*

(F; Macbeth, V. v. 1–7)

In the immediately ensuing lines, we first hear the cry that will echo in Stevens's 'Not Ideas'. Can we escape Macbeth's castle? Yeats's poem makes us see that *Macbeth* like 'The Last Judgment is not Fable or Allegory but Vision' (Erdman: 554), albeit a vision of the end of the decaying kind. The noise that Macbeth hears is to do with the queen's death. I am tempted to ask, which queen is dead? Is our culture dead to Isis, to 'her, the capable' (*SCP*: 471)? If I still believed in source-hunting, then I would be tempted to say that the above lines from *Macbeth*, just before the very darkest moment of the play, are the probably unconscious cause of Yeats's poem.

At least the lines make me see that there are two sets of banners in Yeats's poem. In the sixth line of the first stanza, 'Those banners come not in'. The semicolon that was added to the end of line 5 in the Cuala Press version of 'The Black Tower', which becomes a colon in the various Macmillan editions that include the poem,[9] implies that the banners are those of the enemy. But the earlier, authoritative and '"final" version' of the poem, without the semicolon or colon, suggests the banners could just as well be those of the men of the black tower, hung from its walls, as Macbeth also commands his banners be hung, in response to the banners in the second stanza that are held by the enemy, approaching the tower 'to bribe or threaten'. Fighting mad, Macbeth inverts a siege, making a command that would weaken his castle's defences. His speech is all bombast. Surely it is the soldiers within the besieged castle who 'lye | Till Famine and the Ague eate them up', like the soldiers in Yeats's poem: a besieging army has recourse to supplies, supplies that it cuts off from the castle it besieges. Yeats's poem takes up Macbeth's mad note of defiance and we see his castle darkly in the reflection of 'the old black tower' on the shore.

Bloom argues that 'the truest precursor' (Bloom 1971: 161) to Browning's 'Childe Roland' is a passage from Shelley's Venetian poem, 'Julian and Maddalo'. From a boat they view:

> A building on an island; such a one
> As age to age might add, for uses vile,
> A windowless, deformed and dreary pile;
> And on the top an open tower, where hung
> A bell, which in the radiance swayed and swung;
> We could just hear its hoarse and iron tongue:
> The broad sun sunk behind it, and it tolled
> In strong and black relief.

> (1967: 192)

In his largely dismissive analysis of 'The Black Tower', Bloom does not find 'the associations of the tower with towers in Shelley and Browning, as noted by some critics, very convincing' (1970: 466), but according to his causal model of influence, developed between writing his books on Yeats and Stevens, Shelley's poem also shapes Yeats. Later Bloom would see Shakespeare as inescapable. Moving backwards from Browning to Shelley and then to Milton, like early Bloom, we come closer and closer to the beginning of the unborn kind; we find a strain of immanent Neoplatonism in English literature that is gathered in Yeats's late work. Bloom identifies 'a vision that begins in *Il Penseroso*' as 'What moved most the imagination of the young Yeats' (1970: 9) but the critic unfortunately refuses to take its Neoplatonism very seriously.

As in many of Yeats's poems, Shelley's landscape is at once naturalistic and symbolic, unlike the setting of 'Childe Roland', which is not quite naturalistic and not quite symbolic. Like Yeats, Shelley writes as one well versed in esoteric, especially Neoplatonist, wisdom. Bloom rebuffs Neoplatonism as 'a rather conventional theory of influence' (1975: 30). I would argue that it is the convening power of this undercurrent of perennial wisdom, which makes it, paradoxically, unconventional: it is the 'site of the unspoken statement', which has a 'gathering power', gathering in and preserving 'all it has gathered, not like an encapsulating shell but rather by penetrating with its light all it has gathered, and only thus releasing it into its own nature' (Heidegger 1971: 159–60). Both Shelley and Yeats use the symbol of the tower to write allegories of our official culture's declination from 'age to age', but they also see their poems as charged with divine revelation in time, or tradition, 'Like fabrics of enchantment piled to Heaven' (Shelley 1967: 192), or towers struck by lightning, and they craft their poems so that we may be so charged. For Shelley a funereal bark gliding upon the Venetian Lagoon symbolizes the soul incarnated and afloat on the sea of time and space. The tower becomes, in the hands of a Neoplatonist poet, a potent but ambivalent symbol, facing the world to tell our materialist fable back to us, but also gathering eternity into its explicators or readers, to release each into his own nature. Shelley draws the reader's attention to his technique, or his failure to employ this technique, in the conversation that interrupts his very description with interpretation, a conversation marred, in turn, by the poem:

> 'And such,' – he cried, 'is our mortality,
> And this must be the emblem and the sign
> Of what should be eternal and divine! –
> And like that black and dreary bell, the soul,
> Hung in a heaven-illumined tower, must toll
> Our thoughts and our desires to meet below
> Round the rent heart and pray – as madmen do
> For what? they know not, – till the night of death
> As sunset that strange vision, severeth
> Our memory from itself, and us from all
> We sought and yet were baffled.' I recall
> The sense of what he said, although I mar
> The force of his expressions.

> (1967: 192–3)

'Another emblem there!' (*YCP*: 275), Yeats might well exclaim, but the forlorn bafflement in Shelley becomes defiance in Yeats. How does such a late attitude open up possibilities for his readers? We find the setting of the shore and the tower with the bell ringing already in Milton's 'Il Penseroso', after the speaker has left the dark woods, missing the nightingale, as we might walk out of the setting of 'Cuchulain Comforted' into the setting of 'The Black Tower', or amble between *La Primavera* and *The Birth of Venus*, to catch a glimpse of the moon, symbol of Isis:

> Oft on a Plat of rising ground,
> I hear the far-off *Curfeu* sound,
> Over som wide-water'd shoar,
> Swinging slow with sullen roar[.]

> (*1645*: i. 40)

Milton's lines act as a charm in our canon, charmed as they are from Prospero's speech of renunciation at the end of *The Tempest*. From the seventeenth century onwards later poets have rejoiced 'To heare the solemne Curfewe' (*The Tempest* (V. i. 40), recalling the sense of Shakespeare and Milton to mar the force of their expressions. Milton's idyllic, languorous and crepuscular setting with shore and tower is starkly apocalyptic in Yeats who had long used 'Il Penseroso' to create his own charms.

> Or let my Lamp at midnight hour,
> Be seen in som high lonely Towr,
> Where I may oft out-watch the *Bear*,
> With thrice great *Hermes*, or unsphear
> The spirit of *Plato* to unfold
> What Worlds, or what vast Regions hold
> The immortal mind that hath forsook
> Her mansion in this fleshly nook[.]
>
> (*1645*: i. 40)

With 'Il Penseroso' we find a Neoplatonic counterpart to Macbeth's dark castle, and a way out of the melodramatic performance at the end of the decaying kind that Browning allegorizes at the end of 'Childe Roland' and that Bloom is so adept at describing. We find, in Milton's Neoplatonic symbolism, the beginning of the unborn kind that looks after.

Taylor says the worthy man's 'intellectual light will assiduously shine in the penetralia of his soul, like a lamp secured in a watch-tower, which shines with unremitted splendour, though surrounded by stormy winds and raging seas' (1805: 19). The Psalmist prays:

> Heare my cry, O God, attend unto my prayer. From the end of the earth wil I cry unto thee, when my heart is overwhelmed: leade me to the rocke, that is higher then I. For thou hast bene a shelter for me, and a strong tower from the enemy. (Psalm 61. 1–3)

Is Psalm 61 of the same genre as 'The Black Tower'? The tower is a symbol of watchfulness and ascension. As Raine says, 'for Yeats seeing on all sides the rise of ignorance, the most important thing was that one philosopher should still keep watch in the High Lonely Tower; as Plato, Milton, Shelley and Palmer had kept faith' (1986: 239). The problem is dissemination of this knowledge; perhaps there is for the poet only ever Milton's 'fit audience . . . though few'. Virginia Moore, tracing the Rosicrucian sources of Yeats's work finally admits, 'I can only suggest an interpretation': 'Perhaps, among other meanings, "The Black Tower" points to the fact that Rosicrucianly he was an "oath-bound man": a warning to critics that a fund of material which might help explain his life and views must remain secret' (1954: 439).

The axioms in Yeats's philosophy 'are not axioms until they are proved upon our pulses' (Keats 2002: 88), and it is very well the case that Yeats would have believed current modes of discourse to have no pulse. Has interpretation become the very enemy that seeks to bribe and flatter Yeats's heroically resistant, albeit sleeping, poet soldiers out of the old black tower? Can the academy converse with the old cook? Raine senses the same resistance to criticism in Yeats's last poem as Moore: 'Archetypal symbols have a life of their own apart from and beyond any assigned meaning; and the Tower, whether taken to represent Yeats's own achievement, the nation "half dead at the top" or the empty ruin of "*The Black Tower*" retains its mystery' (1986: 243). The tower must 'withstand the siege of "the savage god" or the flood of modern ignorance'. 'Nevertheless, there is, in the Tower symbol which Yeats made his own, that element of *hybris* reflected in his choice of Self rather than Soul, the human condition rather than release from the wheel of death and birth' (Raine 1986: 244) as we saw in Chapter 1 when we considered the tower symbol in the Tarot pack. Yeats also understood that the Neoplatonist should be struck out of the tower of accumulated wisdom and its ruination is a discovery of 'the rock' within 'that is higher then I': it is only Macbeth who thinks, mistakenly after all, that his castle's 'strength | Will laugh a Siedge to scorne'.

It is fitting, then, that by the time Yeats's experience does 'attain | To somthing like Prophetic strain' (*1645*: i. 44), one of his major mature symbols is the tower ruined at the top. During 'several months of charged creativity' (Brown: 313) from 1927 to 1928, before he fell seriously ill, Yeats was preoccupied with the symbol, composing 'A Dialogue of Self and Soul', which describes the tower's 'broken, crumbling battlement' (*YCP*: 265) and 'Blood and the Moon'. In October he made a short poem, 'Symbols' that condenses his meditations while enumerating the symbols that drive his two very last poems (*YCP*: 270). Yeats had entered his adept phase. Like 'Milton's Platonist', 'Il Penseroso', he had been initiated in various secret rites to attain the status of Magus and he makes his own house within his prized but 'ever-shifting symbol' (Raine 1991: 1):

> A winding stair, a chamber arched with stone,
> A grey stone fireplace with an open hearth,

A candle and written page.
Il Penseroso's Platonist toiled on
In some like chamber, shadowing forth
How the daemonic rage
Imagined everything.
Benighted travellers
From markets and from fairs
Have seen his midnight candle glimmering.

(*YCP*: 227)

Then again, from 1918 to the end of his life Yeats would ironize such activities. As Robartes says in 'The Phases of the Moon', the poem that was to become an integral part of *A Vision*:

that shadow is the tower,
And the light proves that he is reading still.
He has found, after the manner of his kind,
Mere images; chosen this place to live in
Because, it may be, of the candle-light
From the far tower where Milton's Platonist
Sat late, or Shelley's visionary prince:
The lonely light that Samuel Palmer engraved,
An image of mysterious wisdom won by toil;
And now he seeks in book or manuscript
What he shall never find.
Aherne.   Why should not you
Who know it all ring at his door, and speak
Just truth enough to show that his whole life
Will scarcely find for him a broken crust
Of all those truths that are your daily bread;
And when you have spoken take the roads again?

(*YCP*: 184)

By the end of his life Yeats saw the tower as a symbol for our selves, even our wiser selves, which are raised only to be ruined or transformed by the lightning strike of divine revelation, to be conjoined in crisis with Self or 'fearless immortal Spirit'. Yeats writes knowingly after '*Curfeu*', but also after lightning has struck. Like Blake, Yeats sees that the Last Judgement has already occurred, and unfolds gradually in history, if we could but wake up to it, and he wonders whether we should, even if we could, coax the smaller light back to life. 'The Black Tower' is built out of the remains of Macbeth's castle in order to apprehend a vision of Il Penseroso's tower shattered at the top. The Platonist's tower must be ruined as a necessary prelude to spiritual rebirth; his studies should build him high enough for the lightning strike of revelation that razes the everyday self. Climbing the winding stair and then clambering the ruined top of Yeats's tower we have to look before and after, but the gyres run on, our world poised at the end of the decaying kind that precedes the beginning of the unborn kind: 'They also serve who only stand and waite' (*1673*, 'When I consider how my light is spent': i. 59). At the end of the decaying kind, we apprehend a different kind of annihilation that renovates.

From the limited perspective of the towers of our age, we are uncertainly poised at the end of the decaying kind that precedes the beginning of the unborn kind: 'a man's a fool | Who, when his own right king's forgotten, | Cares what king sets up his rule'. A life lived in the absence of 'fearless immortal Spirit', our 'own right king', is an alienated and inauthentic one, regardless of the mundane political 'rule' we live under. Conversely, a man whose everyday self has been joined in crisis to 'age-long memoried self' cannot be touched by worldly tyranny. Blake saw clearly that 'we must All soon follow every one to his Own Eternal House Leaving the Delusive Goddess Nature & her Laws to get into Freedom from all Law of the Members into The Mind in which every one is King & Priest in his own House God Send it so on Earth as it is in Heaven' (Erdman: 784); there is a moment in each day that ruins the self's tower, to open the eternal house of many mansions within the industrious. We may sleep through such a moment, which we might have discovered for ourselves every day of our lives, but that moment will come regardless at the point of death, and we will be judged according to how we will have lived our lives, in industrious freedom of Spirit or in thrall to our everyday selves:

> Only an entity which, in its Being, is essentially **futural** [**zukünftig**] so that it is free for its death and can let itself be thrown back upon its factical "there" by shattering itself against death – that is to say, only an entity which, as futural, is equiprimordially in the process of **having-been**, can, by handing down to itself the possibility it has inherited, take over its thrownness and be **in the moment of vision** for 'its time' ['die eigene Geworfenheit übernehmen und **augenblicklich** sein für "seine Zeit"]. Only authentic temporality which is at the same time finite, makes possible something like fate – that is to say, authentic historicality. (Heidegger 1962: 437; Heidegger 2006: 385)

Such is the task of a life: looking after, it is possible for each to make a soul out of our intelligence that is before us.

What is the relation of the black tower to the cave of the nymphs? They are both symbols of 'thrownness' and possibility. Yeats conjectures that 'so good a Platonist as Shelley could hardly have thought of any cave as a symbol, without thinking of Plato's cave that was the world; and so good a scholar may well have had Porphyry on "the Cave of the Nymphs" in his mind' (*E&I*: 81–2). Yeats moves on from a consideration of Shelley's Porphyrian use of the cave and river, briefly to consider his use of the tower as symbol, another 'very ancient symbol' that

> would perhaps, as years went by, have grown more important in his poetry. The contrast between it and the cave in *Laon and Cythna* suggests a contrast between the mind looking outward upon men and things and the mind looking inward upon itself, which may or may not have been in Shelley's mind, but certainly helps, with one knows not how many other dim meanings, to give the poem mystery and shadow. (*E&I*: 87)

'The Black Tower' suggests a contrast between crypt and tower; 'with one knows not how many other dim meanings', it is made to be a poem of 'mystery and shadow' and its symbols are mixed. The poem suggests another contrast. The first word of the first stanza brings us back to the beginning of *The Iliad*; the chorus with its wind or winds on water at night brings us back to the beginning of Genesis: 'darknesse was upon the face of the deepe: and the Spirit of God mooved upon the face of the waters' (Genesis 1. 2). Porphyry says, 'it was not without reason' that the ancients

> connected winds with souls sinking to generation, and again separating themselves from its stormy whirl: because, according to the opinion of some, souls attract a spirit, and obtain a pneumatic substance. Indeed, Boreas is proper to souls passing into generation: for the northern blasts recreate those who are on the verge of death; and refresh the soul reluctantly detained in the body. On the contrary, the southern gales dissolve life. (Taylor 1969: 313)

In 'The Black Tower' we hear 'the sound of the universe. This is known to all traditions . . . ; "some call it the music of the spheres; some creative sound; others the Holy Spirit" . . . the creative sound to which all is attuned. Wind is an image of the Holy Spirit used in the story of Pentecost' and in Genesis; but such a sound should not be taken figuratively: 'it is a spiritual reality experienced by whoever attains it. Had the author of the Book of Job known this? Had Blake? I leave you merely to reflect that spiritual knowledge is not a matter of information, but of epiphany; and release from suffering can only result from a change of consciousness' (Raine 1991: 139). In 'The Black Tower' the winds roar but they only shake old bones, emblematic of those who can only take winds as an image. These winds are supernatural; 'cold winds blow across our hands, upon our faces, the thermometer falls'. But they also seem to me distinctly northern: such a 'wintry blast' of Boreas also foreshadows yet another life, it is 'proper to souls passing into generation': Yeats is 'content to live it all again', 'A blind man battering blind men' (*YCP*: 267). Can a poem of such ambivalent winds change consciousness so that we begin to hear the sound of the creative Spirit that moves as wind on water? Is 'The Black Tower' merely a poem that describes our 'thrownness' or waste land at the end in the manner of the essentially nostalgic Eliot? Or is it also possessed of a 'fructifying virtue' at the darkest moment before the beginning of the unborn kind?

Much contemporary criticism makes late Yeats sound more like Eliot than Blake. But for all of his love of this world, I would argue that Yeats's late work reveals *'an entity which, in its Being, is essentially **futural'**,* like Blake, *'handing down to itself the possibility it has inherited'* so that it can *'take over its thrownness and be **in the moment of vision** [**augenblicklich**] for "its time"'.* Yeats has a profounder understanding of history than Eliot. The 'Say' that opens 'The Black Tower' hands down to itself the possibility it has inherited; it says with Eckhart that 'If you could do away with yourself for a moment ['einen ougenblik'], even for less than a moment, then you would possess all that [the wilderness of divinity] possesses in itself' (1994: 122; 1993: i. 322): it is oath-bound to 'a Moment' in each day that Blake apprehends Satan cannot find, that renovates every moment of the day, if found and 'rightly placed' by those that awake to become industrious (Blake, *Milton*, plate 35: 283). The wind in 'The Black Tower' also heralds a moment of spiritual change; we may be still asleep but the poem will have simultaneously us and its 'Say': it is movement towards

> a point which is not only unknown, ignored and strange but such that it seems to have no prior reality apart from this movement, yet is so compulsive that narration's appeal depends on it to the extent that it cannot even 'begin' before it has reached it, while it is only the narration and the unpredictable movement of the narration which provide the space where this point becomes real, powerful and appealing. (Blanchot 1992: 62)

The invocation in Book IX of *Paradise Lost* marks its change of genre to tragedy and is of the same climate as Yeats's last poem. 'The Black Tower' would also contain many genres. Milton speaks of a new kind of heroism, the kind that Cuchulain learns in 'Cuchulain Comforted': he will not write of warlike heroes like the Greeks and Romans; 'the better fortitude | Of Patience and Heroic Martyrdom | Unsung' (*PL*, ix. 31–3). Thus he will move away from medieval and contemporary poems about knights and jousts:

> Mee of these
> Nor skilld nor studious, higher Argument
> Remaines, sufficient of it self to raise
> That name, unless an age too late, or cold
> Climat, or Years damp my intended wing
> Deprest, and much they may, if all be mine,
> Not Hers who brings it nightly to my Ear.

> (*PL*, ix. 41–7)

'Cuchulain Comforted' and 'The Black Tower' are poems that remain defiant although they are set in different worlds that become manifest after Milton's 'unless'. Yeats's literal circumstances as he writes these poems intensify even the history of Milton dictating *Paradise Lost*. In 'Cuchulain Comforted' the setting is the dark forest of the next world. In 'The Black Tower' the ailing and elderly Yeats describes our world; figures of 'an age too late, or cold | Climat': we are ruined versions of 'fabl'd' or 'gorgious Knights' (*PL*, ix. 30 and 36). But his intended wing is not depressed because his argument is hers: Yeats's 'Celestial Patroness' (*PL*, ix. 21) is an archetype of Isis who is married to Jesus the Imagination, the Divine Human. The linen makes 'Cuchulain Comforted' unexpectedly a prothalamion, a poem that precedes a marriage that has already happened, if we could but wake up to it.[10] In 'The Black Tower' the marriage seems even further off, its setting mundane, the hierophant less trustworthy. But there can be no shirking the fact, especially in our interpretations of the poem, that it is us who Yeats describes in the dark tower, unless we come to it as its enemy: 'He that is not with me, is against me: and hee that gathereth not with me, scattereth abroad' (Matthew 12. 30). How do we arise from such inauthentic depression, sleeping like Blake's Albion or Yeats's 'hale men', to hear the poem's higher argument, its creative sound? Who is now taking heavenly dictation at her nightly visitation? From our future the theme is pursued by returning to a beginning, or 'a narrative moment logically earlier', but coming after, the end at which 'The Black Tower' would wake us. At the moment, according to Yeats, even the faithful, within an already ruined tower, remain asleep.

'Of Mere Being', or just about alive

In his very last poem, Yeats returned with deliberation to a worldly philosophy, 'established for the ordering of the body and the fallen will': 'the philosophy of soldiers' (*E&I*: 129 and 128). When we move to Stevens's very last poem, 'Of Mere Being', we move to a 'divine' philosophy, 'established for the peace of the imagination and the unfallen will'. We move from the worldly tower, constructed for soldiers, to find 'The palm at the end of the mind' where we 'sympathise with all living things'; we 'come at last to forget good and evil in an absorbing vision of the happy and the unhappy' (*E&I*: 129):

> The palm at the end of the mind,
> Beyond the last thought, rises
> In the bronze decor,
>
> A gold-feathered bird
> Sings in the palm, without human meaning,
> Without human feeling, a foreign song.
>
> You know then that it is not the reason
> That makes us happy or unhappy.
> The bird sings. Its feathers shine.
>
> The palm stands on the edge of space.
> The wind moves slowly in the branches.
> The bird's fire-fangled feathers dangle down.

(OP: 141)

My text of the poem comes from Milton J. Bates's revised and enlarged edition of *Opus Posthumous*. The editor notes, 'This poem apparently survives in only one form, a typescript at the Huntingdon Library. There the final word of line 3 is *decor* rather than, as the first edition of *Opus Posthumous* has it, *distance*' (*OP*: 325). There is no acute accent in Bates's transcription. According to the *OED*, 'décor', with an acute accent, is the 'The scenery and furnishings of a theatre stage. Also transf. and fig., setting, surroundings', or 'The decoration or furnishings of a room, building, etc.; the layout or method of display of an exhibition, etc.'. The first example of this word given is from 1897, and it is used in a literary context. Had 'Of Mere Being' been published under Stevens's supervision, 'decor' might well have had an acute accent since his use of the word comprehends both meanings of 'décor'. Then again, the *OED* includes a separate entry for 'decor', without an acute accent, defining the word as 'Comeliness, beauty, ornament', and providing two examples from the seventeenth century. Both words fit Stevens's poem and both come from the Latin *decor*. According to Stevens's beloved *L&S*, *decor* is '*what is seemly, becoming; comeliness, elegance, grace, beauty, ornament*'. It is a word mainly found in Latin poems, but later it is also frequent in Quintilian. Since 'Of Mere Being' offers the only instance of Stevens's use of 'decor', with or without an acute accent, the pious explicator of the poem would do well to turn to a significant example in *L&S* from Virgil, a poet whose 'works were everywhere held in such reverence and superstitious regard that mysterious powers of prophecy were ascribed to them' (Loane 1928: 185).

In Book V of the *Aeneid* Iris becomes Beroë, 'aged wife of Tmarian Doryclus, who had once had family, fame, and children, and in this form' exhorts 'the throng of Dardan mothers' (Virgil, *Aeneid*, v. 620–3: i. 514–15) weeping for the loss of Anchises:

> Thus speaking, she first fiercely seized the deadly flame, and raising her brand aloft, with full force brandished it and threw. Startled are the minds of the Trojan women, their wits bewildered. At this one from out their throng, and she the eldest, Pyrgo, royal nurse for Priam's many sons, spoke: 'This, look, mothers, is not Beroë; this is not the Rhoeteian wife of Doryclus. Mark the signs of divine beauty ['divini signa decoris'] and the flashing eyes; what fire she has, what lineaments, the sound of her voice, or her step as she moves. I myself but even now left Beroë behind, sick, and fretting that she alone had no part in such a rite, nor could pay to Anchises the offerings due!' So she spoke . . . (Virgil, *Aeneid*, v. 641–53: i. 514–17)[11]

The gold-feathered bird in Stevens's poem sings a foreign song, but without human meaning, without human feeling. In Virgil a goddess speaks through, and so enlivens, an old mother, but with human feeling, although it astonishes the other weeping mothers. Only another old mother can recognize the signs of divine beauty ('divini signa decoris'). Such is the experience of an old poet whose last poem flashes with strange non-allusions to eerily explicative passages from old poems. Stevens is divinely inspired, as Iris, the goddess of the rainbow, speaks through Beroë to exhort the others to burn their ships, cease wandering, and here seek Troy; the old poet is wrapt in a truly wondrous and 'absorbing vision of the happy and the unhappy' here and now:

> 'Nay, come! and burn with me these accursed ships. For in my sleep the phantom of Cassandra, the soothsayer, seemed to give me blazing brands: "Here seek Troy," she said; "here is your home." Now it is time that deeds be done; such portents brook no delay. Lo, four altars to Neptune! The god himself lends the brands and the resolve.' (Virgil, *Aeneid*, v. 635–40: i. 514–15)

By turning to *L&S*, and pursuing the word *decor*, as we know Stevens liked to trace odd Latinate words, we find three women in one; the human-inhuman relation of these figures mirrors the way that Virgil inheres in Stevens: we come upon the more than human it that speaks whenever man speaks. With the voice of an old woman, a goddess speaks as if she is remembering a prophetess in a dream; the old poet Stevens's poem has Virgil flash prophetically through a strange word to recall the divine. 'Of Mere Being' has us play, almost, a version of the *sortes Virgilianae*, where we would seek divine guidance by chance selection of a passage in Virgil; except the intervention of *L&S* means that there is an uncanny set of rules governing the selection of passages. We are dealing here with '*oracular sayings, verses, or sentences* at the opening of a book, selected for the purpose' (*L&S* definition of *sortes Vergilii or Vergilianae*), but Stevens's poem and the examples in *L&S*, rather than chance, dictate the books and the pages at which they are opened. In China the *I Ching* has provided for centuries a more structured version of such bibliomancy, which begins with a throw of coins. The critic must learn to read aright in tradition the coins that the poet throws in each of his poems. Although if I extend this analogy, it becomes more usefully uncertain. It may be that cosmic coins are thrown for a poet only once and each of his poems is an attempt to read the outcome; or it may be that the coins are thrown again each time the poem is read. In any case, I mean to read Stevens as the Chinese might, 'in all directions at once' (*SL*: 828):

> Chinese thinking . . . is, whenever possible, *a thinking in terms of the whole* . . . . This peculiarity can be seen in ordinary conversation with the Chinese: what seems to us a perfectly straightforward, precise

question about some detail evokes from the Chinese thinker an unexpectedly elaborate answer, as though one had asked him for a blade of grass and got a whole meadow in return. With us details are important for their own sakes; for the Oriental mind they always complete a total picture. In this totality . . . are included things which seem to be connected with one another only 'by chance,' by a coincidence whose meaningfulness appears altogether arbitrary. (Jung 1985: 100–1)

I think of this coin throwing, and the contingent consulting of a book, in terms of 'Der Ort', 'the site' of one single poetic statement that Heidegger would 'discuss' through 'clarification' of individual poems, in the dialogue that he establishes between poetry and thinking: 'Originally the word "site" suggests a place in which everything comes together, is concentrated. The site gathers unto itself, supremely and in the extreme. Its gathering power penetrates and pervades everything'; 'Ursprünglich bedeutet der Name "Ort" die Spitze des Speers. In ihr läuft alles zusammen. Der Ort versammelt zu sich ins Höchste und Äußerste. Das Versammelnde durchdringt und durchwest alles' (Heidegger 1971: 159–60; Heidegger 2007: 37). I see this site, as I do Blanchot's *récit*, as the moment and place when and where the coins rest. Perhaps, after all, it is we who are different sets of thrown coins, and the poem, western literature, and tradition, help us half-create and perceive the significance of their outcome. Coins are thrown and a book consulted accordingly, then we half-create and perceive 'Some affluence' (*SCP*: 533). If you permit my extended analogy, our culture is in danger of regarding the thrown coins as merely coins, and of forgetting how to consult the books that have been gathered, or gather themselves, for prophetic purposes, to reveal to us their 'Abundant recompense' (*LB1*: 206) or the 'whole meadow in return'.

I am prepared to follow the game with these refinements because I believe that the playing of *sortes* or literary lots is part of the experience of reading Stevens's late poems. The game can have good and bad outcomes for criticism, and we should take heed that the manifestation of Iris as Beroë hinders, rather than helps, the journeying Trojans. But such an approach is wonderfully unscientific, it is closer to the dangers of practising poetry and magic. If we need any authority for such critical licence, we first hear of this game, in England, in Sir Philip Sidney's *The Defence of Poesie*:

Among the *Romanes* a Poet was called *Vates*, which is as much as a diviner, foreseer, or Prophet . . . ; so heavenly a title did that excellent

> people bestowe uppon this hart-ravishing knowledge, and so farre
> were they carried into the admiration thereof, that they thought in
> the chanceable hitting uppon any of such verses, great foretokens of
> their following fortunes, were placed. Whereupon grew the worde
> of *Sortes Vergilianæ*, when by suddaine opening *Virgils* booke, they
> lighted uppon some verse of his, as it is reported by many, whereof the
> Histories of the *Emperours* lives are full. (1968: sig. B4ᵛ)

Unsurprisingly, since he was writing in the sixteenth century, Sidney
offers a token qualification of his interest in this 'verie vaine and
godlesse superstition, as also it was, to thinke spirits were commaunded
by such verses, whereupon this word *Charmes* deriued of *Carmina*,
commeth'. Nonetheless:

> serveth it to shew the great reverence those wittes were held in, and
> altogither not without ground, since both the Oracles of *Delphos* and
> *Sibyllas* prophesies, were wholly delivered in verses, for that same
> exquisite observing of number and measure in the words, and that
> high flying libertie of conceit propper to the Poet, did seeme to have
> some divine force in it. (1968: sig. B4ᵛ)¹²

  Thomas De Quincey makes a connection between the 'mighty silence'
of infancy, the pure being described in 'Of Mere Being', and versions of
'echo augury':

> These cases of infancy, reached at intervals by special revelations, or
> creating for itself, through its privileged silence of heart, authentic
> whispers of truth, or beauty, or power, have some analogy to those
> other cases, more directly supernatural, in which (according to the
> old traditional faith of our ancestors) deep messages of admonition
> reached an individual through sudden angular deflexions of words,
> uttered or written, that had not been originally addressed to himself.
> (2000–3: xix. 69)

Of these cases 'there were two distinct classes'. The first class is when the
'person concerned had been merely passive'; 'scintillations they are of
what seem nothing less than providential lights oftentimes arresting our
attention, from the very centre of what else seems the blank darkness of
chance and blind accident'; when a passerby notices a casually opened
book and is 'startled by a solitary word lying, as it were, in ambush, waiting
and lurking for him, and looking at him steadily as an eye searching
the haunted places in his conscience'. The second class of message,

'where the inquirer himself cooperated, or was not entirely passive', include the *sortes Virginliniae* and the *sortes Sanctorum* or the *sortes Bibliciae* (2000–3: xix. 69). De Quincey reflects:

> Something analogous to these spiritual transfigurations of a word or a sentence, by a bodily organ (eye or ear) that has been touched with virtue for evoking the spiritual echo lurking in its recesses, belongs, perhaps, to every impassioned mind for the kindred result of forcing out the peculiar beauty, pathos, or grandeur that may happen to lodge (unobserved by ruder forms of sensibility) in special passages scattered up and down literature. (De Quincey 2000–3: xix. 70)

I would argue that Stevens's poems are scattered with passages up and down literature, messages imparted, of both the first and second class, according to De Quincey's distinction, which we can apply to the future life of the poem in explication, and thus to our lives. To illustrate the first class of message, De Quincey misquotes Herbert's sonnet 'Sinne (I)': 'Books ['Bibles' in Herbert] lying open, millions of surprises'. But the Herbert sonnet that I have found to justify my method of explicating 'Of Mere Being' in this chapter is 'The H. Scriptures. II.':

> Oh that I knew how all thy lights combine,
> And the configurations of their glorie!
> Seeing not onely how each verse doth shine,
> But all the constellations of the storie.
>
> This verse marks that, and both do make a motion
> Unto a third, that ten leaves off doth lie:
> Then as dispersed herbs do watch a potion,
> These three make up some Christians destinie:
>
> Such are thy secrets, which my life makes good,
> And comments on thee: for in ev'ry thing
> Thy words do finde me out, & parallels bring,
> And in another make me understood.
>
> Starres are poore books, & oftentimes do misse:
> This booke of starres lights to eternall blisse.

(1968: 50–1)

Herbert finds within the Holy Scriptures the 'site of the unspoken statement', which has a 'gathering power', gathering in and preserving 'all it has gathered, not like an encapsulating shell but rather by penetrating with its light all it has gathered, and only thus releasing it into its own nature'. Pursuing words in the Bible, it turns out that it is we whom are sought: 'there are pow'rs | Which *of themselves* our minds impress' (*LB1*: 184);[13] 'thy words do finde me out': an experience common to explicators is that magical seeming moment when typology becomes tropology, and 'Such are' the book's 'secrets, which my life makes good'. Herbert's poem makes much of the relationship between biblical verse and stars and potions. I am arguing that 'Of Mere Being', like the other poems explicated in this book, has a kind of magic or prophetic power over explication, over our lives. It is a poem that acts as mystical gate-keeper leading us down paths until its words find us out, until the poem comments on us; this is the version of the *sortes* that the poem plays with its readers, although interpreters like to console themselves that it is they who play games with the poem. In reality, once we have made the tenth connection from the third and first, 'Then as dispersed herbs do watch a potion, | These three make up some Christian destinie'. F. E. Hutchinson explains that 'As the verses of Scripture are said to mark one another that they may by combination guide man to salvation, so the scattered herbs are on the watch to be combined in a potion': they would like to cure us. There are 'affinities . . . between the lowly inanimate things of earth and the stars', and words of verse have prophetic powers like stars (1945: 496). Affinities exist too between works of literature, configurations that 'watch' or 'finde' us and determine the future. As Herbert sees that the words of the Bible 'parallels bring' so 'Of Mere Being' draws in other works to prompt us to understand ourselves, and so that we might be understood by a poem that would like to cure us.

In 'Of Mere Being', Stevens's decision not to use an acute accent in 'decor', when he is usually prepared to demarcate inflections, as in 'papier-mâché' in 'Not Ideas', might alert us to the strange game of lots that he will have us play; that he plays, composing his poems. The word 'decor' is presented in its Latinate form and so we naturally turn to *L&S*. But, uncannily, it is unimportant whether Stevens intended us to play the game or not; for now that I have, we perceive the divination: the poem propels us, whether the poet likes it or not, to bibliomancy. Once the game has started, a divine force compels it, orchestrating prophetic relations between what might have been conceived as ill-assorted parts of poems and poems. Something without human meaning begins to speak, through such allusion, this game of *sortes*.

Again a late poem has us move, in our explication of it, beyond modes of discourse usually privileged in literary criticism. Rational, Aristotelian, or socio-politico-historical interpretations never quite suffice when reading late Yeats and late Stevens because these poets came to write more and more according to 'another philosophy, not made by men of action, drudges of time and space, but by Christ when wrapped in the divine essence'. They are 'poets, who are taught by the nature of their craft to sympathize with all living things, and who, the more pure and fragrant is their lamp, pass the further from all limitations, to come at last to forget good and evil in an absorbing vision of the happy and the unhappy' (*E&I*: 129). Even 'The Black Tower', which deliberately evokes 'the philosophy of soldiers', does so, it turns out, in the name of another kind of philosophy. Much criticism tends to talk about poetry in terms of rhetoric and from a historical perspective, but it strikes me that poems can be far more playful and often have far more to do with magic and prophecy. Poems use rhetorical figures and they have historical contexts but what interests me is the ways in which they transmute or escape the limitations of their formal and social circumstances. Noticing that a poem allows us to play a version of the *sortes Virgilianae* is one way of preparing 'pure explication de texte', Stevens's 'principal form of piety': as Stevens advises, 'One should have eyes all the way round one's head and read in all directions at once' (*SL*: 828). After all, an allusion, etymologically, is a kind of game; the playing of *sortes* within a poem, in imitation of classical augury, opens the text to divine influence.

The paragraph after Augustine imagines reciting a psalm in his *Confessions* provides the next text in this chapter that turns from the word 'decor' to the significance of the 'palm' in Stevens's final poem. Again criticism plays a version of the game of lots, but now changing books, and moving, as with the Middles Ages, from the *sortes Virginiae* to the *sortes Sanctorum*. We are playing a game that seems to have a certain inevitability to it:

But because thy loving kindness is better than life itself [Ps. 62. 4], behold my life is a distraction, and thy right hand hath taken hold of me [Ps. 17. 36; 62. 9], even in my Lord the Son of Man, the Mediator betwixt thee that art but one, and us that are many, drawn many ways by many things; that by him I may apprehend him in whom I am also apprehended [Phil. 3. 12–14], and that I may be gathered up from my old conversation, to follow that one, and to forget what is behind: not distracted but attracted, stretching forth not to what shall be and shall pass away, but to those things which are before: not, I say, distractedly but intently, follow I hard on, for the garland of my heavenly calling ['ad palmam supernae vocationis'], where I may hear the voice of thy praise, and contemplate these delights of thine [Ps. 25. 7; 26. 4], which are neither to come, nor to pass away. (Augustine 1912, XI. xxix: ii. 278–81)

We have found the theme of Stevens's last poem: the poem moves 'ad palmam supernae vocationis', to 'the garland of my heavenly calling'; that is, the palm, or 'Abundant recompence', at the end of the mind, is attained in a creative gathering to follow the One, when we are not stretched out and broken in distraction, but extended in reach to retain unity. God exists in the labours of a poet, and so the divine inheres in the style of a poem, whether we find it out by playing a refined version of *sortes* or by more conventional methods of explication de texte, such as the tracing of allusions and the discerning of influence.

Augustine is in fact modifying lines from Philippians: 'ad destinatum persequor ad bravium supernae vocationis Dei in Christo Iesu'; 'I presse toward the marke, for the price of the high calling of God in Christ Jesus' (3. 14): 'not, I say, distractedly but intently, follow I hard on, for the garland of my heavenly calling, where I may hear the voice of thy praise, and contemplate these delights of thine which are neither to come, nor to pass away';[14] 'non secundum distentionem, sed secundum intentionem sequor ad palmam supernae vocationis, ubi audiam vocem laudis et contempler delectationem tuam nec venientem nec praetereuntem'. By also alluding to a line from Psalm 25 (Psalm 26 in KJV): 'ut audiam vocem laudis' (7), Augustine has us recall the next sentence, which reads, 'et enarrem universa mirabilia tua'. With *mirabilia* we find ourselves again in the vicinity of Iris, daughter of wonder: she is the divinity at the edge of Stevens's last poem, the something more than human that speaks at the end, revealed through explication that obeys the *sortes* set up for us to play within the poem. Obeying the rules of that game, following the chanceful allusion, we do well to read the rest of the psalm, especially since Augustine has just pointed out, 'What is now done in this whole psalm, the same is done also in every part of it, yea and in every syllable of it; the same order holds in a longer action too, whereof perchance this psalm is but a part' (Augustine 1912, XI. xxviii: 279):

> Judge me, O LORD, for I have walked in mine integritie: I have trusted also in the LORD; therfore I shall not slide. Examine me, O LORD, and prove me; try my reines and my heart. For thy loving kindnesse is before mine eyes: and I have walked in thy trueth. I have not sate with vaine persons, neither will I goe in with dissemblers. I have hated

the congregation of evill doers: and will not sit with the wicked[.] I will wash mine hands in innocencie: so will I compasse thine Altar, O LORD: That I may publish with the voyce of thanksgiving, and tell of all thy wonderous workes. LORD, I have loved the habitation of thy house, and the place where thine honour dwelleth. Gather not my soule with sinners, nor my life with bloody men. In whose hands is mischiefe: and their right hand is full of bribes. But as for mee, I will walke in mine integritie: redeeme me, and bee mercifull unto me. My foot standeth in an even place: in the congregations will I blesse the LORD.

If not quite the same kind of poem, Psalm 25 and 'Of Mere Being' are parts of 'a longer action'; one exhorts God to Judgement, the other has awoken to Judgement already passed within, 'at the end of the mind'. Like 'The Black Tower' these works are resistant to bribes. Although, fittingly, it remained unpublished at his death, 'Of Mere Being' is Stevens publishing 'with the voyce of thanksgiving': his 'foot standeth in an even place'. After Sidney explains the *sortes Virgilianiae*, he moves on to the Psalms:

> And may not I presume a little farther, to shewe the reasonablenesse of this word *Vatis*, and say that the holy *Davids* Psalms are a divine *Poeme*? If I do, I shal not do it without the testimony of great learned men both auncient and moderne. But even the name of Psalmes wil speak for me, which being interpreted, is nothing but Songs: then that it is fully written in meeter as all learned *Hebritians* agree, although the rules be not yet fully found. Lastly and principally, his handling his prophecie, which is meerly Poeticall. For what else is the awaking his musical Instruments, the often and free chaunging of persons, his notable *Prosopopeias*, when he maketh you as it were see God comming in his majestie, his telling of the beasts joyfulnesse, and hils leaping, but a heavenlie poesie, wherin almost he sheweth himselfe a passionate lover of that unspeakable and everlasting bewtie, to be seene by the eyes of the mind, onely cleared by faith? (1968: sigs B4^v–B4^r)

My contention in this book is that Yeats and Stevens are *Vates*; they are at the end of a tradition that begins around the time of Sidney in England, and with Homer and Hesiod in western literature. A foreign song, without human meaning, without human feeling, sung by the bird in 'Of Mere Being', is like a psalm: 'it is of that unspeakable and everlasting bewtie, to be seene by the eyes of the mind', at the end of the mind. The reader registers the similarity between palm and psalm, a gently comic echo characteristic of late Stevens.

In Book V of the *Aeneid*, the women begin burning the ships, ill incited by Iris disguised as Beroë:

> But at first the matrons were gazing on the ships doubtfully and with jealous eyes, torn between an unhappy yearning for the land now reached and the destined kingdom that beckons them on, when the goddess on poised wings rose through the sky, cleaving in flight the mighty bow beneath the clouds. Then, indeed, amazed at the marvels and driven by frenzy, they cry aloud, and some snatch fire from the hearths within; others strip the altars, and throw on leaves and twigs and brands. With free rein Vulcan riots amid thwarts and oars and hulls of painted pine. (Virgil, *Aeneid*, v. 654–63: i. 516–17)

In my interpretation, which has hopefully not burnt its boats, this divine conflagration beneath a rainbow becomes the bird's fire-fangled feathers, which might also ignite the fronds of the palm: 'frondem ac virgulta facesque | coniciunt' (*Aeneid*, v. 661–2). Stevens's poem moves away from the clamour that Iris incites to an irenic realm 'established for the peace of the imagination and the unfallen will'. By casting lots, by reading other works according to the coins thrown by 'Of Mere Being', playing versions of the *sortes Virgiliniae* and the *sortes Sanctorum* to determine the future of our explication of Stevens's final poem, we establish a strange typology between Virgil and the Psalms. The mischief caused by Iris in the episode from Book V of the *Aeneid* is redeemed in Psalm 25: wonder is reinstated to its rightful beneficience. The desecrated altars in Virgil are compassed in the Psalm: 'That I may publish with the voyce of thankesgiving, and tell of all thy wonderous workes.' Rather than strip an altar to find fronds to burn ships, altars are compassed to publish songs to tell of God's wondrous works: wonder is put to good use. So the song in Stevens's poem makes us see 'God comming in his Majestie', the burning of ships at the end of the decaying kind precedes the singing of wonder in the Psalm at the beginning of the unborn kind. In the happily fortuitous typology we have discovered 'Of Mere Being' compassing, a relationship is made beyond reason, and we read as Roman bibliomancers, and their counterpart augurs, might: 'The bird sings. Its feathers shine'.

Concerning pure existence

For all of my conjectures about the poem's casting of interpretive lots, 'Of Mere Being' has a wonderful syntactic-semantic simplicity.

Its twelve lines are made of seven sentences, five of them beginning with 'The'. The first sentence lasts for its first two stanzas:

> The palm at the end of the mind,
> Beyond the last thought, rises
> In the bronze decor,
>
> A gold-feathered bird
> Sings in the palm, without human meaning,
> Without human feeling, a foreign song.

Like the 'Mere' of the title, signifying at once 'just, only' and 'essential, pure, or very', the words 'end' and 'last', in lines one and two, respectively, have the same two meanings each: both words describe the limit of reason, near death (see Cook 2007: 314). A palm would rise in the distance or decor, 'As if with voluntary power instinct' (*1805*, i. 407), if we were moving towards it, or even away from it under certain circumstances; such a tree symbolizes the end of a pilgrimage. In this poem the journey is made to the end of the mind; in other words, Stevens is talking about the soul's pilgrimage through a life: the speaker has come to the end of the cave that is the world in which we live, as long as 'We say God and the imagination are one'.

If we consider the poems in this book in terms of the Christian calendar then their chronology coincides with the order of events after the Passion; they form a kind of post-passion play for our secular age, expanding the human imagination inwards into the bosom of God: we move from the earliest, Yeats's penultimate poem, 'Cuchulain Comforted', set in the afterlife, following the hero immediately after his Good Friday; through Yeats's last and darkest poem, 'The Black Tower', set at the same time, but in this world, when the king seems dead to those left behind, to those still alive; then with Stevens's last poems, written sixteen years later, we come to an awakening of the king himself, in 'Not Ideas', that opens to the end of the series: 'Of Mere Being' is a celebratory poem that, 'beyond the last thought, rises', in order to imagine an inner Easter Sunday.

As we know from the palms that are carried on Palm Sunday, the week before Easter Sunday, so that we remember, by so prefiguring, Christ's resurrection, 'Palms and branches of foliage are regarded universally as symbols of victory, ascension, regeneration and immortality' (Chevalier and Gheerbrant 1982: 734). They signify belief in the immortality of the soul and the resurrection of the dead. 'Of Mere Being' is of, at once, Palm Sunday and Easter Sunday: it is at the end of the decaying kind but includes a song from the beginning of the unborn kind as all four of the poems in this book must be at once pre- and post-Passion. In Stevens's last poem, we are given the end of a golden bough, rather than string, to lead us in at Heaven's gate, built in Jerusalem's wall, as on Palm Sunday we commemorate Christ's entry into Jerusalem; we are afforded a vision of a tropical and mythological psychopomp that sings a foreign song, our song of the Divine Humanity, on a new kind of Easter Day: the poem says, we have died hereafter, 'at the end of the mind', now Christ is risen within man.

As we move from the darkness of Yeats's final poems to Stevens's lighter last works, we also change guides: we leave the Christian Dante for his own classical guide, Virgil. In Stevens as in Yeats a typological relation is established between classical antiquity and Christianity that we must heed at the end. We find that the ancient poet Virgil is our guide not through uncanny lottery but because of the symbol of the golden palm that rises in 'Of Mere Being'. We turn from Book V of the *Aeneid* to Book VI. The prophetess tells Aeneas of the golden bough that will help him in the underworld:

> There lurks in a shady tree a bough, golden in leaf and pliant stem, held consecrate to nether Juno; this all the grove hides, and shadows veil in the dim valleys. But it is not given to pass beneath earth's hidden places, before someone has plucked from the tree the golden-tressed fruitage. This has beautiful Proserpine ordained to be borne to her as her own gift. When the first is torn away, a second fails not, golden too, and the spray bears leaf of the selfsame ore. Search then with eyes aloft and, when found, duly pluck it with your hand; for of itself will it follow you, freely and with ease, if Fate be calling you; else with no force will you avail to win it or rend it with hard steel. (Virgil, *Aeneid*, vi. 136–48: i. 542–3)

Our cycle of last, or post-and-pre-passion, poems having begun in the gloomy grove of 'Cuchulain Comforted', like Aeneas we find a way out of such a dark wood once we have plucked Stevens's version of the golden bough. From the soldiers' philosophy of 'The Black Tower' we move to another kind of philosophy at the end of Stevens. In 'Of Mere Being' the bird's feathers are golden, fire-fangled and dangling down, like the fronds of a palm. In his very last poem, just before being admitted to hospital for what turns out to be untreatable stomach cancer, the poet has come upon the symbols that will guide his soul through the afterlife: the psychopomp and palm that both burn. Felling trees to make a funeral pyre for Misenus, Aeneas enters the dark wood, the primeval forest, and he remembers the words of the prophetess, and prays that he now find the golden bough. A divine power, which appears at first as chance to mortal eyes, intervenes:

> Scarce had he said these words when under his very eyes twin doves, as it chanced, came flying from the sky and lit on the green grass. Then the great hero knew them for his mother's birds, and prays with joy: 'Be my guides, if any way there be, and through the air steer a course into the grove, where the rich bough overshades the fruitful ground! And you, goddess-mother, fail not my dark hour!' So speaking, he checked his steps, marking what signs they bring, where they direct their course. As they fed, they advanced in flight just so far as a pursuer's eyes could keep them within sight; then, when they came to the jaws of noisome Avernus, they swiftly rise and, dropping through the unclouded air, perch side by side on their chosen goal – a tree, through whose branches flashed the contrasting glimmer of gold. As in winter's cold, amid the woods, the mistletoe, sown of an alien tree, is wont to bloom with strange leafage, and with yellow fruit embrace the shapely stems: such was the vision of the leafy gold on the shadowy ilex, so rustled the foil in the gentle breeze. Forthwith Aeneas plucks it and greedily breaks off the clinging bough, and carries it beneath the roof of the prophetic Sibyl. (Virgil, vi. 190–211: i. 544–7)

There are differences between Virgil and Stevens: no bough is plucked in 'Of Mere Being' and there is only one bird; but both poems use the same motifs. As Vendler says, 'Of Mere Being' is 'iconic' (1984: 42), and we do well to trace the poem's symbols, to enter the dark wood before anagogy, because Stevens has plucked from tradition that which he needs hereafter. J. G. Frazer conjectures that the golden bough in the *Aeneid* is mistletoe:

> If the mistletoe, as a yellow withered bough in the sad autumn woods, was conceived to contain the seed of fire, what better companion could a forlorn wanderer in the nether shades take with him than a bough that would be a lamp to his feet as well as a rod and staff to his hands? Armed with it he might boldly confront the dreadful spectres that would cross his path on his adventurous journey. (Frazer 1933: 707)

The first, two-stanza sentence of 'Of Mere Being' marks at once the end of one kind of story, the kind of adventurous journey that begins with Homer's *Odyssey* and continues through Virgil's *Aeneid* and Dante's *Divine Comedy*, finally to falter in Browning's 'Childe Roland'. But this end-point, at which Stevens's poem arrives, determines the beginning of this story: the movement of the hero's journey is a spiral; the poem's event is 'Ever to come, ever past, ever present in a beginning so sudden that it leaves one breathless, and yet spread out like an eternal return and rebirth . . . ; such is the event the narration would describe' (Blanchot 1992: 65). The two verbs of the first sentence, first 'rises' and then 'sings', occur at the end and the beginning, respectively, of the middle lines of stanzas one and two. The journeying hero has lost volition since it is the palm that rises and he is silent since it is the bird that sings. Each symbol, palm and bird, perfectly counters the other in this symmetrical first half of the poem.

The poem's formal meaning is the foreign song that wells up within it: 'You know then that it is not the reason | That makes us happy or unhappy.' In the second sentence the speaker turns to himself, or to us, 'Beyond the last thought'. 'Received language is to be given over to the demands of another mode of coherence' (Timothy Clark 1992: 50). The exacting step of wonder, a movement forward, but in retreat, as the doves guide Aeneas ever further into the dark wood, is the pressing matter to be thought. Its unfolding is the disposition and subject of the poem, beyond rational discourse. 'The bird sings.' But we do not understand the inhuman subject of its song. 'Its feathers shine.' We must learn to listen and to look in a new way and to make a disciplined step beyond reason before we can experience the world afresh in company of truth and love. The final stanza of the poem is anaphoric, its successive 'The's at the beginning of each one-line-long sentence having a suprarational, paratactic effect, slowing down reason that looks before in order to move incessantly after:

> The palm stands on the edge of space.
> The wind moves slowly in the branches.
> The bird's fire-fangled feathers dangle down.

'Of Mere Being' takes the 'bough that would be a lamp' to check its steps. Marking what signs the poem brings, each directs his or her course: thus engaged we find that such a palm is where a bird sings, hereafter, to guide the journeying soul to our spiritual source at the centre of the earth where each already is. A bird in the hand is worth two in the bush.

At the end of Act IV of his play Hamlet still asks:

> What is a man
> If his chiefe good and market of his time
> Be but to sleepe and feede, a beast, no more:
> Sure he that made us with such large discourse
> Looking before and after, gave us not

> That capabilitie and god-like reason
> To fust in us unusd[.]

(Q 1604; Hamlet, IV. iv. 33–9)[15]

In Act V Hamlet returns a changed man; having come out of the other
end of reason, he sounds more like the speaker of 'Of Mere Being' when
he admits to Horatio, type of the sceptic we saw awoken to new belief
in Chapter 4, in Stevens's 'Not Ideas', 'There's a Divinity that shapes our
ends, | Rough-hew them how we will' (*F*; *Hamlet*, V. ii. 10–11), even if he
is praising rashness to justify the killing of his childhood and university
friends. He obsesses no more with Cicero about the causes of things;
'causas rerum' (2005, I. iv. 11: 12). At his end, when he has moved
beyond the last thought, and is at the end of the mind, 'Had I but time
(as this fell Sergeant death | Is strick'd in his Arrest) oh I could tell you'
(*F*; *Hamlet*, V. ii. 347–8); Hamlet interrupts his own dying words with,
'But let it be'. Shakespeare seems to remember these words at the end of
The Winter's Tale, when Leontes demands to continue gazing on what
he perceives to be the statue of his dead wife:

LEO. Doe not draw the Curtaine.

PAUL. No longer shall you gaze on't, least your Fancie
May thinke anon, it moves.

LEO. Let be, let be:
Would I were dead, but that me thinkes alreadie.
(What was he that did make it?) See (my Lord)
Would you not deeme it breath'd? and that those veines
Did verily beare blood?

POL. 'Masterly done:
The very life seemes warme upon her Lippe.

LEO. The fixure of her Eye ha's motion in't,
As we are mock'd with Art.

PAUL. Ile draw the Curtaine:
My Lord's almost so farre transported, that
Hee'le thinke anon it lives.

LEO. Oh sweet *Paulina*,
Make me to thinke so twentie yeeres together:
No setled Sences of the World can match
The pleasure of that madnesse. Let't alone.

(F; The Winter's Tale, V. iii. 59–73)

Stevens plays with Hamlet's 'But let it be' in his earlier funereal poem, 'The Emperor of Ice-Cream': 'Let be be finale of seem. | The only emperor is the emperor of ice-cream' (*SCP*: 64). When Leontes realizes that the statue of his wife is warm, he says: 'If this be Magick, let it be an Art | Lawfull as Eating'. The contraction that expands Hamlet's 'But let it be', in the final scene of *The Winter's Tale*, is also the subject of 'Of Mere Being', as the poem's title indicates. Reason at the end of Shakespeare's penultimate play has been magicked away when both real and player audiences are spell-bound like the speaker of Stevens's last poem. Then again, we can account, quite reasonably, for what has happened. But let it be. Death is just about being only from pure being. Concerning very existence, it is of mere being.

Epilogue: Songs of Sixpence

In 'Of Mere Being', 'The bird sings' in the palm, at once tree and symbol of the pilgrimage to 'the edge of space'; listening to such 'a foreign song', 'You know then that it is not the reason', the causal quality of discourse, 'That makes us happy or unhappy'. In 'Cuchulain Comforted', the Shrouds decree 'all we do | All must together do', and together sewing, 'Now must we sing and sing the best we can'; by the end of the poem, 'They had changed their throats and had the throats of birds', singing without 'such large discourse' (Q 1604; *Hamlet*, IV. iv. 36) of cause and effect. As we saw in Chapter 3, Dante has another psychopomp, 'l'uccel divino' (*Purgatorio*, ii. 38), the divine bird, pilot his boat of singing souls to the shore of Purgatory:

> 'In exitu Israel de Ægypto,'
> All with one voice together sang, with what
> In the remainder of that hymn is writ.
>
> (Cary: 153)

> *'In exitu Isräel de Aegypto'*
> cantavan tutti insieme ad una voce
> con quanto di quel salmo è poscia scripto.
>
> (*Purgatorio*, ii. 46–8)

At this significant moment in the poem, 'basic patterns and structures of meaning are brought to the fore' (*Purgatorio*: 12). Exodus is of central importance to the allegory of the *Comedy*. According to the fourfold method of interpretation, the senses of Psalm 113 (Psalms 114 and 115 in KJV) 'concern the single most important event of the Jewish prehistory

217

of the faith; the central event of the faith; the effect for each individual in this life; the passage of each soul to the next life. Each implies all the others; all have the same or a closely parallel structure; and together they articulate a causal sequence' (*Purgatorio*: 14). But if interpretation begins with anagogical sense rather than literal sense, as Blake's works begin as 'Vision' to transform history, then the principle of causality cannot adequately describe the relation between all four senses of a work. After Blake, it is envisioned our exodus becomes divine influx.

Attending to Dante's direction of interpretation, which proceeds from the comprehending of literal sense to apprehend eventually anagogical sense, Durling points out that 'Any singing of Psalm 113 (or any psalm) is necessarily situated at some point in this causal sequence, normally on earth, in the present, with "those who believe in Christ" and are presumably "returned to grace"' (*Purgatorio*: 14). What happens when a new kind of song is sung, or poem recited, to 'say God and the imagination are one', in the presence mostly of those who do not believe in Christ? The causal sequence from literal sense through typological and tropological senses to anagogical sense has been disrupted, and according to all four senses. If we are atheist materialists we remain stuck with the literal sense of the work: we are confined by the ideologies of our age and the theories that seek only to foreground those historical, political and social structures and their subjects. If the four senses are reversed so that we apprehend the work as 'Vision' from the beginning, hearing its 'foreign song' by asking about 'the more than human "It" (*das "Es"*) which speaks whenever man speaks' (Caputo 1987: 290), then its senses are connected, not by causality, but by a version of 'the synchronicity principle', which 'asserts that the terms of a meaningful coincidence are connected by *simultaneity* and *meaning*' (Jung 1985: 95), that is, the 'hub' (*U*: 135; Waley 1934: 155) of 'non-being' (Chung-yuan 1975: 30). In his work, Blake would 'open the immortal Eyes | Of Man inwards into the Worlds of Thought: into Eternity | Ever expanding in the Bosom of God, the Human Imagination' (Blake, *Jerusalem*, plate 5: 302) so that his readers can find and rightly place 'a Moment in each day' (Blake, *Milton*, plate 35: 283) that is also 'The Last Judgment' (Erdman: 554). Such a project puts the visionary sense of a work first, to awake us to 'the bright eternal Self that lives in man' (*U*: 135) and so transforms our historical circumstances or worldly premises; it recognizes that 'besides the connection between cause and effect there is another factor in nature which expresses itself in the arrangement of events and appears to us as meaning' (Jung 1985: 95).

The moment of vision that unites all four senses of a work is discovered by Augustine also when he imagines the recitation of a psalm:

> I am about to repeat a psalm that I know. Before I begin, my expectation alone reaches itself over the whole: but so soon as I shall have once begun, how much so ever of it I shall take off into the past, over so much my memory also reaches: thus the life of this action of mine is extended both ways: into my memory, so far as concerns that part which I have repeated already, and into my expectation too, in respect of what I am about to repeat now; but all this while is my marking faculty present at hand, through which, that which was future, is conveyed over, that it may become past: which how much the more diligently it is done over and over again, so much more the expectation being shortened, is the memory enlarged; till the whole expectation be at length vanished quite away, when namely, that whole action being ended, shall be absolutely passed into the memory. (Augustine 1912, XI. xxviii: 276–9)

In this 'the crown jewel' (Ricoeur 1984: 19) of his *Confessions*, Augustine reaches the third and final stage of his argument about the nature of time. 'In the first stage, the idea of a threefold present was proffered in order to resolve the enigma of a being (time) that lacks being. In the second stage, the idea of a distension of the mind was proffered in order to resolve the enigma of the extension of a thing (time) that has no extension' (Severson 1995: 45): Augustine argues, rather than talk of past, present and future, 'it might be properly said, there be three times: a present time of past things; a present time of present things; and a present time of future things. For indeed three such as these in our souls there be; and otherwhere do I not see them' (Augustine 1912, XI. xx: 253). The third stage connects the first two but also establishes an aporia because 'Previously the present was construed in a passive sense'. But now:

> The mind's attention (*intentio praesens*), which is the present component of 'mental time', actively relegates expectations into memories. So the theory of *distentio* (what we measure are impressions that indicate extension in the mind) is joined to that of the threefold present (time can only exist as the present) when expectation and memory are understood both as extensions of the mind and as activities of mental attention. (Severson 1995: 46)

As Ricoeur says, 'The theory of the threefold present, reformulated in terms of the threefold intention, makes the *distentio* arise out of the *intentio* that has burst asunder.' It is as if the tower has been struck by lightning. Ricoeur's thesis is that the *distentio* is related to the passivity of impression in Augustine's passage: 'Therefore, the more the mind makes itself *intentio*, the more it suffers *distentio*' (1984: 19–20 and 21). To adopt partially Yeats's terminology, 'genius', as the crisis that joins 'our trivial daily mind' to 'age-long memoried self' (*Au*: 272), is the paradoxical affluence of dispossession. Ricoeur argues:

> Augustine's inestimable discovery is, by reducing the extension of time to the distention of the soul, to have tied this distention to the slippage that never ceases to find its way into the heart of the three-fold present – between the present of the future, the present of the past, and the present of the present. In this way he sees discordance emerge again and again out of the very concordance of the intentions of expectation, attention, and memory. (1984: 21)

The 'affluence' of my book is a paradoxical process that Ricoeur calls 'slippage'. As he says, 'It is to this enigma of the speculation on time that the poetic act of emplotment replies' (1984: 21–2), an act refined in Blanchot's description of the ceaselessly asymptotic movement of *le récit*. As we saw in Chapter 5, 'The fragile example of the *canticus* recited by heart [Augustine 1912, XI. xxvii, quoted above] suddenly becomes, toward the end of the inquiry, a powerful paradigm for other *actiones* in which, through engaging itself, the soul suffers distension' (Ricoeur 1984: 22). Augustine's passage about reciting the psalm 'goes on to express the series of homologies, of ever-increasing dimension, from the syllabic to the autobiographical to the eschatological' (Freccero 1986: 271):

> What is now done in this whole psalm, the same is done also in every part of it, yea and in every syllable of it; the same order holds in a longer action too, whereof perchance this psalm is but a part; this holds too throughout the whole course of man's life, the parts whereof be all the actions of the man; it holds also throughout the whole age of the sons of men, the parts whereof be the whole lives of men. (Augustine 1912, XI. xxviii: ii. 279)

In Ricoeur's view, 'The entire province of narrative is laid out here in its potentiality, from the simple poem, to the story of an entire life, to universal history'. 'And yet', Ricoeur continues, 'something is missing from the full sense of *distentio animi*, which the contrast with eternity alone can provide' (Ricoeur 1984: 22). Blake finds the eternal in a syllable: his poems begin as vision; they move from the eschatological to vivify the literal: his poems make 'a Moment in each Day' that 'renovates every Moment of the Day if rightly placed' (Blake, *Milton*, plate 35: 283). Ricoeur's point is that 'the theme of *distension* and *intention* acquires from its setting within the meditation on eternity and time an intensification':

> This intensification does not just consist of the fact that time is thought of as abolished by the limiting idea of an eternity that strikes time with nothingness. Nor is this intensification reduced to transferring into the sphere of lamentation and wailing what had until then been only a speculative argument. It aims more fundamentally at extracting from the very experience of time the resources of an internal hierarchization, one whose advantage lies not in abolishing time but in deepening it. (Ricoeur 1984: 30)

Severson points out that these three functions of the interaction between eternity and time trace a movement from creation to redemption; they sketch a change of perspective from speculation about beginnings to attentiveness to endings (see 1995: 48–54). Freccero sees that Augustine's 'discussion of the nature of time conforms exactly to the movement of *terza rima*' (1986: 270). His summary of the 'tautological character' of the *canticum*, which Augustine says is known by heart, brings us to the realm of synchronicity:

> The ending is the beginning, for recitation is the performance, or unfolding, of a text previously known in its entirety. As in the act of speech, we move from the intentionality of the speaker to the performance of the speech, syllable by syllable, until it is completely sounded in time. The silence that follows the speech exactly corresponds to the silence that preceded it. Time, in such a context, is impressed, like syntax, into the service of significance. (1986: 270–1)

Augustine's reasoning brings him to 'another factor in nature which expresses itself in the arrangement of events and appears to us as meaning' (Jung 1985: 95). As Freccero continues, 'This, of course, is the central metaphor of Christian history. God's Word, pre-existing for all time, is recited by all of history until, in the fullness of time, it is made flesh' (1986: 271). The 'slippage' that Ricoeur identifies in Augustine haunts the later work of Yeats and Stevens; their final poems decline themselves in every sense of that verb, just as 'in eternall lines to time' Shakespeare's sonnet 18 'grow'st' as it 'some-time declines, | By chance, or natures changing course untrim'd'. Unorthodox Christianity transforms historical time into poetry, chance and eternity; three kinds of spiritual time to be understood according to the three spiritual senses of the Bible.

Eliade talks of Christianity's

> valorisation of Time – in the final reckoning, its *redemption* of Time and of History. Renouncing the reversibility of cyclic Time, it posits a Time that is irreversible, because the hierophanies manifested in it are no longer repeatable: it is once only that the Christ has lived, has been crucified and has been resurrected. Hence a complete fulfilment of the momentary: Time itself is ontologised: Time is made to *be*, which means that it ceases to become, it transforms itself into eternity. (1991: 169)

If such hierophanies were to be repeated it would be repetition as described by Kierkegaard. We should know:

> That repetition not only *is* for contemplation, but that it is a task for freedom, that it signifies freedom itself, consciousness raised to the second power, that it is the *interest* of metaphysics and also the interest upon which metaphysics comes to grief, the watchword in every ethical view, *conditio sine qua non* for every issue of dogmatics, that the true repetition is eternity . . . that repetition . . . will come to mean atonement[.] (1983: 324)

As Edward F. Mooney explains,

> Take the movement at issue to be a movement toward meaning or value, a gathering of meaning, say, into the present. If this gathering is faced backward we have a Platonic collection (or recollection) of meaning; if this gathering is faced forward toward the future, then we have a repetition, a reception of meaning that is radiating not from one's past but from one's future – towards one's present, offering to receptive agents open fields of possibility. (1998: 287–8)

Such repetition forward is when 'We say God and the imagination are one'; it allows for the kind of chanceful correspondences that I have been tracing in this book made by poets when they are surrounded by 'the daughters of Inspiration' rather than recollecting with 'the Daughters of Memory' (Erdman: 554).

In Chapter 5, I happened upon the first part of the next chapter of Augustine's *Confessions* as the theme of 'Of Mere Being'. The second part is a discovery of 'affluence':

> not, I say, distractedly but intently, follow I hard on, for the garland of my heavenly calling, where I may hear the voice of thy praise, and contemplate these delights of thine, which are neither to come, nor to pass away ['non secundum distentionem, sed secundum intentionem sequor ad palmam supernae vocationis, ubi audiam vocem laudis et contempler delectationem tuam nec venientem nec praetereuntem']. But now are my years spent in mourning [Ps. 30. 11], and thou, my Comfort, O Lord, my Father, art Everlasting; but I fall into dissolution amid the changing times, whose order I am yet ignorant of: yea, my thoughts are torn asunder with tumultuous vicissitudes, even the inmost bowels of my soul; until I may be run into thee, purified and molten by the fire of thy love ['at ego in tempora dissilui, quorum ordinem nescio, et tumultuosis varietatibus dilaniantur cogitationes meae, intima viscera animae meae, donec in te confluam purgatus et liquidus igne amoris tui']. (Augustine 1912, XI. xxix: ii. 278–81)

We have arrived at the realm of anagogy, and we discover a red river running through it, extended in unity to reach a future that gathers being into its essence. The distended end of the decaying kind is countered by the beginning of the unborn kind that unifies. As Chadwick points out, 'Augustine's image of the historical process is that of a flowing river or rivers, with many stormy cataracts', as his translation registers: 'The storms of incoherent events tear to pieces my thoughts, the inmost entrails of my soul'. Below this stormy water that flows to the sea, ancient symbol of time and space, we find the undercurrent of perennial wisdom, as Chadwick's translation continues to register: 'until that day when, purified and molten by the fire of your love, I flow together to merge into you'; 'Underlying this passage is the language of Plotinus . . . about the fall away from the One as a scattering and an extending. Temporal successiveness is an experience of disintegration; the ascent to divine eternity is a recovery of unity' (Augustine 1998: 244). For Plotinus 'multiplicity is a falling away from The Unity':

> Consider the thing that has taken extension; broken into so many independent items, it is now those several parts and not the thing it was; if that original is to persist, the members must stand collected to

their total; in other words, a thing is itself not by being extended but by remaining, in its degree, a unity: through expansion and in the measure of the expansion, it is less itself; retaining unity, it retains its essential being. (1992, VI. vi. i: 615)

As Yeats emblematized with the fisherman, whom we encountered in Chapter 1, the labour of soul-making is upstream, against the flow of history, to its source; Augustine's flowing into God is fiery and upwards, not watery and downwards: 'call it, again and again, | The river that flows nowhere, like a sea' (*SCP*: 533), 'That flows round the earth and through the skies, | Twisting among the universal spaces' (*SCP*: 444). The river, it will be argued, is a topos, a rhetorical commonplace of thinking and poetry; it is also an archetype. In the twentieth century Curtius described the outer aspects of these phenomena, while Jung considered them from within. To compare these approaches is like witnessing Yeats's gyres interlock; in our age we are animated by the difference between conscious activities like imitation or allusion and unconscious influence or chanceful affluence: in late Yeats and late Stevens we witness 'the *distentio* arise out of the *intentio* that has burst asunder'.

Introducing his work, Yeats recalled the Chandogya Upanishad: 'A wise man seeks in Self, those that are alive and those that are dead and gets what the world cannot give' (*E&I*: 509–10; *U*: 109). As Blake knew, 'Swedenborg totally rejected a spatial and temporal and material definition of humanity, and tells of his vision of "the Grand Man of the Heavens", the Divine-Human, who "from a distance" appeared to him as one man, but nearer was seen as an innumerable multitude of human souls' (Raine 1999: 68): 'crowd on curious crowd, || In a kind of total affluence, all first, | All final' (*SCP*: 342). Likewise the four poems at the centre of this book are 'from a distance' by Yeats and Stevens, 'while close at hand they are seen to be made up of multitudes of souls. So every individual spirit is seen to be a part of the universal life' (Raine 1999: 68). Such is the site, soul or slippage of literature, which enters to expand Blake's body of work in his introduction to *Songs of Innocence*, annihilating self to find itself again in *Milton*. As Jonathan Wordsworth says of the climax to Wordsworth's *Prelude*, it is 'imagination' or 'the power that is felt to well up from underlying sources within the individual', 'perfectly imaged in the mounting streams on Snowdon that roar with a single voice, which supports the poet's hope that his own work, "*Proceeding from the depth of untaught things,* | Enduring and creative" may "become | A power like one of Nature's"' (1984: 327).

A book that has the word affluence in its title and makes references to a multitude of other books should end with the same disclaimer as Lao-tsu's:

> True wisdom is different from much learning;
> Much learning means little wisdom.
> The sage has no need to hoard;
> When his own last scrap has been used up on behalf of others,
> Lo, he has more than before!
> When his own last scrap has been used in giving to others,
> Lo, his stock is even greater than before!

> (Waley 1934: 243)

It is hoped that the poetry shows each intent reader the way upon which 'No secondary hand can intervene' (*1805*, xiii. 192). The poems of Blake, Wordsworth, Yeats and Stevens transform earlier works, which are gathered by imitation, allusion, influence and chance. They inspire later works of self-knowledge because each poet is also a gate-keeper, ready to open each reader's heart and mind to that greater Self we share within.

The first line of Yeats's penultimate poem uses epanalepsis, *'eccho sound'* or the figure of 'slow return' (Puttenham 2007: 144), as the poet returns to an early second self. The end of 'Not Ideas' at the end of Stevens's *Collected Poems* relies on anaphora, 'the figure of *Report'* (Puttenham 2007: 142). These rhetorical figures provide themes at the end. Turning to Yeats's and Stevens's very last poems, we find that 'The Black Tower' makes the return seem even slower and 'Of Mere Being' continues the transformation in 'Not Ideas' of hearsay or 'Repetition in the first degree' into repetition as 'consciousness raised to the second power'. In all of these final poems we find birds reporting repetition that has already occurred within but slowly returns to us on earth. 'Cuchulain Comforted' is a nocturne in which bird-like things or shrouds speak and at the end 'They had changed their throats and had the throats of birds'; 'Not Ideas' is an aubade, which incorporates a scrawny cry to herald the dawn chorus. Yeats was enchanted during his final weeks with the same 'foreign song' as Stevens but 'The tower's old cook . . . must climb and clamber | Catching small birds in the dew of the morn'. He is preparing 'at daylight or before' for something as irrefutable as the Song of Sixpence (see *YL*: 922). The paradisal hour of six in the morning at which the speaker awakes in 'Not Ideas' is matched darkly by Yeats's Cuchulain 'that had six mortal wounds'. An age as ironic as Byron might well respond as he reacts to 'the Lakers':

> A nest of tuneful persons, to my eye
> Like four and twenty blackbirds in a pie;
>
> 'Which pie being open'd, they began to sing' –
> (This old song and new simile holds good)
> 'A dainty dish to set before the King,'
> Or Regent, who admires such kind of food.

(Byron 2000, *Don Juan*, 'Dedication'. 7–12: 373)

The banners 'whisper that a man's a fool | Who, when his own right king's forgotten, | Cares what king sets up his rule'. The final poems of Yeats and Stevens are owed to Asclepius. Each dying poet creates for himself that which can guide him to the place of the dead. Their birds are psychopomps that augur. The reader's response to their work depends on a taking up of the end of the linen thread or of the golden bough that could lead us in each day at self-knowledge.

Notes

Prologue: 'Of the planet of which they were part'

1. I adapt the first part of the first line of the last stanza of Yeats's 'Coole Park and Ballylee, 1931': 'We were the last romantics' (*YCP*: 276).
2. Each time Wordsworth published this poem, which was never heavily revised, from the 1798 edition of *Lyrical Ballads* to the final *Poetical Works* of 1849–50, he included a footnote at this point: 'This line has a close resemblance to an admirable line of Young, the exact expression of which I cannot recollect.' Without bothering, during the course of more than fifty years, to look up his source, Wordsworth is admitting something on the cusp of unconscious influence to make it half-knowing allusion. I see this footnote that makes us question Wordsworth's memory and the nature of allusion as integral to the poem.

1 Yeats from *The Tower* to the Last Poems

1. In all of Blake's prose quoted from Erdman, 'Italics within square brackets [*thus*] indicate words or letters deleted or erased or written over. Matter in roman type within square brackets [thus] is supplied by the editor. Angle brackets <thus> enclose words or letters written to replace deletions, or as additions, not including words written immediately following and in the same ink or pencil as deleted matter' (Erdman: xxiv).

3 'Cuchulain Comforted'

1. Pethica has established *NLI* 13,593 (50), 5–6, a two-page revised typescript 'as the "final" version of "Cuchulain Comforted"' (1997: xlv). The date of completion of 'Cuchulain Comforted' ('*January* 13, 1939') appears beneath most of its published versions, as with 'The Black Tower' ('*January* 21, 1939'), although we have no evidence that Yeats himself planned to have their dates printed. My text follows that established by George Yeats and Thomas Mark, which is close to *NLI* 13,593 (50), 5–6 except that in the revised typescript there is no colon at the end of line 11, no period at the end of line 15, no comma in line 16, no comma at the end of line 19, no comma after 'sang' in line 23, and there is a comma instead of a semi-colon at the end of line 24 (see Pethica 1997: 146–7). In the revised typescript some apostrophes and quotation marks are missing.
2. At the climax of Adam's visionary instruction in the final book of *Paradise Lost*, there is an allusion to Dante's *punto*, which, as Milton would have known, is also *segno d'interpunzione*, a stop, full stop, or period: 'So spake th'Archangel *Michael*, then paus'd, | As at the Worlds great period' (*PL*, xii. 466–7).
3. Compare Yeats's diagram of the interlocking gyres (*VB*: 68) with Freccero's illustration of the movement of *terza rima* (1986: 262).

4. 'The main distinction between the literal and spiritual senses', according to Thomas Gilby, is 'an unconscious medieval memory of the Antioch–Alexandria axis', but 'carries no echo of the Pauline contrast between the letter and the spirit' (Aquinas 1964: i. 140; see 2 Corinthians 3. 6).

5. When Northrop Frye passes into anagogy he talks of time only in terms of space (see 1957: 115–28).

6. Blake and the KJV have linen 'clothes', the original plural of cloth. According to modern orthography, Christ's discarded linen cloths becomes visionary clothes for the angels. Does the Resurrection transform cloths to clothes? Can winding-cloths be presented like swaddling-clothes? I retain throughout the original plural form.

7. From Aby Warburg to the Jungians, Botticelli's paintings are open to interpretation. We still conjecture who devised their schemes and for whom they were made. Horne (1908) remains the best guide.

8. For example, Cristoforo Landino, teacher of Angelo Poliziano and Ficino, was capable of allegorical readings to uncover the esoteric senses of texts as well as Aristotelian stylistic analyses. His commentary on Dante's *Comedy* (see Landino 1974) was read by Botticelli, and, as Max C. Marmor points out, 'Landino consistently traces [the soul's moral and spiritual] pilgrimage across recurring tracks of sylvan imagery, interpreting Dante's "selva oscura" at the beginning of the poem as an allegory of the *vita voluptuosa* and the Earthly Paradise at the end of the *Purgatorio* as the setting for the perfected *vita activa*. Finally, Dante ascends to the *vita contemplativa* in the *Paradiso*, receiving the vision of divine perfection' (2003: 205).

9. Ernst H. Gombrich (1945) established Apuleius as a central text for Quattrocento Florentine humanists. The Apuleian thesis has been criticized by E. Panofsky (1960: 194–5). But Gombrich defends a revised version of his essay (1972: 45–64): he is interested in Neoplatonic art as 'solvent'; we witness in Botticelli 'the opening up, to secular art, of emotional spheres which had hitherto been the preserve of religious worship' (1945: 43). Jean Gillies (1981) has argued the importance of Apuleius' description of Isis for Botticelli's *Primavera*.

10. Eliade would have argued that John and Apuleius transmute a common symbol of linen garments, deliberately appropriating older or universal images to help facilitate 'the diffusion' of their messages (1991: 168).

4   'Not Ideas about the Thing but the Thing Itself'

1. Heidegger is explicating the last line from Georg Trakl's poem, 'Jahr': 'Golden eye of the beginning, dark patience of the end'; 'Goldenes Auge des Anbeginns, dunkle Geduld des Endes' (1971: 176; 2007: 56).

2. E. S. Le Comte argues that Milton's lines translate in part lines from Petrarch in *Eclogue IX*: 'late contagia fudit' rendered with 'maximum accuracy' as 'contagion spread' and 'Rot inwardly' as Milton's 'recollection' of 'saniem inclusam' (Petrarch 1974, ix. 67 and 69). In Milton 'The bad air of the plague [in Horton and elsewhere of 1637] is at once the bad air of the shepherd's wretched "songs" or sermons, offered instead of wholesome spiritual food' (Le Comte 1954: 403 and 404). Petrarch's poem also looks upward from its equally topical

subject (the Black Death of 1348–50); as the earthly Philogeus laments the end of the decaying or diseased kind, Theophilus finds the beginning of the unborn or heavenly kind (see Petrarch 1974: 134–5).

3. *Papier-mâché* remains essentially a French word in English, even retaining its accents: it has not become papermashay as it might, had the material itself been first manufactured in England during the age of Shakespeare rather than during the decorous and Francophile eighteenth century. Our English chewing has at least reversed the stress of the French pronunciation of *mâché*, although Stevens himself preferred the French pronunciation of the word as disclosed by the recording of his reading of 'Not Ideas' ('Poems. Selections [Poetry Reading | by Wallace Stevens]' from the studio reading of 6 October 1954 at Harvard University [Cambridge: Woodberry Poetry Room], 1 sound-tape reel [41 min.]: 7½ ips; 7 in., ½-in. tape; also available as part of the Woodberry Poetry Room digital collection of poetry readings at http://nrs.harvard.edu/urn-3:FHCL:1196101 [accessed 29 December 2010]).

4. According to the *OED*, auricular means not only 'Of or pertaining to the ear' but also 'Perceived by the ear; audible' and, consequently, once upon a time, 'Hearsay, oral, traditional'. Auricular and oracular have a more than auricular correspondence.

5. 'Vagitumque Dei' as Milton describes Christ's cries that do not after all occur in 'On the Morning of Christ's Nativity' in 'Elegia Sexta' (*1645*: ii. 34).

6. Could there have been a cock near Stevens's home on Westerly Terrace in the spring of 1954? If there is cock-crow in the poem it is a symbolic cry and the poem should be read for its literal and spiritual senses.

7. As we can see from 'Depression before Spring', Stevens's preferred representation of the crow of the cock is 'ki-ki-ri-ki' not *cock-a-doodle-do* (*SCP*: 63).

8. In Matthew 26. 30, a hymn precedes Christ's dark prophecy: 'Et hymno dicto exierunt in montem Oliveti'; 'And when they had sung an hymne, they went out into the mount of Olives'. And then, in 26. 34, Jesus answers Peter's remonstrance that he will not betray him that night, 'amen dico tibi quia in hac nocte antequam gallus cantet ter me negabis'; 'Verily I say unto thee, that this [n]ight, before the cocke crow, thou shalt denie me thrise'.

9. Wordsworth's 1798 fragment 'Was it for this', the very first draft of *The Prelude*, repeats, as Jonathan Wordsworth has pointed out, 'a rhetorical pattern' (1984: 37) first found in Milton's 'Samson Agonistes': 'For this did the Angel twice descend? for this | Ordain'd thy nurture holy, as of a Plant; | Select, and Sacred' (*1671*: ii. 28). Like two or three pebbles thrown, one after another's ever decreasing ellipses, in the river Derwent, the pattern echoes through the verse: 'Was it for this . . . For this didst thou . . . didst thou . . . Was it for this . . . Was it for this . . . For this . . . For this . . .' (*1798*: 3–5). As Wordsworth traces the birth of his own creativity there may also be a recollecting, in the same manner as Stevens, but backwards, of Milton's repeated 'It was' in the first verse of the hymn in 'On the Morning of Christ's Nativity'. Although I do not mean to hunt for the source of Stevens's 'it was' formula, I seek to discover, by suggesting that 'it was' describes, 'the *hidden* roads that go from poem to poem' (Bloom 1973: 96): to apprehend prophecy by following the paths of hearsay.

10. Heidegger discusses the site of Trakl's 'unspoken statement', the origin of all of his poetry, through clarification of Trakl's individual poems only. I would

argue that the discussion of Stevens's unspoken poetic statement must first pass through the explication of his *and others'* individual poems.

11. Wordsworth provides the link between the two different kinds of gaudiness: 'Readers accustomed to the gaudiness and inane phraseology of many modern writers, if they persist in reading this book to its conclusion, will perhaps frequently have to struggle with feelings of strangeness and aukwardness' (*LB1*: i–ii).

12. I think of the poems as espoused not least because each talks of waking as a union of man and promised wife. At the end of 'Depression before Spring', 'no queen comes | In slipper green' (*SCP*: 63) whereas the 'dweller in the dark cabin' in 'Hymn from a Watermelon Pavilion' is told, 'A feme may come, leaf-green, | Whose coming may give revel | Beyond the revelries of sleep' (*SCP*: 89).

13. Discovering for us the sound of the real, the 'Howls hoo' in 'hotel' that is transmuted in the sound of 'hymns': the 'Who's there?' (I. i. 1) that opens *Hamlet* and its first scene of hidden hymns.

14. Mimicking the 'mimic hootings' and the owls' 'long halloos' of Wordsworth's 'There was a boy' (*LB2*: ii. 14).

15. Bloom cannot decide 'Whether or not there is an allusion to Blake' (1977: 367).

5   The Very Last Poems

1. Blake is annotating a passage in Swedenborg's *Heaven and Hell*: '. . . That the Hells are so many and various, appears from it's being given me to know, that under every mountain, hill, rock, plain, and valley, there were particular Hells of different extent in length, breadth, and depth. In a word, both Heaven and the World of Spirits may be considered as convexities, under which are arrangements of those infernal mansions. So much concerning the Plurality of Hells' (1784, para. 588: 389).

2. The order of the last poems in *YCP* was arranged by Thomas Mark, in consultation with George Yeats. For Yeats's different draft Contents, created possibly late on 26 January 1939, not very long before he finally lost consciousness, see Pethica 1997: 466. Pethica sees that Yeats's proposed ordering of the last poems balances 'seriousness and self-ironization' (1997: xxxvi).

3. Pethica has established *NLI* 30,200 (1), an undated typescript draft of the poem (incorporating one revision made in black ink, probably by Yeats, inserting 'that' in line 21) as 'the "final" version of "The Black Tower"': 'If the traditional idea of "authorial intention" were to be followed strictly here, future editions would have to print the poem without punctuation it not only needs, but which Yeats's "authorial expectation" clearly presumed it would get from his wife and Thomas Mark' (1997: xlv). My text follows that established by George Yeats and Mark. But it should be noted that *NLI* 30,200 (1) has no punctuation in the choruses, apart from a period at the end of each, and only the following punctuation during the stanzas: comma after 'spent' in line 3, comma at the end of line 3, comma at the end of line 4, period at the end of line 6, period at the end of line 14, question mark at the end of line 16, and period at the end of line 26 (see Pethica 1997: 138–41).

4. In his Divine Comedy Illustrations, Blake represents the tower before the Stygian lake, across from the light of the gate tower of Dis, in Canto VII of *Inferno*, as a ziggurat (plate 17).

5. 'The suggestion arises that there is some kind of equation to be made between metre and the archetypal plane of self' (Wenthe 1997: 43). Wenthe quotes Yeats in 'Per Amica': 'a vision, whether we wake or sleep, prolongs its power by rhythm and pattern, the wheel where the world is butterfly' (*M*: 341); accordingly, by the late poems, 'Metre is . . . "an unconscious norm" that manifests, through nondiscursive "measure" rather than discursive statement, a permanent, archetypal domain of existence' (45). But I am not so sure that there is such a simple correspondence between metrical regularity and the realm of archetypes in Yeats as Wenthe makes out.

6. Patrick Diskin has argued (1961: 107–8) that 'The Black Tower' is founded on Yeats's remembrance of an episode in Standish O'Grady's 1892 *Finn and his Companions*. W. J. Keith proposes an Arthurian source (1960: 120), quoting E. K. Chambers's *Arthur of Britain*: 'Beneath the Castle of Sewingshields, near the Roman wall in Northumberland, are vaults where Arthur sleeps with Guinevere and all his court and a pack of hounds. He waits until one blows the horn which lies ready on a table, and cuts a garter placed beside it with a sword of stone. Once, a farmer, knitting on the ruins, followed his clew of wool which had fallen to a crevice and found the vault. He cut the garter and Arthur woke, but as he sheathed the sword, fell asleep again, with the words – "O woe betide that evil day | On which this witless wight was born | Who drew the sword – the garter cut, | But never blew the bugle horn"' (1927: 224). It strikes me that Yeats would have been interested in the witless farmer, not sewing like the Shrouds in 'Cuchulain Comforted', but knitting, and who follows the end of his own clew of wool into the labyrinth, when the poet would wind the end of Blake's golden string into a ball to find the way out. The farmer is a type, corresponding to the swineherd Eumaeus in *The Odyssey*, Bottom in *A Midsummer-Night's Dream*, the swineherd in 'Cuchulain's Fight' and the old cook in 'The Black Tower'.

7. An enemy of the poem would read it in a deliberately limited way, trying to bribe or threaten meaning out of it by imposing upon it preordained political or ideological theories. To read it as an oath-bound man is to accommodate oneself to the cryptic, carefully to listen to the style of the poem in order to discover its secret meanings without any arbitrary expectations, usually fabricated out of prevailing materialist or metaphysical systems of thinking.

8. Bloom would call this '*Apophrades* or The Return of the Dead' (1997: 139). I also hear, in 'The Black Tower', Arthur Hugh Clough's 'Say not the struggle nought availeth', which Winston Churchill had broadcast in 1941.

9. Probably added after Yeats's death when George Yeats typed out the poem.

10. As Raine says we are 'of an age whose great longing is for some new heavenly marriage that shall produce a new divine child to save us from impending apocalypse' (Jung 2002: quotation on front endpaper).

11. The passage echoes the old nurse's recognition of Odysseus on his return home (*Odyssey*: xix).

12. As Geoffrey Shepherd notes, 'The practice of opening Virgil at random and applying the passage on which the eye first fell to the particular circumstances

of the inquirer developed in imperial Roman times; see examples in *Sex scriptores historiae Augustae: Life of Emperor Hadrian*, II, 8, *Life of Alexander Severus*, XIV, 5, and *Life of Clodius Albinus* [V, 2] (by Julius Capitolinus)' (Sidney 1973: 151). For a comprehensive discussion of classical and later instances of the practice of taking lots from Virgil, see Loane 1928.

13. De Quincey's italics and spelling, when he quotes these lines from Wordsworth's 'Expostulation and Reply' in which the cases of infancy that he describes are first noted (De Quincey 2000: ix. 69).

14. William Watts's translation registers Augustine's modification of Philippians. But Henry Chadwick does not convey Augustine's change of *bravium* to *palmam*, preferring to keep his translation of *palmam* the same as the translation of *bravium* in modern spelling editions of the KJV: 'I "pursue the prize of the high calling"' (Augustine 1998: 244).

15. The *locus classicus* is Cicero: 'But the most marked difference between man and beast is this: the beast, just as far as it is moved by the senses and with very little perception of past or future, adapts itself to that alone which is present at the moment; while man – because he is endowed with reason, by which he comprehends the chain of consequences, perceives the causes of things, understands the relation of cause to effect and of effect to cause ['per quam consequentia cernit, causas rerum videt earumque praegressus et quasi antecessiones non ignorat'], draws analogies, and connects and associates the present and the future – easily surveys the course of his whole life and makes the necessary preparations for its conduct' (2005, I. iv. 11: 12–13).

Bibliography

Abrams, M. H. (1965) 'Structure and Style in the Greater Romantic Lyric' in Frederick W. Hilles and Harold Bloom (eds) *From Sensibility to Romanticism* (New York: Oxford University Press).

Albright, Daniel (ed.) (1994) *W. B. Yeats: The Poems* (London: Dent).

Altieri, Charles (2008) 'Why "Angel Surrounded by Paysans" Concludes *The Auroras of Autumn*', *Wallace Stevens Journal* 32: 151–70.

Ambrose (1992) *Ambroise de Milan: Hymnes*, ed. Jacques Fontaine (Paris: Éditions du Cerf).

Apuleius (1922) *The Golden Asse*, trans. William Adlington (London: Simpkin, Marshall, Hamilton, Kent and Co.).

——— (1989) *Metamorphoses*, trans. J. Arthur Hanson (Cambridge: Harvard University Press).

Aquinas, Thomas (1964) *Summa theologiæ*, trans. Thomas Gilby, 61 vols (London: Eyre and Spottiswoode).

——— (2010) *Commentary on the Gospel of John*. trans. Fabian R. Larcher and James A. Weisheipl, 3 vols (Washington: The Catholic University of America Press).

Auerbach, Erich (2003) *Mimesis* (Princeton: Princeton University Press).

Augustine (1848–9) *Homilies on the Gospel according to St. John and his first Epistle. In Evangelium Iohannis tractatus*, 2 vols (Oxford: John Henry Parker).

——— (1912) *Confessions*, trans. William Watts, 2 vols (Cambridge: Harvard University Press).

——— (1998) *Confessions*, trans. Henry Chadwick. (Oxford: Oxford University Press).

Baird, James (1992) '"Preface" to *Ishmael*. Jungian Psychology in Criticism: Some Theoretical Problems' in Richard P. Sugg (ed.) *Jungian Literary Criticism* (Illinois: Northwestern University Press).

Bayley, Harold (1912) *The Lost Language of Symbolism*, 2 vols (London: Williams and Norgate).

Belsey, Catherine (1985) 'Constructing the Subject: Deconstructing the Text' in Robert Con Davis and Ronald Schleifer (eds) (1998) *Contemporary Literary Criticism* (London: Longman).

Blanchot, Maurice (1971) *Le livre à venir* (Paris: Gallimard).

——— (1992) *The Sirens' Song*, trans. Gabriel Josipovici (Brighton: Harvester).

Bloom, Harold (1970) *Yeats* (New York: Oxford University Press).

——— (1971) *The Ringers in the Tower* (Chicago: University of Chicago Press).

——— (1973) *The Anxiety of Influence* (New York: Oxford University Press).

——— (1975) *Kabbalah and Criticism* (New York: Seabury Press).

——— (1977) *Wallace Stevens* (Ithaca: Cornell University Press).

——— (1997) *The Anxiety of Influence*, 2nd edn (Oxford: Oxford University Press).

Brooke, Nicholas (ed.) (1990) *William Shakespeare: The Tragedy of Macbeth* (Oxford: Oxford University Press).

Brown, Terence (1999) *The Life of W. B. Yeats* (Oxford: Blackwell).

Browning, Robert (1940) *The Poetical Works* (Oxford: Oxford University Press).

Budge, E. A. Wallis (trans.) (2008) *The Book of the Dead* (London: Penguin).

Byron (2000) *The Major Works*, ed. Jerome J. McGann (Oxford: Oxford University Press).

Caputo, John D. (1987) *Radical Hermeneutics* (Bloomington and Indianapolis: Indiana University Press).

Carey, John (ed.) (1997) *John Milton: The Complete Shorter Poems*, 2nd edn (London: Longman).

Chambers, E. K. (1927) *Arthur of Britain* (London: Sidgwick).

Chaucer, Geoffrey (1987) *The Riverside Chaucer*, ed. Larry D. Benson, 3rd edn (Oxford: Oxford University Press).

Chevalier, Jean and Alain Gheerbrant (1982) *Dictionary of Symbols*, trans. John Buchanan Brown, 2nd edn (London: Penguin).

Chung-yuan, Chang (1975) *Tao: A New Way of Thinking* (New York and London: Harper and Row).

Cicero (2005) *De Officiis*, trans. Walter Miller (Cambridge: Harvard University Press).

Clark, Lorraine (1991) *Blake, Kierkegaard, and the Spectre of Dialectic* (Cambridge: Cambridge University Press).

Clark, Timothy (1992) *Derrida, Heidegger, Blanchot: Sources of Derrida's Notion and Practice of Literature* (Cambridge: Cambridge University Press).

Clarke, Edward (2006) 'Ariel among the Second Selves: Wallace Stevens and William Wordsworth in Creative Conversation', *Wallace Stevens Journal*, 30: 30–44.

Coleridge, Samuel Taylor (1956–71) *Collected Letters*, ed. E. L. Griggs, 6 vols (Oxford: Clarendon Press).

———— (2001) *Poetical Works*, ed. J. C. C. Mays, 3 vols (Princeton: Princeton University Press).

Conte, Gian Biagio (1986) *The Rhetoric of Imitation* (Ithaca: Cornell University Press).

Cook, Eleanor (1988) *Poetry, Word-Play, and Word-War in Wallace Stevens* (Princeton: Princeton University Press).

———— (1998) *Against Coercion* (Stanford: Stanford University Press).

———— (2007) *A Reader's Guide to Wallace Stevens* (Princeton: Princeton University Press).

Curtin, Jeremiah (1890) *Myths and Folk-Lore in Ireland* (Boston: Little, Brown).

Curtius, Ernst Robert (1990) *European Literature and the Latin Middle Ages*, trans. Willard R. Trask (Princeton: Princeton University Press).

Daiches, David (1960) 'The Opening of *Paradise Lost*' in Frank Kermode (ed.) *The Living Milton* (London: Routledge).

Dante (1990) *Dante's Il convivio (The banquet)*, trans. Richard H. Lansing (New York: Garland).

———— (1920) *Dantis Alagherii epistolae. The letters of Dante*, ed. and trans. Paget Toynbee (Oxford: Clarendon Press).

Daruwala, M. (1998) 'Yeats and the Ghost of Wordsworth', *Yeats Annual*, 13: 197–220.

Davis, Robert Con and Ronald Schleifer (eds) (1998) *Contemporary Literary Criticism* (London: Longman).

de Man, Paul (1984) *The Rhetoric of Romanticism* (New York: Columbia University Press).

De Quincey, Thomas (2000–3) *The Works of Thomas De Quincey*, 21 vols (London: Pickering and Chatto).

Diskin, Patrick (1961) 'A Source for Yeats's "The Black Tower"', *Notes and Queries*, 8: 107–8.

Eagleton, Terry (2008), *Literary Theory: An Introduction*, anniversary edn (Oxford: Blackwell).

Eckhart (1993) *Werke*, ed. Josef Quint and Ernst Benz, 2 vols (Frankfurt: Verlag).
——— (1994) *Selected Writings*, trans. Oliver Davies (London: Penguin).

Edmonds, J. M. (trans.) (1928) *Greek Bucolic Poets*, rev. edn (Cambridge: Harvard University Press).

Eliade, Mircea (1958) *Patterns in Comparative Religion*, trans. Rosemary Sheed (London: Sheed and Ward).
——— (1991) *Images and Symbols*, trans. Philip Mairet (Princeton: Princeton University Press).

Emerson, Ralph Waldo (1883–4) *The Complete Works of Ralph Waldo Emerson*, 12 vols (London: Routledge).

Finneran, Richard J. (with G. M. Harper, and W. M. Murphy) (ed.) (1977) *Letters to W. B. Yeats*, 2 vols (London: Macmillan).
——— (1990) *Editing Yeats's Poems: A Reconsideration* (New York: St. Martin's Press – now Palgrave Macmillan).
——— (ed.) (1997) *W. B. Yeats: The Poems*, 2nd edn (New York: Scribner).

Fort, Paul (1921) *Selected Poems and Ballads of Paul Fort*, trans. John String Newberry (New York: Duffield).

Fowler, Alastair (ed.) (1998) *John Milton: Paradise Lost*, 2nd edn (London: Longman).

Frazer, J. G. (1933) *The Golden Bough*, abridged edn (London: Macmillan).

Freccero, John (1986) *Dante: the Poetics of Conversion* (Cambridge: Harvard University Press).

Fredman, Stephen (1990) *Poet's Prose*, 2nd edn (Cambridge: Cambridge University Press).

Frye, Northrop (1957) *The Anatomy of Criticism* (Princeton: Princeton University Press).
——— (1992) 'The Archetype of Literature' in Richard P. Sugg (ed.) *Jungian Literary Criticism* (Illinois: Northwestern University Press).

Gelpi, Albert (1987) *A Coherent Splendour* (Cambridge: Cambridge University Press).

Gillies, Jean (1981) 'The Central Figure in Botticelli's "Primavera"', *Woman's Art Journal*, 2: 12–16.

Gombrich, Ernst H. (1945) 'Botticelli's Mythologies: A Study in the Neoplatonic Symbolism of His Circle', *Journal of the Warburg and Courtauld Institutes*, 8: 7–60.
——— (1972) *Symbolic Images* (London: Phaidon).

Gould, Warwick (1996) 'The Definitive Edition: a History of the Final Arrangement of Yeats's Work' in A. Norman Jeffares (ed.) *Yeats's Poems*, 3rd edn (Basingstoke: Palgrave Macmillan).

Graham, Daniel W. (ed. and trans.) (2010) *The Texts of Early Greek Philosophy* (Cambridge: Cambridge University Press).

Graves, Robert (1999) *The White Goddess*, ed. Grevel Lindop (London: Faber and Faber).

Heaney, Seamus (1980) *Preoccupations* (London: Faber and Faber).

———— (1984) 'A New and Surprising Yeats', *The New York Times*, 18 March.
———— (ed.) (2000) *W. B. Yeats: Poems selected by Seamus Heaney* (London: Faber and Faber).
Heidegger, Martin (1962) *Being and Time* (Oxford: Blackwell).
———— (1971) *On the Way to Language*, trans. Peter D. Hertz (San Francisco: Harper).
———— (2002a) *The Essence of Truth*, trans. Ted Sadler (London: Continuum).
———— (2002b) *Off the Beaten Track*, ed. and trans. Julian Young and Kenneth Haynes (Cambridge: Cambridge University Press).
———— (2006) *Sein und Zeit* (Tübingen: Verlag).
———— (2007) *Unterwegs zur Sprache* (Stuttgart: Klett-Cotta).
Herbert, George (1968) *The Temple (1633)* (Menston: Scolar).
Hesiod (2006) *Theogony. Works and Days. Testimonia*, ed. and trans. Glenn W. Most (Cambridge: Harvard University Press).
Hollander, John (1981) *The Figure of Echo* (Berkeley: University of California Press).
Horne, Herbert (1908) *Alessandro Filipepi, commonly called Sandro Botticelli, painter of Florence* (London).
Hutchinson, F. E. (ed.) (1945) *The Works of George Herbert* (Oxford: Clarendon Press).
Jacobus, Mary (1976) *Tradition and Experiment in Wordsworth's Lyrical Ballads, 1798* (Oxford: Clarendon Press).
Jeffares, A. Norman (1996a) *W. B. Yeats: Man and Poet*, 3rd edn (London: Kyle Cathie).
———— (1996b) *Yeats's Poems*, 3rd edn (Basingstoke: Palgrave Macmillan).
Jones, David (1974) *The Sleeping Lord* (London: Faber and Faber).
Jung, C. G. (1951) 'Foreword' in *The I Ching or Book of Changes*, trans. Richard Wilhelm and Cary F. Baynes (London: Routledge).
———— (1963) *Mysterium Coniunctionis, an Inquiry into the Separation and Synthesis of Psychic Opposites in Alchemy*, trans. R. F. C. Hull, 2nd edn (London: Routledge).
———— (1985) *Synchronicity*, trans. R. F. C. Hull (London: Routledge).
———— (2002) *Answer to Job*, trans. R. F. C. Hull (London: Routledge).
———— (2010) *The Undiscovered Self*, trans. R. F. C. Hull (Princeton: Princeton University Press).
Keats, John (1820) *Lamia, Isabella, The Eve of St Agnes* (London: Printed for Taylor and Hessey).
———— (2002) *Letters*, ed. Robert Gittings, rev. Jon Mee (Oxford: Oxford University Press).
Keith, W. J. (1960) 'Yeats's Arthurian Black Tower', *Modern Language Notes*, 75: 119–23.
Kennelly, Brendan (1975) 'High Talk. The Philosophical Poetry of W. B. Yeats. By Robert Snukal', *The Review of English Studies*, New Series, 26. 101: 99–100.
———— (1994) *Journey into Joy: Selected Prose*, ed. Åke Persson (Newcastle upon Tyne: Bloodaxe Books).
Kermode, Frank (2002) *The Romantic Image*, new edn (London: Routledge).
Kierkegaard, Søren, (1983) *Fear and Trembling. Repetition*, ed. and trans. Howard V. Hong and Edna H. Hong (Princeton: Princeton University Press).
———— (1989) *The Concept of Irony*, ed. and trans. Howard V. Hong and Edna H. Hong (Princeton: Princeton University Press).

—— (1998) *The Point of View*, ed. and trans. Howard V. Hong and Edna H. Hong (Princeton: Princeton University Press).

Landino, Cristoforo (1974) *Scritti critici e teorici*, ed. Roberto Cardini (Rome: Bulzoni).

Lansing, Richard (ed.) (2010) *The Dante Encyclopedia* (New York: Routledge).

Le Comte, E. S. (1954) '"Lycidas", Petrarch, and the Plague', *MLN*, 69: 402–4.

Lemprière, John (1801) *Bibliotheca classica*, 4th edn (London).

Loane, Helen A. (1928) 'The Sortes Vergilianae', *The Classical Weekly*, 21. 24: 185–9.

Lovelace, Richard (1930) *The Poems of Richard Lovelace*, ed. C. H. Wilkinson (Oxford: Clarendon Press).

Mackail, John William (1915) 'Introduction' in Charles Lancelot Shadwell (trans.) *The Paradise of Dante Alighieri* (London: Macmillan).

Marmor, Max C. (2003) 'From Purgatory to the "Primavera": Some Observations on Botticelli and Dante', *Artibus et Historiae*, 24. 48: 199–212.

Mooney, Edward F. (1998) '*Repetition*: Getting the world back' in Alastair Hannay and Gordon D. Marino (eds) *The Cambridge Companion to Kierkegaard* (Cambridge: Cambridge University Press).

Moore, Virginia (1954) *The Unicorn* (New York: Macmillan).

Newlyn, Lucy (1993) *Paradise Lost and the Romantic Reader* (Oxford: Clarendon Press).

—— (2000) *Reading, Writing, and Romanticism: The Anxiety of Reception* (Oxford: Oxford University Press).

—— (2006) 'Foreword' in Damon Walford Davies and Richard Marggraf Turley (eds) *The Monstrous Debt: Modalities of Romantic Influence in Twentieth-Century Literature* (Detroit: Wayne State University Press).

Olney, James (1975) 'The Esoteric Flower: Yeats and Jung' in George Mills Harper (ed.) *Yeats and The Occult* (London: Macmillan).

O'Neill, Michael (2007) *The All-Sustaining Air* (Oxford: Oxford University Press).

Panofsky, E. (1960) *Renaissance and Renascences in Western Art* (London: Paladin).

Payne, Mark (2007) *Theocritus and the Invention of Fiction* (Cambridge: Cambridge University Press).

Pethica, James (ed.) (1997) *Last Poems: Manuscript Materials by W. B. Yeats* (Ithaca: Cornell University Press).

Petrarch (1974) *Bucolicum Carmen*, trans. T. G. Bergin (New Haven: Yale University Press).

Plato (1997) *Complete Works*, ed. John M. Cooper (Indianapolis: Hackett).

Plotinus (1992) *The Enneads*, trans. Stephen Mc Kenna (New York: Larson Publications).

Porphyry (1983) *On the Cave of the Nymphs*, trans. Robert Lamberton (New York: Station Hill Press).

Preminger, Alex and T. V. F. Brogan (eds) (1993) *The New Princeton Encyclopedia of Poetry and Poetics* (Princeton: Princeton University Press).

Prudentius (1949–53) *Prudentius*, ed. and trans. H. J. Thomson, 2 vols (Cambridge: Harvard University Press).

Puttenham, George (2007) *The Arte of English Poesie* (Teddington: The Echo Library).

Raine, Kathleen (1970) *William Blake* (London: Thames and Hudson).

——— (1974) *Death-in-life and life-in-death: 'Cuchulain Comforted' and 'News for the Delphic Oracle' (New Yeats Papers)* (Dublin: The Dolmen Press).

——— (1986) *Yeats the Initiate* (London: George Allen and Unwin Limited).

——— (1991) *Golgonooza: City of Imagination* (Ipswich: Golgonooza Press).

——— (1992) 'C. G. Jung: A Debt Acknowledged' in Richard P. Sugg (ed.) *Jungian Literary Criticism* (Illinois: Northwestern University Press).

——— (1999) *W. B. Yeats and the Learning of the Imagination* (Ipswich: Golgonooza Press).

——— (2002) *Blake and Antiquity* (New York: Routledge).

Richardson, Joan (1988) *Wallace Stevens: The Later Years* (New York: William Morrow).

Ricks, Christopher (ed.) (1996) *T. S. Eliot: Inventions of the March Hare* (New York: Harcourt Brace and Company).

——— (1998) 'Eliot's Sources and "a cumulative plausibility"', *ANQ*, 11. 3: 4–11.

——— (2002) *Allusion to the Poets* (Oxford: Oxford University Press).

Ricoeur, Paul (1984) *Time and Narrative*, trans. Kathleen McLaughlin and David Pellaver (Chicago: University of Chicago Press).

Rilke, Rainer Maria (2006) *Sonnets to Orpheus*, trans. M. D. Herter Norton (New York: Norton).

Rumi (1995) *Selected Poems*, trans. Coleman Barks (London: Penguin).

Seneca (1917–25) *Epistles*, trans. Richard M. Gummere, 3 vols (Cambridge: Harvard University Press).

Severson, Richard James (1995) *Time, Death and Eternity: Reflecting on Augustine's Confessions* (London: Scarecrow Press).

Shakespeare, William (1891) *The Works of Shakespeare*, ed. William George Clark and William Aldis Wright, 'The Globe Edition' (London: Macmillan).

Shelley, Percy Bysshe (1967) *Poetical Works*, ed. Thomas Hutchinson (London: Oxford University Press).

——— (2003) *The Major Works*, ed. Zachary Leader and Michael O'Neill (Oxford: Oxford University Press).

Sidney, Philip (1968) *The Defence of Poesie (1595)* (Menston: Scolar).

——— (1973) *An Apology for Poetry, or The Defence of Poesy*, ed. Geoffrey Shepherd (Manchester: Manchester University Press).

Sinclair, John D. (trans.) (1961) *The Divine Comedy of Dante Alighieri*, 3 vols (Oxford: Oxford University Press).

Stevens, Wallace (1950) *The Auroras of Autumn* (New York: Knopf).

Struck, Peter (2004) *Birth of the Symbol* (Princeton: Princeton University Press).

Swedenborg, Emanuel (1784) *Heaven and Hell* (London).

Taylor, Thomas (1805) *Miscellanies in Prose and Verse* (London).

——— (1969) *Thomas Taylor the Platonist: Selected Writings*, ed. Kathleen Raine and George Mills Harper (London: Routledge).

Tyndale, William (trans.) (2008) *The New Testament: a Facsimile of the 1526 Edition* (London: The British Library).

Vaughan, Henry (1957) *The Works of Henry Vaughan*, ed. L. C. Martin, 2nd edn (Oxford: Clarendon Press).

Vendler, Helen (1980) 'Stevens and Keats' "To Autumn"' in F. Doggett and R. Buttel (eds) *Wallace Stevens: A Celebration* (Princeton: Princeton University Press).

——— (1984) *Wallace Stevens: Words Chosen Out of Desire* (Cambridge: Harvard University Press).

—— (2007) *Our Secret Discipline: Yeats and Lyric Form* (Oxford: Oxford University Press).

von Balthasar, Hans Urs (1968) *Man in History* (London: Sheed and Ward).

Waley, Arthur (1934) *The Way and Its Power* (London: Unwin).

Wellesley, Dorothy (1964) *Letters on Poetry from W. B. Yeats to Dorothy Wellesley* (Oxford: Oxford University Press).

Wenthe, William J. (1997) '"It Will be a Hard Toil": Yeats's Theory of Versification, 1899–1919', *Journal of Modern Literature*, 21: 29–48.

Whiting, Anthony (1996) *The Never-Resting Mind: Wallace Stevens' Romantic Irony* (Michigan: University of Michigan Press).

Whitman, Walt (1860) 'Bardic Symbols', *Atlantic Unbound*, v. xxx: 445–7.

Wilhelm, Richard (1922) *Chinesische Lebensweisheit* (Darmstadt: Reichl).

Wilson, F. A. C. (1958) *Yeats and Tradition* (New York: Macmillan).

—— (1960) *Yeats's Iconography* (London: Gollancz).

Wind, Edgar (1958) *Pagan Mysteries in the Renaissance* (London: Faber and Faber).

Wordsworth, Dorothy (2002) *The Grasmere and Alfoxden Journals*, ed. Pamela Woof (Oxford: Oxford University Press).

Wordsworth, Jonathan (1984) *The Borders of Vision* (Oxford: Oxford University Press).

—— (1991) *Ancestral Voices* (Poole: Woodstock).

—— (ed.) (1995) *The Prelude: The Four Texts* (London: Penguin).

Wyatt, Thomas (1969) *Collected Poems*, ed. Kenneth Muir and Patricia Thomson (Liverpool: Liverpool University Press).

Yeats, W. B. (ed.) (1936) *The Oxford Book of Modern Verse* (Oxford: Oxford University Press).

—— (1938) *New Poems* (Dublin: Cuala Press).

—— (1939) *Last Poems and Two Plays* (Dublin: Cuala Press).

—— (1949) *The Poems of W. B. Yeats*, 2 vols (London: Macmillan).

Zolla, Elémire (1990) *Verità segrete esposte in evidenza* (Venice: Marsilio).

Index